HOLDING THE MEDIA ACCOUNTABLE

Holding the **MEDIA** *Accountable*

CITIZENS,

ETHICS,

AND

THE LAW

Edited by David Pritchard

Indiana
University
Press

BLOOMINGTON AND INDIANAPOLIS

This book is a publication of
Indiana University Press
601 North Morton Street
Bloomington, IN 47404-3797 USA

http://www.indiana.edu/~iupress

Telephone orders 800-842-6796
Fax orders 812-855-7931
Orders by e-mail iuporder@indiana.edu

The paper used in this publication meets the minimum requirements
of American National Standard for Information Sciences—
Permanence of Paper for Printed Library Materials, ANSI
Z39.48-1984.

Manufactured in the United States of America

Library of Congress Cataloging-in-Publication Data

Holding the media accountable : citizens, ethics, and the law / edited
  by David Pritchard.
       p.   cm.
  Includes bibliographical references and index.
    ISBN 0-253-33662-7 (cloth : alk. paper). — ISBN 0-253-
21357-6 (pbk. : alk. paper)
    1. Mass media—Moral and ethical aspects—United States.
2. Journalism—Moral and ethical aspects—United States.
3. Mass media and public opinion—United States. 4. Mass
media—Law and legislation. 5. Responsibility.   I. Pritchard,
David Hemmings.
  P94.H65   2000
  174'.9097—dc21   99-37764

1 2 3 4 5 05 04 03 02 01 00

CONTENTS

ACKNOWLEDGMENTS / vii

ACKNOWLEDGMENTS

Journalism and mass communication programs in the United States routinely teach media law and ethics as subjects of High Philosophy. Media law generally is taught as the study of constitutional law as revealed by decisions of the Supreme Court of the United States. Media ethics often is the study of how the thought of great ethicists of the western world might be applied to current media controversies. These approaches are not without merit, but neither takes into account the day-to-day realities of media law and ethics in the lives of ordinary media people and their audiences.

Holding the Media Accountable hopes to help fill that gap. I got the idea for the book several years ago, when I was on the faculty of the School of Journalism at Indiana University in Bloomington. I was reading an innovative compilation of studies about non-judicial dispute resolution titled *No Access to Law: Alternatives to the American Judicial System.*[1] I was surprised to learn that the authors of the chapters were, for the most part, undergraduate or master's students in anthropology who had done their research under the supervision of Laura Nader, the University of California–Berkeley anthropology professor who edited the book.

The research in *No Access to Law* was quite good, I thought, but no better than the research that graduate students in my seminars on media law and ethics had been producing. I began thinking of the seminar papers and theses my students were writing as possible chapters in a book. I shared the idea with colleagues at Indiana University, who were enthusiastic. A small grant from the IU Bureau of Media Research made possible the initial selection and editing of the chapters.

Life, of course, delayed the completion of *Holding the Media Accountable.* Since receiving the BMR grant, I have spent a year as a Fulbright scholar in Canada, left Indiana to take a faculty job in my home state of Wisconsin, and was unexpectedly drafted to be chair of my department during a difficult period in its history. My father died of a lingering illness; my first child was born.

Along the way, the students who wrote the chapters completed their degrees and got jobs of their own. They learned a lot from being willing to take a fresh look at how media law and ethics operate in the real world; *Holding the Media Accountable* is intended to share the learning with others. If nothing else, the book shows the value of seeing media law and ethics as routine behavior rather than High Philosophy.

A number of colleagues provided useful advice about this project. Foremost among them is David H. Weaver, Roy W. Howard Professor at the IU School of Journalism, whose unwavering support has meant more to me than I suspect he realizes. Others who made valuable comments include Dan Berkowitz, David Boeyink, Robert Drechsel, Linda Lawson, Jeremy Lipschultz, Karen Riggs, and Kathy Rogers.

My thanks to all.

NOTE

1. Laura Nader, ed., *No Access to Law: Alternatives to the American Judicial System* (New York: Academic Press, 1980).

HOLDING THE MEDIA ACCOUNTABLE

1

Introduction:
The Process of Media Accountability

DAVID PRITCHARD

Much of what people know about the world beyond their own experience comes from the mass media. In a variety of direct and indirect ways, media content influences what people believe, what they think about, and how they act.

The media's potential to influence large numbers of people makes conflict over media content inevitable. In some cases the conflict deals with broad issues, such as violence on television or possible bias in news about public affairs, while in other cases the conflict may be local and individualized, as when a newspaper publishes information that harms the reputation of an ordinary citizen.

Holding the Media Accountable: Citizens, Ethics, and the Law is about these kinds of conflicts. The book, which presents eleven studies of how citizens and media organizations deal with conflict, is the first collection of empirical research into the process of media accountability.

Holding the Media Accountable differs from other books in the area of media accountability in that it contains no analyses of legal doctrine, nor does it propose ethical principles for media organizations to follow. The authors whose work is represented in these pages believe that media law and ethics have concrete meaning only in the context of accurate knowledge about media accountability in day-to-day life. What legendary jurist Oliver Wendell Holmes, Jr., said about law—"The life of the law has not been logic: it has been experience"[1]—also is true of media accountability. Although media accountability can be discussed in the abstract, it cannot truly be understood without examining how the process actually works.

THE PROCESS OF MEDIA ACCOUNTABILITY

The phrase "media accountability" is often used but seldom defined. Some writers think of media accountability in terms of news credibility. Others see it in terms of legal obligations and prohibitions. Still others discuss media accountability without defining it at all. The confusion led two influential scholars to declare a few years ago that discussion of media accountability was a "conceptual muddle."[2] Shortly afterward, another scholar wrote that "the whole question of accountability remains one of the great unresolved issues of contemporary journalism."[3]

Clarifying the conceptual muddle is important; we need a definition of media accountability that is precise, yet broad enough to encompass a range of formal and informal activity. *Holding the Media Accountable* uses the following definition: *Media accountability is the process by which media organizations may be expected or obliged to render an account of their activities to their constituents.*[4]

An account is an explanation or justification of a media worker's or a media organization's conduct. A constituent is an individual, group, or organization whose good will is important to the media organization. A media organization can have many constituents, including audience members, advertisers, news sources, peers in other media organizations, and regulatory agencies such as the Federal Communications Commission.

It is important to stress that media accountability is a process. It is behavior over a period of time. It is not a set of legal doctrines, ethical rules, or complaint procedures written on paper, though such norms may affect how people behave throughout the accountability process. Accountability can be informal and individual, as when a public official asks a journalist to explain or justify the previous day's news judgment. The process also can be formal and organizational, as when a multinational corporation sues a major television network for libel.

Just as media systems reflect the characteristics of their communities and nations,[5] so do forms of media accountability. In the United States, site of most of the research reported in this book, the ideology of press freedom militates against a strong role for government in media accountability. Lacking an integrated system of government-imposed rules and procedures, the American system of media accountability is fragmented, informal, and diverse. To the extent that rules and formal procedures are part of the system of media accountability in the United States, they have roots in various established sets of norms, including professional practices, journalism ethics, and media law.

It is important to keep in mind, however, that media accountability is a process, not a set of normative prescriptions. Although accountability may take place in the shadow of various kinds of legal and ethical norms, norms by themselves cannot provide a clear understanding of a system of media accountability.[6] Such an understanding comes only from careful research into the actual workings of the media accountability process. The importance of focusing on experience to understand the functioning of normative systems such as media law and ethics was noted by the late Thomas Emerson, one of the twentieth century's most influential theoreticians in the area of free expression:

> It is not enough merely to formulate the broad principles or simply to incorporate them in general rules of law. It is necessary to develop a framework of doctrines, practices, and institutions which will take into account the actual forces at work and make possible the realistic achievement of the objectives sought.[7]

Examining the "actual forces at work" in media accountability is a prerequisite to the achievement of a system of media accountability that enhances the quality of social and political life. *Holding the Media Accountable* is part of that necessary process of examination.

NAMING, BLAMING, AND CLAIMING

Before a media constituent (an individual, group, or organization) makes an accountability demand to a media organization, the constituent must first be dissatisfied. Disputes must take root and grow before they bloom into demands for accountability. Understanding how unhappy media constituents behave before an accountability demand is made is important to understanding media accountability as a whole.

Every day, untold thousands of constituents perceive deficiencies in some form of media content such as a newspaper story or a radio show. Many of these constituents have low expectations of media content, and thus may not be upset by the perceived deficiencies. Other constituents, though, are bothered by them. When such constituents become aware of their dissatisfaction, they have *named* a problem. The naming need not be public; they may have named the problem only to themselves. The important point is that there can be no demand for accountability unless someone first names a problem. Naming is the first step in the accountability process.

People who name a problem with media content may or may not *blame* the media organization for the problem. Blaming is the second step in the accountability process. Naming and blaming are distinct phenomena. People who name a problem with media content do not necessarily blame a media organization for it. News sources unhappy with how a news organization portrayed them, for example, may blame themselves for the unsatisfactory story, perhaps because they think they failed to communicate clearly with the reporter. Or they may simply believe that they have no right to second-guess journalists' judgments about how to portray people.

People who name a problem and who blame the media for it may decide to activate the media accountability process by making a *claim*. Claimants seek some kind of remedy or recompense from the media organization they deem responsible for the problem. Claimants may be satisfied with a simple explanation, or they may want more: a correction, an apology, or some form of financial reparation for harm they believe was caused by the offending media content.[8] Claiming, the first time the media organization is alerted to a possible problem, is the third step in the accountability process.

Media organizations may provide satisfaction to many claimants. Claimants who are not satisfied, however, may decide to engage in public disputing behavior by taking their claim to a judicial or governmental regulatory body (a court or an agency such as the Federal Communications Commission), by using mechanisms of media self-regulation such as press councils or news ombudsmen, or by seeking public support for their cause. The path a dispute takes after the claiming stage depends on a host of factors, including the media organization's response to a claim,[9] the nature of the relationship between the claimant and the media organization,[10] the kinds of disputing forums available,[11] and how accessible such forums are to unsatisfied claimants.[12]

CITIZENS AND ACCOUNTABILITY

So much of the writing about media accountability has focused on formal rules such as laws and ethics codes or formal procedures such as libel lawsuits and press councils that it is easy to forget the people on the front lines of media accountability: the people who produce media content and the citizens who must name, blame, and claim to set the accountability process in motion. Chapters 2 through 4 of *Holding the Media Accountable* examine their behavior.

Chapter 2 documents the routine use of deception by the members of the news staff of a network-affiliate television station in a small Midwestern market. The study, based on observation and on interviews with journalists at the station, found that viewers were almost never informed of deceptive techniques, perhaps because the journalists at the station used deception without much thought. The undisclosed deception posed an accountability dilemma: How can a news organization's constituents even consider asking for an account if they are not aware of the methods used to gather news? The study was conducted at a station typical of those where television journalists have their first jobs, which raises questions about whether the casual use of deception documented in chapter 2 is destined to become the norm in television news.

Chapter 3 attempts to fill a gap in knowledge about the early stages of the media accountability process. What kinds of problems do people who have been mentioned in the news name, whom do they blame for the problems, and what kinds of claims do they make? The chapter approaches those questions via a series of interviews with people who had been mentioned in stories published by a typical American newspaper. About half of the people perceived errors in the stories that mentioned them. From a journalistic point of view the errors were trivial, but most of the citizens who perceived errors felt that their reputations had been damaged. None of them filed lawsuits or complained to editors, so their complaints were invisible to the newspaper. Their concern about damage to their reputations was real, however, and they took active steps to repair the damage.

Although none of the citizens interviewed in the study in chapter 3 complained to the newspaper, some people do contact news organizations to complain. Chapter 4 reports a study of how a typical American newspaper deals with complaints about news content. The research is based on extensive observation in the newsroom, as well as on interviews with newspaper staff members. Chapters 3 and 4 are linked because they both deal with the same community and with complaints about the same newspaper.

MEDIA SELF-REGULATION

Chapters 5 through 7 move from a focus on citizens' naming, blaming, and claiming to an examination of accountability via media self-regulation. Sadly, the record is mixed at best.

On the theory that it is in news organizations' self-interest to be as accountable as possible to their audiences, some newspapers in the United States have created the position of ombudsman. Duties vary from newspaper to newspaper, but all ombudsmen receive and investigate complaints about news content and journalism ethics. Chapter 5 assesses the workings of the ombudsman at the *Louisville Courier-Journal,* the first newspaper in the United States to have an ombudsman. The chapter, based on several weeks of newsroom observation and on a survey of *Courier-Journal* staff members, comes to cautiously optimistic conclusions about the potential effectiveness of the ombudsman as an agent of media accountability.

Other forms of media self-regulation do not fare so well. Fifty years ago the Hutchins Commission on Freedom of the Press urged "vigorous, mutual criticism" as a key to media accountability.[13] Chapter 6 explores whether journalism reviews provide enough such criticism to serve as effective forms of professional self-regulation. The specific focus of the chapter is the *St. Louis Journalism Review,* one of the oldest such publications in the United States. The chapter is based on an analysis of the content of the review, on a survey of journalists whose work has been the focus of comment in the review, and on interviews with several journalists. The verdict? The review's influence is marginal.

Chapter 7 is an examination of press council decision-making during a period of high political tension in Canada: the 1980 referendum in the French-speaking province of Quebec about whether it should secede from Canada. The study found that the Quebec Press Council's decisions applied ethical principles inconsistently. In addition, the QPC had a disturbing tendency to give undue preference in its decisions to media and political institutions to which it had actual or prospective financial ties. The study, based on archival research in Quebec, raises troubling questions about the ability of agents of media self-regulation to judge media behavior impartially.

LAW, LAWYERS, AND MEDIA ACCOUNTABILITY

Chapters 8 through 12 look at the role of lawyers and law in media accountability, with a specific focus on the behavior of people involved in disputes.

Chapter 8 looks at what can happen when citizens organize to bring their complaints about media content to a government regulatory body. The chapter is a case study of efforts by an Indianapolis-based group to influence the Federal Communications Commission to take action against a popular (and controversial) radio show in Indianapolis. The research is based on interviews and on analysis of the 155 personal letters of complaint sent to the FCC. Although the study deals with complaints about a radio show that was more entertainment than news, the lessons that can be derived from chapter 8 would be equally applicable to complaints about news.

Like chapter 8, chapter 9 looks at regulation of controversial entertainment content. But while chapter 8 was a case study of federal regulation, chapter 9 examines local regulation—specifically, the workings of obscenity and indecency law as applied to municipal cable access television. The study's observation and interviews found that decision-making on the local level was arbitrary. Managers of the access channel were uncertain how to apply legal standards, producers had few clues about what constituted acceptable program material, and at least some producers were not aware of their legal right to appeal censorship of their programs.

Despite the frequent ambiguity of legal standards and the sometimes arbitrary nature of enforcement, there is no denying that many journalists and other media workers are quite concerned about running afoul of the law. Sociologist Gaye Tuchman found as much in her classic study of newswork. Tuchman wrote:

> In my first interview with a newsworker, the vice-president of news at NEWS [a television station Tuchman studied], I quickly learned the importance of credibility. My initial question was, "What should I know to study news?" I was given a text on libel law.[14]

Media workers' fears of being sued, however, probably are exaggerated. Although there are more than 120,000 journalists in the United States,[15] for example, in any given year fewer than a hundred libel lawsuits are filed against U.S. journalists and media organizations.[16] What's more, the media end up winning the vast majority of the lawsuits.[17] Of course, it is possible to become enmeshed in legal questions without actually being sued or suing someone else.

Chapter 10 approaches these issues with a study of how eight Indiana newspapers use lawyers. The merits of *Holding the Media Accountable*'s empirical approach are especially apparent in this chapter. Traditional legal research would review relevant statutes and court decisions in a law library, and would conclude that press law is uniform throughout Indiana. Chapter 10's interviews, by contrast, revealed that press law in action differs tremendously from community to community. Newspapers in large communities use lawyers quite differently than do newspapers in small communities. The results of the study suggest that perceptions of legal problems may depend on community characteristics.

Chapter 11 looks at a state press association and how newspaper managers use it to help them define their newspapers' legal rights. Every state has a press association, but their role in helping shape interpretations of the law had never been studied. The results of the chapter are provocative: Newspapers had three times as many questions about access to information (public records and open meetings) as about libel, for example. The study is based on interviews with press association staff, on internal press association memoranda, and on a survey of editors.

Chapter 12 deals with the intriguing issue of what happens to libel disputes after the U.S. Supreme Court has resolved the constitutional issues the cases present. The overviews of the cases in media law textbooks generally end with the decision of the Supreme Court, but in truth most cases are sent back to lower courts for further proceedings. Chapter 12 reveals that the party who won the legal battle at the Supreme Court level does not always win the legal war in the end. Americans may believe that the Supreme Court is the "court of last resort," but most libel cases live on long after the Supreme Court has dealt with them. The chapter is based on interviews with plaintiffs, defendants, and lawyers in twenty-two libel cases that were dealt with by the U.S. Supreme Court between 1964 and 1990.

A NOTE ON METHOD

All but one of the eleven empirical chapters in *Holding the Media Accountable* are case studies of media accountability in specific communities or regions (the exception is chapter 12, the study of libel cases after they leave the U.S. Supreme Court). The case study method relies heavily on firsthand observation and on information obtained directly from participants in the process under study (e.g., interviews, documents). No such study, by itself, is generalizable in the usual social-science sense.

One of the studies focuses on a Canadian province. The other nine deal with phenomena from the American Midwest, including six studies of media accountability in Indiana alone. The regional nature of the research raises the question of whether the phenomena the case studies explore are widespread. There can be no definitive answer to the question without a survey of media accountability in hundreds of communities of various kinds, and the authors of the chapters make no claim to pure representativeness or absolute generalizability.

That said, many readers will find the situations described in the empirical chapters to be quite familiar. The research was done in the Midwest because that's where the researchers were, but the specific settings were chosen because of their ordinariness. The goal was not to strain to find communities that were perfectly representative—no such community exists—but rather to find communities and states that were "not so atypical as to be unique."[18] If readers hear echoes of their own communities as they move through the chapters, the choices of research settings will have been justified.

THE FUTURE OF MEDIA ACCOUNTABILITY

Although it reveals problems with North American systems of media accountability, *Holding the Media Accountable* is at its core an optimistic book. The scholars whose work it presents believe that the first step in improving a system is to learn about its flaws. The next step is to build on the knowledge of a system's flaws to propose reforms that will "make possible the realistic achievement of the objectives sought," to use Emerson's phrase.

Toward that end, *Holding the Media Accountable* closes with a chapter that synthesizes the results of the empirical chapters and assesses the future of media accountability. The chapter outlines the conditions required for systems of norms such as law and ethics to be useful tools of media accountability, and focuses on the role of citizens in activating such systems. The authors of the studies in *Holding the Media Accountable* view an efficient, accessible system of media accountability as an inherent part of democracy. Their goal is to contribute to the quality of democratic life by research that enhances citizen participation in media accountability.

NOTES

1. Oliver Wendell Holmes, Jr., *The Common Law* (Boston: Little, Brown, 1881), p. 5.
2. Everette E. Dennis and Donald M. Gillmor, "Introduction," in Everette E. Dennis, Donald M. Gillmor, and Theodore L. Glasser, eds., *Media Freedom and Accountability* (New York: Greenwood Press, 1989), p. viii.

3. Peter Desbarats, *Guide to Canadian News Media* (Toronto: Harcourt Brace Jovanovich Canada, 1990), p. 172.

4. David Pritchard, "The Role of Press Councils in a System of Media Accountability: The Case of Quebec," *Canadian Journal of Communication* 16 (February 1991): 73–93.

5. With respect to the influence of community characteristics on media systems, see Phillip J. Tichenor, George A. Donohue, and Clarice N. Olien, *Community Conflict and the Press* (Beverly Hills, Calif.: Sage Publications, 1980). With respect to differences among countries, see David H. Weaver, "The Press and Government Restrictions: A Cross-National Study over Time," *Gazette* 23 (1977): 152–170, and David H. Weaver, Judith M. Buddenbaum, and Jo Ellen Fair, "Press Freedom, Media, and Development, 1950–1979: A Study of 134 Nations," *Journal of Communication* 35 (Spring 1985): 104–117.

6. There is some question whether legal or ethical norms regarding expression have any systematic influence at all. Legal standards regarding expression do not necessarily determine outcomes. See David Kairys, "Freedom of Speech," in David Kairys, ed., *The Politics of Law* (New York: Pantheon Books, 1982), pp. 140–171, and Thomas Streeter, "Beyond Freedom of Speech and the Public Interest: The Relevance of Critical Legal Studies to Communications Policy," *Journal of Communication* 40 (Spring 1990): 43–63. Ethical norms fare no better than law as regulators of journalistic conduct. See David Pritchard and Madelyn Peroni Morgan, "Impact of Ethics Codes on Judgments by Journalists: A Natural Experiment," *Journalism Quarterly* 66 (Winter 1989): 934–941.

7. Thomas I. Emerson, *The System of Freedom of Expression* (New York: Random House, 1970), p. 4.

8. For a more in-depth treatment of the initial stages of disputing, see William L. F. Felstiner, Richard L. Abel, and Austin Sarat, "The Emergence and Transformation of Disputes: Naming, Blaming, Claiming . . . ," *Law & Society Review* 15 (1980–81): 631–654, and David Pritchard, "A New Paradigm for Legal Research in Mass Communication," *Communications and the Law* 8 (August 1986): 51–67.

9. Randall P. Bezanson, Gilbert Cranberg, and John Soloski, *Libel Law and the Press: Myth and Reality* (New York: The Free Press, 1987).

10. Richard V. Ericson, Patricia M. Baranek, and Janet B. Chan, *Negotiating Control: A Study of News Sources* (Toronto: University of Toronto Press, 1989), pp. 308–313.

11. Louise Williams Hermanson, "News Council Complainants: Who Are They and What Do They Want?" *Journalism Quarterly* 70 (Winter 1993): 947–970.

12. Robert Martin, "Libel and Class," *Canadian Journal of Communication* 9 (Spring 1983): 1–14.

13. Commission on Freedom of the Press, *A Free and Responsible Press* (Chicago: University of Chicago Press, 1947), p. 94.

14. Gaye Tuchman, *Making News: A Study in the Construction of Reality* (New York: The Free Press, 1978), p. 83.

15. David H. Weaver and G. Cleveland Wilhoit, *The American Journalist in the 1990s: U.S. News People at the End of an Era* (Mahwah, N.J.: Lawrence Erlbaum, 1996).

16. Bezanson, Cranberg, and Soloski, *Libel Law and the Press,* chap. 6; Donald M. Gillmor, *Power, Publicity, and the Abuse of Libel Law* (New York: Oxford University Press, 1992), p. 135.

17. Bezanson, Cranberg, and Soloski, *Libel Law and the Press,* p. 5; Don R. Pember, *Mass Media Law,* 6th ed. (Madison, Wis.: Brown and Benchmark, 1993), pp. 115–116.

18. Malcolm M. Feeley, *The Process Is the Punishment: Handling Cases in a Lower Criminal Court* (New York: Russell Sage Foundation, 1979), p. xx.

2

The Routine Nature of Journalistic Deception

TOM LULJAK

JOURNALISTS AND THEIR CRITICS PRODUCE A SEEMINGLY END-
LESS OUTPOURING OF OPINION THAT EITHER PRESCRIBES HOW
JOURNALISTS SHOULD ACT IN SITUATIONS THAT RAISE ETHICAL
CONTROVERSIES OR THAT CRITICIZES HOW JOURNALISTS DID ACT
IN A GIVEN CONTROVERSY. ALL TOO OFTEN LOST IN THE HUBBUB IS
THE REALITY OF HOW ORDINARY JOURNALISTS ORDINARILY ACT.

CHAPTER 2 IS ONE OF THE FEW EXISTING STUDIES OF ORDI-
NARY NEWS ETHICS IN ACTION. THE CHAPTER REPORTS THE RE-
SULTS OF AN OBSERVATIONAL STUDY AT A WELL-REGARDED TELE-
VISION NEWS DEPARTMENT IN A SMALL MARKET IN THE MIDWEST.
THE AUTHOR FINDS THAT THE USE OF DECEPTION IN NEWSGATH-
ERING IS CASUAL AND ROUTINE, SO MUCH SO THAT THE JOURNAL-
ISTS HARDLY EVEN THINK OF IT AS DECEPTION.

THE CHAPTER HELPS ESTABLISH TWO IMPORTANT POINTS RE-
LATED TO ACCOUNTABILITY. THE FIRST IS THAT EVEN SMALL NEWS
ORGANIZATIONS IN SEDATE MARKETS ENGAGE IN QUESTIONABLE
BEHAVIOR FOR WHICH THEY COULD BE, AND PERHAPS SHOULD BE,
CALLED TO ACCOUNT. THE SECOND IS THAT THE JOURNALISTS
TEND NOT TO SEE THE BEHAVIOR AS QUESTIONABLE, WHICH SUG-
GESTS THAT THEY MIGHT NOT BE RECEPTIVE TO ANY DEMANDS FOR
ACCOUNTABILITY THAT ARE MADE.

TOM LULJAK KNOWS TELEVISION NEWS INTIMATELY. HE SPENT
TWO DECADES AS A TELEVISION JOURNALIST IN WISCONSIN BE-
FORE MOVING INTO CORPORATE COMMUNICATIONS. AN EARLIER
VERSION OF THIS CHAPTER, WHICH WAS PART OF THE RESEARCH
FOR LULJAK'S MASTER'S THESIS AT THE UNIVERSITY OF WIS-
CONSIN–MILWAUKEE, WAS PRESENTED TO THE ASSOCIATION FOR
EDUCATION IN JOURNALISM AND MASS COMMUNICATION. AT THIS
WRITING, LULJAK IS DIRECTOR OF CORPORATE COMMUNICATIONS
FOR UNITED WISCONSIN SERVICES, INC., AND BLUE CROSS AND
BLUE SHIELD UNITED OF WISCONSIN.

The constant quest for more readers or viewers is a staple of journalism in the United States. News organizations have high regard for journalists who can create news stories that attract and hold audience members' attention.

Information provided by individuals and groups is the raw material of journalism. The raw information is not news until a journalist has fashioned it into a story. Sources' motives for providing information to journalists can be quite diverse, but rarely do they include increasing the size of a news organization's audience. In contrast, prominent among the interests journalists keep in mind as they put together stories is the need to attract and maintain an audience.

Journalists' interest in audience size is at times inconsistent not only with the interests of the people who provide the raw material of the news, but also with various people's perceptions of the public interest. The dominance of news organizations' interest in audience size contributes to doubts about the ethical status of journalism.

Media critic Janet Malcolm, for example, concluded that journalistic work is built upon a foundation of deception. In a widely discussed essay, she wrote:

> Every journalist who is not too stupid or too full of himself to notice what is going on knows that what he does is morally indefensible. He is a kind of confidence man, preying on people's vanity, ignorance, or loneliness, gaining their trust and betraying them without remorse.[1]

Malcolm's assertion begs for confirmation. Is deception common in journalism, or is it rare? Under what conditions does deception occur?

This chapter addresses those questions by reporting the results of an observational study of newswork at a commercial television station in the Midwest. The results suggest that various forms of deception may be a routine component of journalistic work.

BACKGROUND

Sissela Bok describes deception generally as when "we communicate messages meant to mislead [others], meant to make them believe what we ourselves do not believe." According to Bok, "we can do so through gesture, through disguise, by means of action or inaction, even through silence."[2]

In the specific context of journalism, deception "can take many forms, from outright lying, to deceiving, or misleading, or misrepresenting, or merely being less than forthright," according to the authors of an ethics handbook for the Society of Professional Journalists. They added that "all of these actions are intended to cause someone to believe what is not true."[3]

Journalists may justify using deception in a variety of ways. In some cases, they may argue that deception is necessary to obtain information which is a vital public service, such as exposing wrongdoing by government officials or informing consumers of fraudulent business practices. In other cases, the rationales for deception are related more to the news organization's private interest than to the public interest. News organizations compete for audiences. A news organization may perceive that deception will provide it with information that will give it a competitive edge.

Journalists also may make personal decisions to engage in deception, possibly for reasons of convenience, perhaps to protect sources from embarrassment or to try to obtain sensational information that may put the journalist in the spotlight.

There is considerable disagreement among journalists over whether deception in journalism is defensible. In 1977 Ben Bradlee, at the time executive editor of the *Washington Post,* defended the Pulitzer Prize board's decision to deny an award to the *Chicago Sun-Times* for its undercover exposé of municipal corruption, which included the newspaper's buying a tavern and having its journalists operate it for four months.

"In a day in which we are spending thousands of man-hours uncovering deception, we simply cannot deceive," said Bradlee, a member of the Pulitzer Prize board.[4]

Many journalists are more open-minded than Bradlee about deception, however. A national survey of more than a thousand journalists in the early 1990s, for example, found that 60 percent of all journalists, and 90 percent of television journalists, thought using hidden microphones or cameras sometimes may be justified. Television journalists also were more likely than journalists for other media to be open to the use of false identifications in the newsgathering process.[5] Television journalists' high tolerance for deceptive reporting practices has been documented in other surveys, as well.[6]

One of the rare studies that dealt with the actual frequency of questionable reporting methods was a survey of newspaper journalists in the 1980s. It found that 72 percent of the journalists said that at least once a year they used reporting techniques which raised ethical questions. In a book based upon the survey, journalism professor Philip Meyer reported that "the news business is following an unconscious rule that offhand, casual deception is okay, but elaborate and carefully planned deceptions are wicked."[7]

One of the difficulties with using surveys to understand journalists' ethics is that they are based on standardized questionnaires. The problem is that ethical decisions are not standardized. Frank McCulloch noted that the practice of ethics is "inescapably situational. This is the case simply because every situation is so complex and so laden with variables that it is impossible to conceive of anything resembling a common solution."[8]

If the ethical decision-making process in journalism truly is "inescapably situational," then a researcher who wants to focus on the process itself should study journalists in a single situation, thus eliminating factors related to differences between news organizations that can conceal the real forces at work.

The study reported in this chapter used personal observation to gather data among the journalists at a single television station. The method has been used often in a variety of journalism environments by sociologists and other researchers interested in newswork. The findings of such research suggest strongly that journalistic work follows predictable routines.[9] The observation was conducted at a network-affiliate commercial television station in the Midwest. The station consistently topped its competitors in ratings while maintaining a long-standing reputation for quality news. It had received several national and regional awards for journalistic excellence in recent years. I spent fourteen hours over two days meeting with and observing the journalists at the station. The station's news director had granted unlimited access to the news operation, including permission to observe story planning meetings, telephone conversations, meetings between reporters and sources, and private conversations among members of the news staff. I also had the opportunity to interview staff members about their news philosophies and reporting techniques.

The news director was told that the purpose of the study was to investigate various aspects of decision-making in a newsroom, particularly as to ethical concerns. I did not specifically state that I would be looking for instances of deception, although I would have shared that information if anyone had asked. No one did.

From the beginning of the research, the station's news director repeatedly stated that he did not wish to place any constraints on my recording or reporting of the information I gathered. Despite the willingness of the news director to allow his station and his staff members to be identified, I have decided to disguise the name of the television station and the identities of its journalists. I did not ask individual staff members whether they wanted to be identified. Whether or not they would have consented to be identified, I believe that exposing identities could lead to unproductive speculation about the foibles of individuals, the station, or the community that would blur this study's focus on the process of ethical decision-making in journalism.

Accordingly, the names of all individuals at the station have been altered, as have the locations and circumstances of some news stories that might identify the station, which is located in Madison, Wisconsin. I will call the station WSML-TV.

In the course of my fieldwork I observed a variety of behaviors that I classified as deception. The types of deception included a willingness to broadcast misleading information, misrepresentation of motives, concealment of one's role as a reporter, surreptitious recording, misleading of sources, and staging of news events.

I use narrative to describe the deceptive behaviors and the journalists' rationales for them. My goal is to illustrate the differing contexts in which journalists use deception. In some cases, journalists gave quite a bit of thought to the act of deception. In others, journalists used deception with such ease that they apparently had not given much consideration to the ethics of their actions.

THE WSML-TV NEWS STAFF

In television news there is a constant battle over which stories will be told on the air. At WSML the fight over the content of the day's news begins at 9:30 in the morning when an assortment of reporters, producers, and editors—nine people in all—crowds into the small office of news director Bill Benson. They come together to decide what stories the WSML staff will cover during the day. Although the list of story assignments changes throughout the course of a day, the 9:30 A.M. meeting sets the tone for much of the day's decision-making.

As the meeting began on the first day of this study's observation, Benson—a veteran news director—was sparring with his crime reporter, Tim Vaughn. Vaughn was unhappy because one of the local hospitals had refused to release the names of dozens of local university students injured in an accident. Vaughn wanted to push harder to get the information. Benson wasn't so sure.

"I'm on the side of truth," Benson told Vaughn. "But do you want to sit at home and find out your kid is in the hospital while watching TV?"

Vaughn remained unconvinced. Leaning forward, he responded: "What happens if next time it's a plane crash? Who's going to release the names then?"

"The authorities," Benson told his reporter. "That's their job."

In an interview later in the day, Benson said that Vaughn "is a good, solid reporter who pushes hard for what he believes in." But Benson, once a reporter himself, added, "I've been around long enough to know that withholding information for a while is not always a bad thing. I know that rushing ahead can do more harm than good."

Benson's statement was important because, as this study will demonstrate, there sometimes is a contradiction between what journalists say they believe and how they actually behave. The disagreement between Benson and Vaughn over how hard to push for the names of injured students was especially interesting, because in other situations observed during this study Benson attempted to justify a deception designed to broadcast *more* information than authorities desired while Vaughn was willing to cooperate with authorities in a deception that could have resulted in his transmitting inaccurate information to the public.

HELPING SOURCES DECEIVE

"You burn 'em once and you're done."
—Tim Vaughn, police reporter

With cropped hair and a rough complexion, thirty-four-year-old Tim Vaughn did not look like a television news reporter when he walked through Madison's public safety building. If he had been wearing a cheaper suit, he could have been mistaken for one of the cops he spent much of his time covering.

As was clear during his debate with news director Benson, Vaughn could be passionate about seeking complete and accurate information. Vaughn's vision of journalism had another side, though.

Like most police reporters, Vaughn was heavily dependent on law-enforcement sources. For several weeks before my observations at WSML, the Madison police department had been investigating the death of a local man whose body had been found in Chicago. Authorities in Chicago had declared the death a suicide, but a deputy sheriff whom Vaughn met as I accompanied him during his daily reporting at the public safety building was convinced that the man had been murdered. The deputy said police were looking for a way to convince three Madison men that authorities had enough evidence to consider charging them with the murder, even though, the deputy admitted, police did not have sufficient evidence. He told Vaughn he would be willing to do an on-camera interview about the murder investigation if Vaughn agreed to certain conditions.

Dropping his voice to a near-whisper, the deputy suggested that Vaughn assist police by allowing an investigator to use a television interview to broadcast misleading statements in hopes that the three suspects would see them. "We want these guys to think we know more than we really do," the deputy said. Vaughn readily agreed to broadcast misleading information and urged the deputy to notify him when he was ready to put out the message.

Later, explaining why he was willing to cooperate with the deputy in broadcasting a statement that Vaughn knew wasn't true, Vaughn said, "It's a great story. They get the guys and I get the story." Vaughn said he thought that the authorities were correct in their belief that the local suspects committed the murder. The implicit value judgment Vaughn made was that the harm of misleading viewers would be outweighed by the possible arrest of individuals responsible for committing a serious crime. It was not entirely clear how the police officer thought that broadcasting a misleading statement might help solve the crime. During the observed conversation with the officer, Vaughn did not raise the question.

Vaughn believed that his relationship with law-enforcement authorities was important to his success as a reporter. "I'm pretty tight with some of them. There's a bond there of mutual respect," he said. "It's not that I consider them friends. It's just that I don't look at my relationship with them as adversarial."

Despite Vaughn's willingness, the deceptive on-camera interview never took place.

MISREPRESENTATION OF MOTIVES

> *"I realized I've got to loosen her up in order to get any help."*
> —Tim Vaughn, police reporter

WSML's police reporter also was involved in a second form of deception during the time I was at WSML: he misrepresented his motives to a news source.

Among the sources that Vaughn cultivated in the public safety building were the members of law-enforcement agency support staffs. He acknowledged that he paid special attention to the clerks and secretaries, most of them female, who had access to information that could set his stories apart from those of the other television stations in town.

"A lot of the women [clerks] here are bored with their jobs," Vaughn said. "They're nice people who don't mind getting some attention. So I try to have a good relationship with them and it can pay off."

On one of the mornings of this study's observation, the object of Vaughn's attention was a stern-looking female clerk in the sheriff's office. Vaughn was trying to learn more about the participants in an overnight domestic dispute that resulted in a woman stabbing her husband.

"I need some information on one of your old boyfriends," Vaughn told the woman.

Looking up, the clerk said, "*My* boyfriend?"

"Yeah," Vaughn responded, "another one of those ne'er-do-wells you used to date." The woman laughed and asked Vaughn which case he was referring to.

"The guy told his wife he didn't love her anymore and then went to sleep," Vaughn said. "So she *forked* him!"

As Vaughn waited for the clerk to produce a mug shot and a computer printout of the criminal record of the couple involved in the incident, he confided that his banter with the clerk was calculated to win favor with her. When he began covering the office, the woman "hated reporters," he said. "It took me two years to get her trust. I realized I've got to loosen her up in order to get any help. That's why I talk dirty to her."

Whether or not the clerk was aware of Vaughn's selfish motives, it is clear that he intentionally tried to form an emotional bond with her during his daily visits so that he could have greater access to police information. Ethicist Deni Elliott argues that insincere empathy of the kind Vaughn used constitutes serious deception that "plays havoc with the very trust they [journalists] need to maintain their business."[10]

MISREPRESENTATION OF IDENTITY

> *"That was the story and we needed to get it."*
> —Bill Benson, news director

> *"From a résumé perspective, it will be great to have this experience on my tape!"*
> —Laura Cole, student intern reporter

Laura Cole was the youngest and least experienced reporter in the WSML newsroom. She was a senior at the University of Wisconsin–Madison, where she was studying journalism. As part of her final year in school, she was spending a semester as a reporter-intern on the WSML news staff. Because of her inexperience, Benson had not allowed Cole to appear on camera or record the narration track on stories for the first two months of the internship. Cole's lack of air time meant that the general public did not know what she looked like. That made her an ideal reporter to conceal her identity to gain access to a place from which the media had been banned.

Officials at UW–Madison had designated the student seating section at the university's football stadium off-limits to members of the media after a near-tragedy the week before, when dozens of students were seriously injured during a post-game celebration. Some had to be resuscitated after being crushed against a fence adjacent to the football field. Fearful that fan rowdyism would erupt again, the university decided to ban reporters from entering the student seating section of the stadium during the next game.

As soon as he learned of the ban, news director Benson protested to university officials. But despite his contention that the public had a right to know exactly what was happening in the student section, the university denied Benson's request for access. He recalled going to lunch that day thinking, "We have to get that story." That was when he decided that his unknown student intern would be the lead reporter on the story. He determined that the only way to gather the information he believed his viewers should have was to use deception.

The first part of the deceptive scheme concocted by Benson involved having Cole use her student ID card to purchase a ticket for the student section of the stadium, the one which had been declared off-limits to reporters. Cole said she would not have attended the game if she had not been on assignment as a reporter. When buying the ticket, Cole did not tell university authorities that she planned to use it for reporting purposes.

The second part of the scheme involved the use of a hidden recording device. Benson gave Cole a wireless microphone that she concealed under her jacket when she entered the student section. During the game Cole used the microphone to capture the audio portion of interviews she conducted with students. University officials stationed at the entrances to the student section were unable to see the microphone and so could not enforce their no-media policy.

Benson knew that Cole had violated the university's ban on reporters entering the area, but he defended the deception. "That was the story and we needed to get it," he said.

Cole, who acknowledged that she had been nervous about her involvement in the project, was surprised to be doing a story with significant ethical issues so early in her career. She was concerned, however, that her participation in the deception could anger university officials to the extent that they might take some kind of disciplinary action against her.

"I was doing something they didn't want me to do," she said. However, neither Cole nor Benson thought they were doing anything illegal. "Legally, I had the right to be there in the stands," said Cole, adding that "having the news director behind me helped me know I was right."

When questioned about the appropriateness of using deception to gather her interviews, Cole agreed with Benson that the public's right to know how students reacted following the previous week's disturbance overrode any ethical concerns about the reporting techniques. Besides, Cole said, "it gave us video the others didn't have."

Only the audio portions of Cole's interviews were made with equipment concealed from university officials. The video accompanying her interviews was recorded by a cameraman positioned on the stadium sidelines in front of the student section. Because the wireless microphone transmitted the audio on a radio frequency, the cameraman was able to get video even though he was standing hundreds of feet away from Cole and the students she was interviewing. University officials apparently were unaware that the interviews were being videotaped and did nothing to stop them.

In the stands, Cole identified herself to students as a reporter from WSML. She encountered no difficulty in obtaining interviews. "Students like to break the rules," she noted, adding that the "kids all said this is *so* cool."

In reviewing the experience, Cole said that her biggest apprehension about the day's events surrounded news director Benson's decision to identify her in the introduction to her report as a student intern. Cole was concerned that viewers watching her report might be more critical of her on-air performance if they knew that she was still a student and not a full-time professional. "I don't think the average viewer needed to know" that she was an intern, Cole said.

Despite her fear of losing credibility with the audience because she was a student, Cole believed that the experience could prove to be important to her career. "I'd do it again," she said. "From a résumé perspective, it will be great to have this experience on my tape!"

Asked if she had any second thoughts regarding the deception, Cole responded: "I wouldn't do it all the time. People may become apprehensive wondering if we are doing something sneaky. Also, the university may make it more difficult to do any coverage in the future."

Benson, who described himself as extremely conservative in the use of hidden recording techniques, said it was unlikely that the episode would lead to an increase in such reporting by his staff. But he did reserve the right to use undercover procedures again. "There are times when you need it to capture reality," Benson said. "So, there is a place for it, but it can be abused."

Using deception to get a reporter into the student section of the stadium clearly was appropriate because "that's where the news was," Benson said. He added, "The fact that we let the university know we could be ingenious—that doesn't bother me either."

DECEPTION IN "SOFT" NEWS

> *"I view my stories as the P.R. job of the station. It's not our job
> to make them look bad."*
> —Roger Holms, anchor/feature reporter

Sitting at his desk along the back wall of the newsroom, Roger Holms quietly surveyed the activity around him. The pace was quickening for fellow staffers preparing the noon newscast. With less than forty-five minutes before air time, there were scripts to write and videotape to edit. But Holms, one of the most experienced members of the news staff, was not involved in the last-minute work for the noon newscast. It was a good time to talk about his work, he said.

Holms, an anchor of the five o'clock newscast, would not be shifting into high gear for several more hours. Like all anchors, Holms spent most of his working hours in the newsroom instead of out in the community. He and his co-anchor took the lead in selecting stories and writing copy for the top-rated early evening newscast. But although the program included a summary of the hard news of the day, it was best known for the casual, conversational style that the two anchors brought to the show. Their easy banter helped differentiate the five o'clock newscast from the rest of the news programs on WSML.

The softer touch suited Holms just fine. A fifteen-year veteran at WSML, Holms had worked his way into the anchor chair after having covered a wide variety of hard news stories as a general assignment reporter. At the time of the study, the only regular field reporting Holms did involved the production of features, a form of "soft" news. His regular "On the Road" reports had become popular with WSML viewers. Typically, Holms's features focused on an individual who had either an unusual hobby or job or a unique personality.

"I get kidded a lot by the other reporters covering hard news," said Holms. "When they see me working on one of my stories they'll say, 'Who did you talk to this week? A manic-depressive or someone with another compulsive disorder?'"

The teasing didn't bother Holms, though. He said: "I consider myself a journalist. And I think other reporters appreciate my work. They know and I know that you can't do features if you don't do [hard] news."

For Holms the distinction between the two types of stories was important not only because of differences in content but because Holms believed that feature reporting allowed journalists to use a different set of rules. Specifically, Holms believed that hard news stories required a journalist always to "get the other side." As a feature reporter, though, "I don't ever approach a story that way." When he wrote about the personalities his feature stories focused on, he said he "just presents their story."

However, what "their story" actually was sometimes was not the story

Holms ended up reporting to his viewers. He acknowledged that he sometimes engaged in deceptive practices to produce stories that were positive and upbeat.

Ideas for Holms's stories came from a variety of sources. Letters and telephone calls from viewers and stories from small-town newspapers provided a steady stream of information about interesting "characters," as Holms referred to his subjects. Holms screened potential interview subjects by phone and said he usually could pick "good" subjects.

Occasionally, though, when Holms arrived to interview his subject, he discovered that the individual was what he called a "loser." By that, Holms meant that the person he had decided to feature was not the sympathetic or inspiring personality that was the hallmark of his reports. Holms said that the discovery that his subject was a "loser" rarely prevented him from going ahead with a story that ended up portraying the interview subject in a favorable light, even if he believed that such a portrayal was undeserved.

"Sometimes my photographer and I will walk away from a shoot and say, 'This will look good—*on TV,*'" Holms said.

Holms defended his practice of putting a positive spin on interview subjects even when it meant misleading the audience.

"Even if people [the interview subjects] aren't bright, I still try to make them look smart in my story," he said. "I don't want them to look like fools. It's not our job to make them look bad."

Holms, who stopped doing hard news stories because he found them to be "mundane and routine," said he views his feature beat "as the P.R. job of the station." His stories help give newscasts a "human touch," he added.

In addition to deleting material that might create an unsympathetic picture of interview subjects, Holms used another form of deception. Sometimes, he acknowledged, he and his photographer mislead the sources themselves.

"We will roll on everything," he said, referring to the technique he and his photographer used to capture subjects on videotape in unguarded moments. The interviewees were aware that they were going to be the subject of a television story, so Holms said he didn't "feel bad" about recording their actions and comments even if a subject believed the camera was turned off. "It's not like it's undercover camera work," he said.

If Holms were to return to hard news, he believed he would have to change his reporting techniques. "I would have to sit people down for an interview and tell them I was recording," he said.

Covering hard news also would have altered Holms's attitude toward his interview subjects.

"I would become more cynical and skeptical," he said. Hard news reporters "don't take people's word, because [in hard news] it matters." According to Holms, information in hard news stories should be viewed differently than that in features.

STAGING NEWS EVENTS

"Come on, we'll just shoot it tight, so no one will know it is you."
—Anne Marshall, news anchor

Shifting uneasily in her chair, the anchorwoman leaned forward and protested: "I am so uncomfortable with this. I'm used to asking the questions." But Anne Marshall, who co-anchored the noon and 6 P.M. newscasts on WSML, agreed to continue talking about the decision-making process she participated in each day.

Suddenly, Marshall spotted someone leaving an editing room near her desk. Interrupting the interview, Marshall shouted, "Bobbi, can you blow your nose?" Bobbi Janski, a veteran producer at the station, seemed surprised by the question. "What do you want?" she asked.

With a wide grin Marshall explained that she was working on a feature story about a local professor who was trying to find a cure for the common cold. To illustrate the story Marshall was looking for pictures of people suffering the effects of a cold. Janski seemed dubious.

"Come on," Marshall told the producer. "We'll just shoot it tight, so no one will know it is you." Marshall handed a tissue to Janski while one of the staff photographers, who had been standing nearby, aimed his camera and zoomed in for a tight shot of an embarrassed Janski dabbing at her nose.

After the "action" was captured on videotape Marshall told the photographer to walk around the newsroom to obtain video of other members of the staff blowing their noses or sneezing. The photographer protested, telling Marshall, "You better help me with this. People are going to think I'm stupid asking them to do this." Marshall smiled and agreed to accompany the photographer later. Other than discussing their embarrassment, neither Janski nor the photographer challenged Marshall about whether the staged sniffling was an appropriate way to illustrate a news story.

Because of her anchor duties, Marshall did not have many opportunities to go into the field to report stories. Although she said she enjoyed hard news, she did not mind working on the feature story about the possible cold cure. "All of these things are important—what people need to know and what they want to watch," she said.

According to Marshall, the broadcast news industry had changed sharply from what it had been like only a few years earlier. She believed it was no longer possible for broadcast journalists to operate in the revered Edward R. Murrow style.

A heavy reliance on news consultants in the 1990s had led to programming in which "all the superficial elements are highlighted," she said. "News is married to sales because we are there to provide information and sell air time."

DISCUSSION

Two days of observation of the news staff at a commercial television station in the Midwest uncovered direct evidence of several episodes of deception.

The police reporter was involved in two of the episodes. He was willing to broadcast an interview containing information he knew to be false, and he misrepresented his motives for engaging in good-natured (if mildly salacious) banter with a female clerk.

The veteran news director concocted a fairly elaborate scheme that involved a student intern not only concealing her role as a reporter to gain access to student seating in the university stadium but also using a hidden microphone to capture interviews.

A male anchor acknowledged both that he suppressed information that he thought would be embarrassing to the subjects of his feature stories and that his photographer routinely videotaped subjects when the subjects thought the camera was turned off.

A female anchor persuaded co-workers to pretend to be suffering from colds to help her illustrate a story about medical research.

Some of the journalists used deception for reasons of convenience. That was the apparent justification for the police reporter's insincere banter with the female clerk (he wanted to have easier access to information) and for the female anchor's decision to illustrate her story with co-workers (she wouldn't have to leave the newsroom to get pictures of cold sufferers).

Offering viewers the kinds of stories they would find pleasant was the rationale for the anchor who consciously fashioned stories to fit his notion of small-town pastoralism, even when the reality he encountered in the field was at odds with the notion. According to sociologist Herbert Gans, romantic and pleasantly nostalgic themes such as pastoral values are highly prized in news stories because they are so pleasing to audiences.[11] The anchor also did his best to make sure that his carefully sculpted reports did nothing to embarrass their subjects. He was not wrong in saying that his feature reporting served as "the P.R. job of the station."

Journalists in this study justified other episodes of deception in terms of public service, although they also were mindful of the competitive advantages they believed deception could bring. Police reporter Tim Vaughn was willing to broadcast an interview containing false information because he thought it might lead to the capture of murderers, a clear public service. But he was mindful that his willingness to cooperate in the police scheme could land him an exclusive story. "They get the guys and I get the story," he said. The surreptitious reports from the student seating section in the football stadium allowed the public to know what was going on there and also "gave us video the others didn't have," as student intern Laura Cole noted. Cole also was honest about her self-interest: "From a résumé perspective, it will be great to have this experience on my tape!"

Clearly, considerations other than public service played prominent roles in the deception observed at WSML. The need to attract a larger share of the available audience, either by besting other stations or by airing features that consciously stressed pastoral values, loomed large. However, audience considerations were not the only forces at work; convenience and notions of public service also influenced decisions to engage in deception.

Some of the decisions to engage in deception were the result of careful thought and planning. The elaborate scheme involving the student intern reporter and the football game was an example. Other decisions, in contrast, involved little or no discussion. The police reporter's eagerness to air what he knew to be a misleading police statement and the anchor's snap decision to illustrate her story about colds with staged sniffling were examples. Although it is impossible to make broad generalizations based on fourteen hours of observation in one newsroom, it seems clear that many members of the WSML news staff considered small-scale deception to be a legitimate journalistic strategy that did not pose ethical questions serious enough to merit debate.

That so much deception was encountered in the fourteen hours of field research suggests not only that deception is a legitimate journalistic strategy at WSML, but that it is a routine strategy. This conclusion is consistent with the research that has found that journalistic work follows predictable routines. What had not been previously realized is the extent to which deception can be part of the routine.

The frequent occurrence of deception in such a short period was striking because the journalists had an incentive to conceal deceptive practices from an outside observer. Deception in journalism is massively unpopular with the public, and revealing that a station's journalists routinely engage in deception could have had drastic consequences for the station's ratings. If anything, then, this study may under-report the extent of deception at WSML.

In addition to its findings, this study validated the use of observation and in-person interviews as means of learning about journalistic behavior. Surveys using standardized questionnaires certainly have their uses, but it is unlikely that they could have uncovered the extent of deception at WSML, perhaps because the activity is so routine that the journalists do not consider it deceptive.

The frequency of deception raises important questions about the ethical behavior of journalists. A key question is whether deception is always wrong. The wide variety of deceptive practices observed during this study and the significant debate that has taken place within the journalistic community suggest that there is no easy yes-or-no answer to the question. Instead, journalists who think about the issue of deception are likely to focus on when deception can be justified and whether it can be avoided by using different reporting methods that will still produce the desired information.

Such discussions were rare in this study, however. News director Benson and student intern reporter Cole believed that surreptitious recording was the only way to show the public what was happening in the student seating section of the football arena that had been ruled off-limits to reporters. Although they captured exclusive video, neither was able to cite the value the surreptitious recording ultimately had on the public's understanding of the issue.

Reporter Tim Vaughn, covering the police and court beat, spoke proudly of his ability to gather information from sometimes reluctant sources and described his willingness to broadcast misleading material that might lead to the arrest of criminal suspects. Like Benson, Vaughn was pleased with the exclusive nature of his reports but never really considered alternate, nondeceptive methods of gathering the information.

While Benson and Vaughn used deception in connection with public policy or public safety stories, the two other examples of deception that were observed involved feature-oriented news material. In such cases no public-service rationale for deception was even advanced.

The wide variance in the amount of discussion that occurred among members of the news staff before a deceptive act is one of the most important findings of this study. Although some of the deceptions occurred only after extensive debate within the newsroom, other deceptions were used by journalists who appeared to have given little prior thought to their actions.

By not considering alternatives, reporters run the risk of making deceptive reporting techniques a standard form of journalistic behavior. The result may be a quicker and more convenient process for gathering the news. But it also may lead to an erosion of public confidence in the news media as a responsible and trusted source of information, particularly if the journalist does not share with viewers the fact that deception was used in the newsgathering process and the rationale for the deception.

The irony is that journalistic deception, often inspired by a desire to gain the biggest possible share of the available audience, over time may undermine public confidence in the integrity of a station's newsgathering process, thus reducing the size of the audience for its news programming.

NOTES

1. Janet Malcolm, *The Journalist and the Murderer* (New York: Knopf, 1990), p. 1.

2. Sissela Bok, *Lying: Moral Choice in Public and Private Life* (New York: Random House, 1978), p. 13.

3. Jay Black, Bob Steele, and Ralph Barney, *Doing Ethics in Journalism* (Greencastle, Ind.: Society of Professional Journalists, 1992), p. 109.

4. Quoted in David Shaw, *Press Watch: A Provocative Look at How Newspapers Report the News* (New York: Macmillan, 1984), p. 139.

5. David Weaver and G. Cleveland Wilhoit, *The American Journalist in the 1990s: U.S. News People at the End of an Era* (Mahwah, N.J.: Lawrence Erlbaum, 1996).

6. K. Tim Wulfmeyer, "Defining Ethics in Electronic Journalism: Perceptions of News Directors," *Journalism Quarterly* 67 (1990): 984–991.

7. Philip Meyer, *Ethical Journalism* (Lanham, Md.: University Press of America, 1987), p. 81.

8. Frank McCulloch, *Drawing the Line: How 31 Editors Solved Their Toughest Ethical Dilemmas* (Washington, D.C.: ASNE Foundation, 1984), p. v.

9. See, e.g., Gaye Tuchman, *Making News: A Study in the Construction of Reality* (New York: The Free Press, 1978); Herbert J. Gans, *Deciding What's News* (New York: Random House, 1979); and Mark Fishman, *Manufacturing the News* (Austin: University of Texas Press, 1980).

10. Deni Elliott, "Journalistic Deception," in Peter Y. Windt, Peter C. Appleby, Margaret P. Battin, Leslie P. Francis, and Bruce M. Landesman, eds., *Ethical Issues in the Professions* (Englewood Cliffs, N.J.: Prentice-Hall, 1989), p. 144.

11. Gans, *Deciding What's News*, pp. 48–50.

3

Why Unhappy Subjects of News Coverage Rarely Complain

DAVID PRITCHARD

CHAPTER 2 DOCUMENTED HOW JOURNALISTS SOMETIMES CUT
ETHICAL CORNERS, EXHIBITING A SURPRISING READINESS TO EN-
GAGE IN BEHAVIOR THAT THEIR SOURCES AND AUDIENCE MEM-
BERS MIGHT FIND QUESTIONABLE. ONE WOULD EXPECT SUBJECTS
OF SUCH NEWS COVERAGE TO BE UNHAPPY WITH JOURNALISTS'
BEHAVIOR AND TO DEMAND AN EXPLANATION OR JUSTIFICATION
FOR IT.

CHAPTER 3 CONFIRMS THAT MANY SUBJECTS OF ORDINARY
NEWS STORIES ARE UNHAPPY WITH THE STORIES. HOWEVER,
DESPITE THE FACT THAT THEY HAVE NAMED PROBLEMS WITH HOW
THEY WERE PORTRAYED AND OFTEN HAVE BLAMED THE NEWS OR-
GANIZATION FOR THE PROBLEMS, THE UNHAPPY SUBJECTS RARE-
LY MADE A CLAIM TO THE NEWS ORGANIZATION. THEIR FAILURE
TO MAKE CLAIMS MEANT THAT THE ACCOUNTABILITY PROCESS,
WHICH DEPENDS ON CLAIMS, NEVER INVOLVED THE NEWS ORGANI-
ZATION.

THAT THE UNHAPPY SUBJECTS DIDN'T MAKE CLAIMS TO THE
NEWS ORGANIZATION DOES NOT MEAN THAT THEY REACTED PAS-
SIVELY TO WHAT THEY CONSIDERED TO BE THE NEWS ORGANIZA-
TION'S FLAWED PORTRAYAL. RATHER, INTERVIEWS SHOWED THAT
UNHAPPY SUBJECTS OFTEN TOOK ACTIVE STEPS TO ASSESS HOW
FRIENDS, CO-WORKERS, AND FAMILY MEMBERS REACTED TO THE
NEWS STORY. IF THE OTHERS WEREN'T UPSET WITH THE STORY
—AND THAT WAS THE TYPICAL CASE—THEN THE PERSON WHO
HAD BEEN THE SUBJECT OF THE STORY WASN'T UPSET EITHER. IF
SOMEONE WAS UPSET, HOWEVER, THE SUBJECT OF THE STORY
WENT TO GREAT PAINS TO REPAIR THE DAMAGE.

EARLIER VERSIONS OF THIS RESEARCH WERE PRESENTED
TO NATIONAL MEETINGS OF THE LAW AND SOCIETY ASSOCIATION
AND THE ASSOCIATION FOR EDUCATION IN JOURNALISM AND MASS
COMMUNICATION. THE CHAPTER'S AUTHOR, DAVID PRITCHARD, IS
A PROFESSOR IN THE DEPARTMENT OF JOURNALISM AND MASS COM-
MUNICATION AT THE UNIVERSITY OF WISCONSIN–MILWAUKEE.

Media accountability research to date has focused principally on people who have made active decisions to try to hold the media accountable by doing such things as writing letters to the editor, complaining to a news ombudsman or press council, or suing a news organization. No studies have examined the behavior of people who believed they had been wronged by the media, but who did not pursue the accountability process by making a complaint.

This chapter fills that gap, highlighting interviews with ordinary people who had been featured in stories in a typical American daily newspaper. Although almost half the subjects[1] perceived inaccuracies or other problems in the stories, none sought a remedy or even an explanation from the newspaper. That is not to say that the subjects were passive or stoic in the face of what they considered to be inaccuracy. Indeed, most took active steps to repair the damage they feared the news stories had caused to their relationships with friends, family, or co-workers—essentially, to their reputations. Because these reputations were private, the repair work was private. Having had one encounter with the newspaper turn out badly, the "victims" of inaccuracies in routine news stories preferred to assess and repair the reputational damage themselves, without any assistance from the newspaper.

In terms of the accountability process outlined in chapter 1, the present study examines people who name a problem with media content, who may or may not blame the media for the problem, and who do not make a claim to the media for a remedy. The research focuses not on well-known politicians and celebrities who deal with the media so often that the experience for them is commonplace. Instead, the study looks at ordinary people in a Midwestern town, many of whom tend to think that having the local paper mention them in a story is a pretty big deal.

REFERENCE GROUPS AND REPUTATION

Reference groups are sets of people or organizations to which a person owes allegiance and from which the subject takes cues for behavior.[2] The reputations of people who are not public figures are limited largely to their reference groups: their families, friends, and co-workers. Individuals generally try to influence how they are perceived by members of their reference groups; they hope to control the nature of the messages about them that circulate within their social networks. Individuals who become subjects of news stories, though, cede a certain amount of control to the journalists who prepare the stories.

This loss of control can cause problems, because reporters experience routine news stories quite differently than do the stories' subjects. Reporters write lots of routine stories, investing relatively little time and energy in any single one. For the ordinary citizen, in contrast, taking part in a news story can be a memorable experience. Especially in smaller communities, members of a subject's reference groups are quite likely to pay attention to the news story, and the subject awaits their comments as eagerly as Broadway actors await reviews of an opening-night performance.

The wait for "reviews" can be stressful for subjects of news coverage, who experience uncertainty about how family members, friends, and co-workers will react to the newspaper's portrayal. Subjects wonder whether reference group members will blame them for any perceived deficiencies in the story.

Subjects of a news story may define a news story as deficient for any number of reasons. They may find a story to be unflattering, or they may think that the story should have emphasized themes that the reporter did not highlight. Even if a story contains no errors of unambiguous fact, subjects and members of their reference groups may define the story as inaccurate. Surveys of subjects of news coverage reveal that roughly half of all news articles contain what subjects consider to be errors.[3]

Just as news is socially constructed,[4] so is inaccuracy. Some perceived errors are clear mistakes of objective fact (e.g., incorrect addresses, misspelled names), but subjects of news coverage also tend to define as an error any deviation from their conception of what the story should be.[5] That subjects and reporters often have different ideas about how a story should turn out may help account for the fact that reporters disagree with as many as 80 percent of subjects' claims of error.[6] William Tillinghast concluded that "error is largely a state of mind," with subjects of coverage "matching published information not only against their knowledge but also against their expectations."[7]

The nature of the relationship between the subject and the reporter also influences perceptions of error. Newsmakers who are personally acquainted with someone who works at the newspaper are less likely to perceive errors than are people who do not know a newspaper employee. When they do perceive errors, they consider them to be less serious than do people who are not personally acquainted with a newspaper employee.[8]

In addition, subjects of news coverage vary in their ability to predict and control what will be published. That is, subjects vary in their ability to minimize the deviation between the story they hoped to see published and the story that actually was published. The greater the subject's ability to control what is published, the less likely the subject is to perceive error.[9] Similarly, the greater a subject's ability to control what is published, the less stress the news story is likely to cause within the subject's reference groups.

In general, subjects who represent legitimated organizations and who have experience with the press are better able than other subjects to control how they are portrayed.[10] When a subject has had frequent previous dealings with a reporter, the subject has a fair amount of control over the stories the reporter writes. In such cases, the mutually beneficial continuing relationship between subject and reporter suggests a community of interest that the reporter will be careful not to disturb. If, however, there is no continuing relationship between subject and reporter, the subject will have less influence over the content of the story—in part because the reporter may treat the story more casually.

METHOD

This study's data come from interviews with people who were mentioned in news stories in an Indiana newspaper typical of American dailies in size (about 30,000 circulation Monday through Saturday, 45,000 circulation Sunday) and patterns of news coverage. Attempts were made to contact all local residents who were quoted or mentioned significantly in staff-written, bylined stories in the main news section of the newspaper during an initial two-week period several years ago and a one-week period four years later.[11] Telephone interviews with sixty-one subjects of news coverage, about half of the total number of subjects for the two time periods, were completed.[12]

The first questions in the interviews were designed to determine whether respondents were aware that the newspaper had published a story that mentioned them and whether they were satisfied with the story. All respondents were aware that the newspaper had published a story mentioning them. If they claimed to be very satisfied, they were asked to evaluate the story's fairness and accuracy before the interview was terminated. Respondents who indicated anything less than total satisfaction were asked a variety of questions about why they were not satisfied (i.e., why they had named a problem), whether they blamed the newspaper for the problem(s) with the story, whether they had contacted anyone at the newspaper about the problem with the story, and what other actions the story caused them to take. The dissatisfied respondents also were asked to evaluate the story's fairness and accuracy.

The interviews, which were tape-recorded and then transcribed, ranged from four to forty-five minutes in length. Some of the interviews were short because the people mentioned in the newspaper did not find the story to be deficient in any way. Other interviews were long, largely because respondents who had found the news story deficient did not respond passively to the questionnaire. Instead, they tended to use the first few questions of the survey as a springboard into often-lengthy appraisals of their encounter with the press— what the reporter could have done differently, what they (the subjects) could have done differently.

The result was that the interviews were less rigidly structured than initially intended. The respondents' eagerness to talk sometimes disrupted the orderly administration of the questionnaire, but that lack of tidiness was more than offset by the richness of their comments in what often turned out to be semi-structured conversations with the interviewers. It was apparent that many of the respondents had given a lot of thought to the experience of being the focus of press attention. A rough indication of the salience of the experience for the respondents was the fact that none of them refused to be interviewed for this study.

About half (28) of the 61 subjects found the newspaper stories that mentioned them to be deficient in some respect, and most of them (26) were able to name a specific problem with the content. Fifteen of the 26 who named a problem also blamed the newspaper for the problem. Most of those 15 people thought about asking the newspaper to remedy the problem, generally by publishing a correction or clarification, but none of them ever contacted the newspaper to make a claim for corrective action. Instead, they initially assessed the level of damage to their reputations within their reference groups. In some cases, they learned that the damage was minimal or nonexistent, so no further action was necessary. In other cases, the damage was significant to them. In such instances the subjects of the news story negotiated the meaning of the perceived deficiency in the story with members of their reference groups. In every case the negotiation was at least partially successful, repairing their reputations and thus eliminating the need for making a claim to the newspaper.

Subjects' attitudes toward the news stories that mentioned them were directly related to how they thought members of their reference groups would react. Initially, the subjects who named a problem with the news story perceived a threat to their relationships with members of their reference groups. They then worked to shore up relationships by constructing a meaning of the experience that was satisfactory not only to them but to their reference groups. After that process was successful, the subjects felt little or no continuing sense of grievance against the newspaper, and thus made no claim.

Some of this study's subjects had agreed to cooperate with the newspaper on a story with the intention of enhancing their position in their social network. These subjects apparently hoped that their positive mentions of reference group members would be published and would please the reference group members. Several subjects who had seen the news story as a way to enhance their status were bothered by seemingly trivial inaccuracies or omissions in news stories. Their major concern was that family, friends, or co-workers would blame them for the inaccuracies or omissions. Subjects whose ongoing relationships were threatened in this fashion were angry at the newspaper until others in their social network indicated that they weren't upset by the inaccuracies or omissions. The case of a retired foundry worker was typical:

Were you satisfied with the story?

Yeah. The only thing was, he [the reporter] said we had eight grandsons, but we've got seven grandsons and one granddaughter. The thing that kind of got me, my granddaughter was here Sun-

> day—they'd seen the paper down to her grandfather's, her mother's mom and dad—and she said, "Now, Grandpa, don't you worry about that." Well, I said I wish they'd mentioned her because she was the only girl in our family.
>
> *Did the story do anything like make you cancel your subscription to the paper or tell your friends that the paper was inaccurate?*
>
> Well, no; I get a lot of compliments on the story. Yeah, there's a lot of 'em. They call me the celebrity!

The former foundry worker had been upset that his granddaughter hadn't been mentioned in the story. After she said she wasn't upset, the subject was pleased with the story; he could revert to the role of celebrity within his network of family and friends.

In general, subjects who perceived errors in stories were quick to assess the possibility of damage. A reporter who interviewed a woman at a pro-choice rally managed to misquote her in the story about the rally. The woman thought about asking the newspaper for a correction but didn't after she realized that her family and friends weren't upset. She said: "My husband told me it didn't sound that bad, so I said, 'O.K.' Everybody else said, 'Great quote!' They were glad I was in there [in the story]."

Some subjects hoped to satisfy both organizational and personal goals by talking with a reporter. An American Legion member active in planning for Memorial Day celebrations, for example, liked the fact that the Legion was getting some ink in the local paper.

> *Were you satisfied with the story?*
>
> Well, I had to be satisfied because it was talking about the veterans doing things for the community and so forth and so on. That was the big idea, right there.

But his pleasure at that organizational success was tempered by the reporter's failure to mention one of the subject's friends, who the subject thought deserved credit for helping plan the festivities. Several days after the story appeared, the subject had a chance encounter with the reporter who wrote the story. Here's what the subject said about his conversation with the reporter:

> I told her, like I just told you, that I liked it [the story] 75 percent, but she forgot to mention the name of a very specific thing. She said, "Well, I didn't get that note." I said, "I know something happened; that's a good excuse, as far as I'm concerned, but you got me in trouble with one of my friends." That was the end of the conversation.

He described his efforts to repair his relationship with his friend this way:

> This other person that I'm speaking of, he's thought about it and taken it in good grace and I'm trying my best to make it up to him. He's a heck of a nice fella and I just hate it in the worst way. Originally, he was a little curious—why was it done that way? I said, "Well I didn't do it, that's the way it was reported." Now that he's thought about it, he's slept on it, he's over it now and it's a joking matter now. We're not worried about it. We don't get serious about something like that; it's not a life or death situation. But this young lady [the reporter], she goofed it!

The subject's friend apparently had been upset at not being mentioned, so much so that the subject complained about the omission in his chance encounter with the reporter. Although the friend finally came to terms with the omission, it was still important to the subject that others know that the reporter "goofed it."

Subjects whose motive for cooperating with the newspaper was to strengthen relationships with family and friends often focused on small errors and omissions; subjects who cooperated with the newspaper as part of an organizational strategy were much more concerned with the overall tone of the story. Such sources, who typically represented established organizations and who had previous experience with reporters, tended to overlook errors of fact and reporter-source etiquette so long as the gaffes did not cast the source's organization in a bad light.

Sources who represent legitimate organizations in a small community can manipulate press coverage with relative ease.[13] Such coverage often is scripted by the organization, with full cooperation from the reporter. Not surprisingly, the organizational representatives in this study claimed to be pleased with the reporters who were so cooperative and with the resulting stories, even when the stories contained clear errors. Such claims by news sources may reflect more a desire to declare success than actual success, but there was no denying that there were many actual successes.

The county planner, for example, was the sole source for a story outlining her efforts to win support in rural parts of the county for a controversial land-use plan to control growth. The planner said she was "very satisfied" with the story, which was written by a reporter who, she believed, was a willing participant in her strategy to win approval for the plan.

> I'm working pretty closely with the reporter on this plan, and it's essential that it get publicized in, with the proper attitude, let's say, and he's very aware of that and he's been extremely helpful.
>
> *Did you think the story was fair?*
>
> Oh yeah—it was exactly what I wanted.

The planner thought the story was fair because it was "exactly what I wanted." Opponents of the proposed plan, whose existence was not even hinted at in the story, may have had a different view of the fairness of the story. For purposes of this study, though, the important point is the perfect fit between the story the planner expected and the story that was published. The planner perceived no deficiency, no errors, in the story.

In a similar vein, the local school superintendent, who was frequently mentioned in the newspaper, said he had no complaints at all about news coverage of his activities.

> In three years, I've never had an unfair news story. Oh, sometimes, because of editorial needs, they'll have to cut out some meaningful comments, but I've had excellent accuracy in their reporting.

Now, it is barely conceivable that a daily newspaper did not make a single factual error in three years of intense coverage of the public schools. What was important to the superintendent was the tone of the coverage, which was overwhelmingly positive. A clue to the reason for the positive nature of the coverage came from the reporter who covered the schools during most of the superintendent's three-year tenure. The reporter said that he had been "very impressed" with the superintendent from the start, and acknowledged that his coverage undoubtedly reflected that assessment.

The county planner and the school superintendent represented important local government agencies. Representatives of nongovernmental organizations who were hoping that coverage would enhance their groups' image were generally less media-wise, but equally satisfied with how their organizations were portrayed.

A woman who was one of several people trying to organize a local chapter of Mothers Against Drunk Driving, for example, was happy with a newspaper feature about the effort.

> Really, I thought it was an excellent article. She [the reporter] was accurate, she quoted everyone, you know, what they said, accurately, she did a lot of research into, you know, more than what we were able to tell her about especially one accident in particular, and she even called the parties involved and got a quote from them and she called several people in the county and I think she did a real good job.

A story about the local hospital's plan to offer incentives to attract nurses to certain high-need areas illustrates these processes in more depth. Although the story contained errors, it did portray the hospital as taking active steps to solve the serious problem of a shortage of nurses. In many ways the story was a journalistic disaster, but the hospital's vice president of patient care thought it was a positive story anyway:

> The hospital is pleased with the article. We were unhappy with a couple of kind of background items. One is that—I was very im-

pressed with the gal who interviewed me; I thought she did a very nice job, except her equipment didn't work. She had a tape recorder, which did not work, which is not a negative to her, except she hadn't taken notes because the tape recorder had started out working, and I felt it would have been appropriate to check the quotes, since they weren't real quotes.

So she kind of tried to remember what the quotes were when she got back to the newspaper office?

Right. We knew that the equipment had been down and I had encouraged her to call back. I would have appreciated that. The other item was that the hospital's media policy is that we certainly will make our employees available to talk to media concerning issues, but the media policy wasn't followed in this example. One of my staff members was interviewed, and the hospital was not aware that was happening.

The interviewer knew that the reporter (a student intern at the newspaper) and the staff member (a nurse) had been classmates in a recently completed course at the local university. He mentioned the fact to the hospital administrator, who had not known it. Despite the fact that the two young women (the reporter and the nurse) had been classmates, the administrator continued to say that the nurse should have refused to talk to the reporter without first getting clearance from the hospital's public relations department.

In the story, the nurse said that the reality of working in a hospital was quite different from what she had thought it would be. "I was very idealistic in the beginning and became very realistic—almost cynical," the reporter quoted the nurse as saying. "As soon as you see a patient die or have to chop off another patient's leg because he is not responsive to antibiotics, that shoots your idealism in the rear end."

The hospital administrator was bothered by the quote not because she doubted that it accurately reflected the nurse's feelings, but rather because she thought the nurse should have given a more positive portrayal of hospital life.

> She was speaking as a hospital nurse, and her comments were kind of, you know, we're sensitive to that. People don't come in and get their legs chopped off every day, and for that to be in the paper—kind of sensationalism—that's something that's very rare.

The nurse's quote was the only thing about the story that the administrator perceived as a problem. The reason? The quote focused on some of the ugly things, such as deaths and amputations, that happen in hospitals. The story's factual errors and garbled quotes, in contrast, did not portray the hospital in a negative light. In fact, the administrator defined the story as accurate.

> *Despite the fact that the quotes weren't exact, that the story er-*
> *roneously called a nursing consultant a staff nurse, and that the*
> *reporter didn't ask permission to talk to the nurse, was the story*
> *accurate?*

It was very accurate. There wasn't anything in there that was questionable. Oh, she gave me some years on my life, but nobody cared
about that but me. She [the reporter] said I graduated from high
school in the '60s [actual graduation date: 1974]. But that didn't
really make any difference; that didn't matter to anyone but me.

From the administrator's point of view, the important thing was that the
hospital be portrayed in a positive light. Factual inaccuracies and semifabri-
cated quotes were less serious than what hospital officials considered to be a
true but sensational comment from a nurse.

Interestingly, the nurse who had been quoted took a similar view. As noted
earlier, the nurse and the reporter had been classmates at the local university.
Their acquaintance made it easy for the reporter to seek out the nurse as a
source, difficult for the nurse to refuse, and difficult for the nurse to blame the
reporter for any problem with the story. When the nurse heard informally that
"someone in the hierarchy" at the hospital was displeased with her, she blamed
herself for the problem.

> *Were you satisfied with the story?*

Well, she quoted me accurately—I wish she hadn't, but she did.

> *What kinds of problems did you see with the story?*

Well, they were self-induced. They were things that I had said that
I thought I could have said better. Where I said chopping off a
patient's leg really kicks your idealism in the rear end—I've gotten
several comments on that. I probably could have phrased that a
little bit better.

> *But that's what you really think?*

Well, yes.

The nurse's conflict stemmed from the competing interests of two distinct
reference groups. A desire to enhance her status within her university reference
group led her to grant the interview; her loss of status within her hospital reference group led her to regret having given it. The fact that the nurse's quote
was honest, accurately reported, and highly relevant to the story did not prevent
the nurse, like the hospital administrator, from defining publication of the quote
as a problem. The nurse blamed herself for the problem, though, so she never
considered making a claim to the newspaper for corrective action.

Subjects' difficulty controlling what gets published no doubt adds to many citizens' skepticism of the press. Such skepticism was much in evidence in this study. For example, the American Legion member who had wanted his friend to be mentioned in a story said, "I don't trust them reporters any further than I can throw 'em, as far as that goes. Every time you talk to a reporter, you get in trouble. They don't print it word for word, and you've got an argument on your hands the next day."

The woman who was active in the effort to organize a MADD chapter had such skepticism about the press that she said she was surprised that her encounter with the reporter had worked out so well.

> I was real pleased; I was surprised.

> *Why?*

> Well, I hear that a lot of reporting that goes on in the paper that's inaccurate. I guess maybe more on the statewide and national levels, but I guess the local writers are closer to home and they would maybe have to, you know, face up to anything that was printed incorrectly.

The fact is, however, that very few journalists ever did have to "face up" to anything. Twenty-six of the sixty-one subjects in this study named a problem, and fifteen blamed the newspaper for the problem, but none of the subjects contacted someone at the newspaper to make a claim for some sort of remedy.

Whether or not the subjects blamed the newspaper for the problem did not seem to be the key factor in how they reacted to the problem. When relationships were threatened by the newspaper story, subjects acted quickly to limit the damage. When relationships were not threatened, subjects simply let the matter slide. A high-school senior who spoke at her school's graduation ceremonies, for example, noted that the portion of the story that summarized her speech contained inaccuracies.

> I thought it was an O.K. article, except there's some things [in the story] that I didn't even mention. Like, they say I talked about poverty and I never once mentioned poverty. I mean, I wasn't upset about it, but I mean I didn't mention anything even close to poverty. It was kind of funny. I thought maybe they didn't pay really close attention, but I wasn't upset.

Finally, a physician, an AIDS specialist who said that the newspaper's report of a speech he gave about AIDS contained a glaring factual error about a basic medical fact, also decided not to seek a correction.

> It is possible that I misstated it at that moment. I cannot rewind my internal tape recorder and know with accuracy what I actually said, but I had tried to make that point so clearly.

Did you contact the newspaper to ask for a correction?

No, I did not.

Why not?

Because I felt that the public reading that would in all likelihood not understand the correction. I decided it wasn't worth it.

The doctor added that people in the medical community who knew him—members of his professional reference group—would realize that he wasn't responsible for the mistake. He was far more concerned about what fellow AIDS specialists thought about him than the fact that readers of the news story had been misinformed.

In general, the subjects in this study were more interested in assessing the damage to their reputations within their reference groups, and repairing it if necessary, than in correcting inaccurate or misleading information that the newspaper had disseminated to tens of thousands of people.

DISCUSSION

This study explored what people do when newspaper stories cause problems for them. The results suggest that, although many people experience problems after being mentioned in routine newspaper stories, they are unlikely to ask the newspaper to help them solve the problems.

About half of the people mentioned in local news stories perceived problems with the stories, problems that they often defined as inaccuracies. Some stories did contain unambiguous errors of fact, but subjects of news coverage also tended to define as errors any omission of information they wanted included or inclusion of information they did not want to see in the story, even if they had furnished it. None of the dissatisfied subjects, however, asked the newspaper to publish a correction or clarification. In terms of the accountability process outlined in chapter 1, the subjects named problems, and they often blamed the newspaper for the problems. But none of them made a claim to the newspaper. The accountability process, which depends on claims, never involved the newspaper.

This is not to say, however, that the subjects of news coverage were passive. Just the opposite: they were quite active in assessing the impact of the problematic news stories on their reputations with their friends, family, and co-workers and, if necessary, taking steps to repair their reputations. From the subject's point of view, satisfactory news stories were those that didn't damage relationships with members of their reference groups. Strict factual accuracy was a secondary consideration for ordinary citizens and organizational representatives alike.

For journalists, in contrast, factual accuracy is vital. Indeed, the credo of the newspaper in this study, published daily on its masthead, was: "The policy of this newspaper is to strive for accuracy! Like perfection, total accuracy may be unattainable; however, it will remain our primary goal and we will not feel satisfied until it is within our grasp."

Told of the results of this study, the newspaper's editor was surprised to learn that stories caused problems for almost half of the people they mentioned. He had been assuming that most people who were unhappy with how they had been portrayed either called him or wrote a letter to the newspaper. In fact, he considered himself to be very accessible to people who had complaints about the newspaper's performance. Every week he reserved two hours to take phone calls from people who wanted to talk about the newspaper; this "Call the Editor" program was regularly publicized with a large display ad in the newspaper. In addition, virtually all the letters sent to the editor were published on the editorial page. But none of the subjects in this study called the editor, wrote letters, or contacted the newspaper in any way.

It is important to note that the newspaper did not go out of its way to displease any of the twenty-six unhappy subjects in this study. None of the stories was nasty or adversarial. Many of the stories that caused problems were factually accurate; the errors in other stories were clearly unintentional, and in most cases seemed trivial to an outsider.

To someone on the inside of a social network, though, "trivial" errors may create uncertainty that leads to strained relationships. When that happens, subjects work to repair relationships. If, as this study and the newspaper accuracy studies cited above suggest, approximately half of all newspaper stories contain what subjects consider to be errors, then the type of damage-control behavior described above may be quite common. In fact, if half of all newspaper stories fail to satisfy subjects, then it may occur thousands or tens of thousands of times a day.

Each perceived error is fairly minor, each bit of damage control fairly easy to accomplish. The phenomenon is invisible to journalists because, as this study has shown, unhappy subjects rarely complain about perceived errors. In the aggregate, though, the accumulation of perceived error may have serious long-term implications for citizens' trust in the news media.

NOTES

The author is indebted to Dan Berkowitz, David Boeyink, Bob Drechsel, Linda Lawson, Karen Riggs, and Kathy Rogers for insightful comments on various portions of this research, and to John Barr for conducting the second set of interviews.

1. This study uses the word "subject" to mean people who have been prominently

mentioned in a news story. "Subject" is a more apt word than "source," because some subjects are not sources; i.e., they do not provide information directly to the news organization. Similarly, some sources are not subjects; they provide information to a news organization, but are not mentioned in the resulting stories. For example, a person involved in an automobile accident would be a subject, but not a source, if a news organization produced a story about the accident from information gleaned solely from police reports. The police officer who granted access to the reports, in turn, would be a source, but not a subject.

2. John Dimmick, "The Gate-Keeper: An Uncertainty Theory," *Journalism Monographs* 37 (1974). See also Sally Falk Moore, "Law and Social Change: The Semi-Autonomous Social Field as an Appropriate Subject of Study," *Law & Society Review* 7 (1973): 719–746, and Dianne Lynne Cherry, "Newspaper People's 'Significant Others': Ethics as a Function of Reference Groups," *Newspaper Research Journal* 6(3) (1985): 33–46.

3. Mitchell V. Charnley, "Preliminary Notes on a Study of Newspaper Accuracy," *Journalism Quarterly* 13 (1936): 394–401; Fred C. Berry, "A Study of Accuracy in Local News Stories of Three Dailies," *Journalism Quarterly* 44 (1967): 482–490; William C. Blankenburg, "News Accuracy: Some Findings on the Meaning of Errors," *Journal of Communication* 20 (1970): 375–386; Hal Marshall, "Newspaper Accuracy in Tucson," *Journalism Quarterly* 54 (1977): 165–168; Michael Ryan and Dorothea Owen, "An Accuracy Survey of Metropolitan Newspaper Coverage of Social Issues," *Journalism Quarterly* 54 (1977): 27–32; William A. Tillinghast, "Newspaper Errors: Reporters Dispute Most Source Claims," *Newspaper Research Journal* 3(4) (1982): 15–23.

4. Harvey Molotch and Marilyn Lester, "News as Purposive Behavior: On the Strategic Use of Routine Events, Accidents, and Scandals," *American Sociological Review* 39 (February 1974): 101–112; Gaye Tuchman, *Making News: A Study in the Construction of Reality* (New York: The Free Press, 1978); Mark Fishman, *Manufacturing the News* (Austin: University of Texas Press, 1980).

5. Gary C. Lawrence and David L. Grey, "Substantive Inaccuracies in Local News Reporting," *Journalism Quarterly* 46 (1969): 753–757; William A. Tillinghast, "Source Control and Evaluation of Newspaper Inaccuracies," *Newspaper Research Journal* 5(1) (1983): 13–24.

6. Tillinghast, "Newspaper Errors."

7. Tillinghast, "Source Control," p. 22.

8. Lawrence and Grey, "Substantive Inaccuracies"; Blankenburg, "News Accuracy."

9. Tillinghast, "Source Control."

10. Tuchman, *Making News;* Richard V. Ericson, Patricia M. Baranek, and Janet B. L. Chan, *Negotiating Control: A Study of News Sources* (Toronto: University of Toronto Press, 1989).

11. Interviews were conducted by the author during the first time period. The additional interviews four years later were conducted by one of the author's graduate students. The second set of interviews was intended to check whether the processes noted during the first round of interviews could be identified among different subjects by a different interviewer in a context of different local issues. The two data sets turned

out to be entirely consistent with each other, and have been combined in this article's analyses.

12. Subjects were contacted within three days of when the story that featured them was published. Three attempts were made to reach each eligible subject of news coverage. If a subject was mentioned in more than one news story that met the criteria for inclusion in the study, he or she was asked about the most recent story. The survey was limited to bylined stories so that the identity of the reporter who wrote the story could be ascertained. The survey was limited to local residents because it is unlikely that subjects living elsewhere would have seen the newspaper's portrayals of them.

13. Leon V. Sigal, *Reporters and Officials: The Organization and Politics of Newsmaking* (Lexington, Mass.: D. C. Heath, 1973); Tuchman, *Making News;* Oscar H. Gandy, *Beyond Agenda Setting: Information Subsidies and Public Policy* (Norwood, N.J.: Ablex, 1982).

4

How a Typical American Newspaper Handles Complaints

NEIL NEMETH

CHAPTER 3 DOCUMENTED HOW ORDINARY NEWS COVERAGE
CAUSES A VARIETY OF DIFFICULTIES FOR THE PEOPLE IT POR-
TRAYS. DESPITE THE PROBLEMS, HOWEVER, UNHAPPY SUBJECTS
ARE UNLIKELY TO ADDRESS A CLAIM TO THE OFFENDING NEWS
ORGANIZATION.

NONETHELESS, NEWS ORGANIZATIONS DO RECEIVE COM-
PLAINTS; PEOPLE WHO HAVE NAMED A PROBLEM AND BLAMED THE
NEWS ORGANIZATION FOR IT SOMETIMES DO MAKE CLAIMS. IN
CHAPTER 4, NEIL NEMETH REPORTS THE RESULTS OF AN OBSERVA-
TIONAL STUDY THAT EXAMINED HOW A TYPICAL U.S. NEWSPAPER
RESPONDS TO SUCH CLAIMS. CONDUCTING HIS RESEARCH IN THE
SAME COMMUNITY THAT WAS THE FOCUS OF CHAPTER 3, NEMETH
FOUND THAT UNHAPPY READERS—INCLUDING, BUT NOT LIMITED
TO, SUBJECTS OF NEWS COVERAGE—CONTACTED THE NEWSPAPER
VIRTUALLY EVERY DAY. CURIOUSLY, THOUGH, THE NEWSPAPER
SEEMED INDIFFERENT TO MANY OF THE COMPLAINTS. THE EXCEP-
TIONS WERE COMPLAINTS FROM SOURCES WITH HIGH SOCIAL OR
POLITICAL STATUS, WHICH TENDED TO BE DEALT WITH QUICKLY.

THE CHAPTER, A REVISED VERSION OF A PAPER WRITTEN FOR
A GRADUATE SEMINAR AT INDIANA UNIVERSITY, SUGGESTS THAT
TYPICAL NEWS ORGANIZATIONS MAY NOT RESPOND EFFECTIVELY
TO ACCOUNTABILITY DEMANDS FROM ORDINARY CITIZENS. AT THIS
WRITING, NEMETH IS ON THE FACULTY OF THE DEPARTMENT OF
COMMUNICATION AT PURDUE UNIVERSITY–CALUMET.

The news industry has come up with a variety of mechanisms (e.g., ethics codes, news ombudsmen, media criticism, and press councils) designed to
make news organizations more accountable to their audiences. At a fundamental level, however, media accountability is a simple process, one that occurs
countless times every day without the benefit of formal mechanisms of media
accountability. Whenever someone asks a news organization to explain or jus-

tify one of its decisions, the media accountability process has been set into motion.[1]

The process can be successful only if the news organization in some way addresses the concerns of the person who sought the explanation. How responsive a news organization is to people who request explanations (i.e., who make an accountability demand) may influence how likely the requesters are to sue the news organization.[2]

Compared to the number of accountability demands news organizations receive, very few people sue the media.[3] This is not to suggest that news organizations which ignore accountability demands pay no price for their indifference (or arrogance). People unsatisfied with how a news organization responds may well try to harm the news organization in any of a number of ways. They may minimize future dealings with the news organization by canceling a subscription, refusing future interviews, or declining to buy advertising space. Or they may attempt to damage the news organization's credibility by telling friends and acquaintances about their unsatisfactory experience.[4]

Available evidence suggests that large news organizations may not do a good job of handling routine accountability demands.[5] News organizations in small towns might be expected to do better, if only because they are less bureaucratic and more accessible to their constituents. This chapter examines how a newspaper in a small U.S. city deals with basic demands for accountability—complaints or criticism from readers about news decisions.

BACKGROUND

In the United States, virtually all news organizations are privately owned businesses. Although very little research has explored how news organizations handle complaints, there is a body of literature about how businesses handle consumer complaints. Because most news organizations are, in a fundamental sense, businesses, understanding how businesses respond to customers who complain provides a context for understanding how news organizations deal with audience members who complain.

Complaints represent an early part of the disputing process. Marc Galanter visualized this process as a pyramid divided into two parts: the lower layers where disputes come into being and evolve, and the upper levels where fully developed disputes are taken over by lawyers and resolved in the courts.[6] One of the ways a dispute can begin is when a consumer is unsatisfied with a product he or she has purchased. The consumer may feel "injured" by the problem with the product, and may complain to the seller. A complaint evolves into a dispute only after the party perceived to be responsible for the injury is blamed, a claim is made against the allegedly responsible party, and the claim is rejected in whole or in part.[7]

For a variety of reasons, most complaints are either settled or dropped before they arrive at the upper levels of the disputing pyramid. Complainants can stop the disputing process at any of a number of points, ranging from a refusal to begin disputing (e.g., as when a consumer unhappy with a product refuses to complain) to the withdrawal of a claim when offered an acceptable settlement.

Interestingly, many news organizations have experience helping audience members process complaints against businesses. Consumer affairs reporters, often with a flashy title such as "Action Line," solicit calls from people who are unhappy with products or services they have purchased. The reporters then try to arrange a settlement of the problem that is satisfactory both to the consumer and to the business before publishing or broadcasting a story about the complaint and the resolution. Several studies have examined "Action Line" journalism, concluding that it stresses consensual outcomes largely because local news organizations prefer not to offend businesses.[8]

We know much less about the methods news organizations use to handle complaints about their own performance. Readers who have problems with the way they are portrayed in routine news stories may be unlikely to make their claims known to newspaper personnel. Instead, as David Pritchard's study of subjects of newspaper attention in chapter 3 shows, they often try to repair damage by themselves without making any accountability demand to the news organization that offended them.

Nonetheless, it is clear that news organizations do receive a considerable number of accountability demands in the form of complaints about their journalistic performance. If existing research about consumer disputing can be adapted to media-related disputing, we can expect a variety of factors to influence the course these complaints take. Key among these factors are social forces such as the nature of the relationship between the consumer (or reader) and the business (or news organization), the consumer's social status, and the consumer's ability to articulate the complaint effectively.[9]

This chapter examines how one newspaper handled complaints. Data for this study were gathered by several methods, including thirty hours of observation of newsroom behavior at the *Bloomington (Indiana) Herald-Times,* interviews with key *Herald-Times* personnel responsible for handling complaints, and analysis of written complaints received by Bob Zaltsberg, editor of the newspaper.

The *Herald-Times* is a morning newspaper with a daily circulation of about 30,000 and a Sunday circulation of about 45,000. In terms of circulation size, the *Herald-Times* was fairly average among the 1,600 or so daily newspapers in the United States. In terms of patterns of news coverage, the *Herald-Times* also was unexceptional.

At the time of the study, the newspaper, owned by Schurz Communications of South Bend, Indiana, had just converted from afternoon to morning publication and changed its name from the *Herald-Telephone* to the *Herald-Times*. About 85 percent of the newspaper's circulation was in Monroe County, which includes the city of Bloomington and Indiana University.

Key complaint-handling personnel at the newspaper included editor Zaltsberg, who started as a reporter in 1977 and worked his way up to managing editor before being named editor in 1985; city editor Bill Strother, who supervised twelve staff members, including news reporters; and switchboard operator Sheila Corbin, who joined the *Herald-Times* in 1989 after working as a night switchboard operator at Bloomington Hospital.

Complaints came to the *Herald-Times* principally through three different channels: the "Call the Editor" program, telephone calls to newsroom personnel, and letters to the editor.

THE "CALL THE EDITOR" PROGRAM

Late one Tuesday afternoon, his eyes glued to the computer terminal lodged inside his bookcase, *Herald-Times* editor Bob Zaltsberg waited for readers to take him up on an offer he hoped they would not be able to refuse: to call him with their gripes, their concerns, or even their praise. The telephone, poised atop a stack of telephone books, sat ready for the first call.

The "Call the Editor" program had been conceived as a way for the newspaper to be more accessible to its readers. Under the program, Zaltsberg took telephone calls in his office on Tuesdays from 4:30 to 6 P.M. His direct telephone number was publicized so that callers could reach him without going through the switchboard operator.

However, the program had not been heavily promoted since Zaltsberg had begun working on converting the newspaper from an afternoon to a morning publishing cycle, and incoming calls were few. At the time of the study, the most recent pitch for the program had appeared in a *Herald-Times* advertising supplement more than a week earlier.

"We simply stopped promoting it when I got involved in the planning for the a.m. conversion," Zaltsberg said. "It wasn't that we didn't think it was important, it was just that the conversion became more important when it came to allocating time."

Finally, Zaltsberg's telephone rang at about 5:15 P.M., forty-five minutes after the "Call the Editor" period had started. The caller was a caseworker from a local training center for disabled people with a story suggestion. The suggestion concerned a man with Down's syndrome who worked in an Indiana University dining hall. Zaltsberg indicated that the story had news value and would likely be handled in one of two ways: as a human interest story by one of the newspaper's reporters or as part of a larger story about disabled people and training programs in the Bloomington area.

While waiting for more telephone calls, Zaltsberg typed away at his computer terminal and talked about why the "Call the Editor" program had not realized its potential.

"I think the thing we learned here is that this [the program] needs to be aggressively promoted with ads in the paper," he said. "When we aggressively promoted it, I would get anywhere from eight to sixteen calls each day."

Zaltsberg also suggested that the program's afternoon time slot may not have been best for readers, who might be more likely to complain in the morning, immediately after receiving the newspaper (and perhaps being offended by something in it). Whatever the reason, few people contacted Zaltsberg during the ninety minutes set aside every week for the "Call the Editor" program. On the day of observation, for example, the call from the caseworker at the training center for disabled people was the only one Zaltsberg received.

DAY-TO-DAY TELEPHONE COMPLAINTS

Sheila Corbin was a woman in a big hurry. Seated behind the front desk that dominated the main entrance to the *Herald-Times* building, she was running a race with time.

First, it was a beeping switchboard control panel. Next, it was greeting a series of visitors who wanted to pay their advertising bills. And, finally, it was helping the business department staff get out monthly billings. Sometimes Corbin had a hard time getting everything done at once.

"You have to answer the telephone first because it's beeping," she said. "The people who are waiting are aware that you aren't paying full attention to them."

Corbin said her procedure for handling complaints about news was straightforward. "If the caller asks to speak to someone [specific], I put them through," she said. "If I get a general question or complaint, I give it to [city editor] Bill Strother." If Strother and editor-in-chief Zaltsberg were unavailable to take a call about a general question or complaint, Corbin transferred the call to Zaltsberg's secretary.

Corbin acknowledged that callers who asked to speak to a specific person in the newsroom sometimes got lost in the shuffle, largely because Corbin had no way to be sure who was in the newsroom to answer the calls.

"I don't really know who's back there [in the newsroom]," Corbin said. "It's pretty much hit or miss. We've had situations where I didn't know reporters were out of town, and I took messages and told them [callers] that the call would be returned. Bill Strother and Bob Zaltsberg have worked on that, and it's improved. I know there's room for improvement, but the reporters really do try."

Really "hot" complaints went to either Strother or Zaltsberg, but Corbin said such complaints were rare. "A lot of people who call don't want to talk to anybody in particular," she said. "They just want to make sure their complaint is registered."

When a "hot" complaint did arrive, city editor Strother thought it was important that either he or Zaltsberg get involved.

"When somebody calls and says we've gotten something wrong that's defamed someone and hurt their business and ruined their reputation and they're wanting to sue us, then the reporters tell me or Bob [Zaltsberg]," Strother said.

"Whenever libel comes into the conversation, it's an immediate concern," Strother added. "I don't handle the situation any differently, though. I tell them we'll check the error. I try to keep as many [callers] as I can away from Bob. He has other things to do. But if they're not satisfied after I have talked to them, I give them to Bob."

A story written by Mike Leonard, the *Herald-Times*'s local columnist, about a Bloomington-area husband and wife who made and starred in hard-core pornographic movies provided a good example of how the system works.

Zaltsberg received six telephone calls complaining about Leonard's story. Three were anonymous calls that expressed disappointment and/or disgust at what the callers considered to be bad taste. "Why do we need to glorify something of this nature?" one asked. The three callers who identified themselves by name voiced similar complaints.

Zaltsberg also received several pieces of mail about the story. One envelope included a clipping of the story from someone who had drawn devil's horns on a picture of one of the filmmakers.

"A few people called, and I talked to some of them," Zaltsberg said. "These were angry, emotional people who didn't want smut being run in the paper. I told them this was a story about people who live and work in the community who were engaged in legal professions, even if they were unusual."

Overall, Zaltsberg said he received about a dozen complaint calls and letters, and a handful of supportive calls.

Zaltsberg said he struggled with how to respond to the criticism. He decided not to write a column explaining the newspaper's reasons for running the story, although he had received a number of angry letters to the editor. However, because all of the letters were unsigned, none were published.

In addition to the calls and letters directed to Zaltsberg, Leonard estimated that he received between eight and ten calls on the issue. "A lot of people who called thought that the newspaper endorsed it [the pornographic movie making] just because we ran a story on it," Leonard said.

Complaints of a more general nature were funneled to Strother, the city editor. An example of how the system worked occurred about 11:30 A.M. the day the *Herald-Times* published a story about an accident in which three persons were injured and the siding of a house was damaged.

A telephone call came from a "friend of the victims" who was concerned that a quotation in the story emphasized that the owners of the house would need to replace the siding after the accident. The caller was upset that the siding of the house seemed more important in the story than the health of the accident victims.

"I think she [the caller] was reading more into the story than was there," Strother said. His explanation convinced the caller that no offense was intended.

The incident showed that phoning the newspaper can be an effective way of obtaining an explanation of its behavior—but only if the caller reaches someone who knows why the newspaper acted as it did. Often, complainants' calls failed to reach the appropriate journalist.

Incoming calls (except for the "Call the Editor" program) came to the main switchboard, where Sheila Corbin answered them. Corbin's uncertainty about who was in the newsroom at any given time was borne out by observation. Strother was often away from his desk as he circulated around the newsroom to consult with his reporters. And on a typical day, he was out of the newsroom having lunch between 1:30 and 2:30 P.M. When Strother was away from his telephone, it was often answered by copy editor and TV editor Doug Wenrich, whose desk was located near Strother's.

Wenrich answered what questions he could, but often had to acknowledge that the caller needed to talk with Strother. In such cases, Wenrich either offered to take a message or suggested that the caller try to contact Strother later. It's unclear whether such callers ever ended up talking with Strother. During this study's thirty hours of newsroom observation, Wenrich answered about two dozen calls that had been directed to Strother.

Not all complaints came directly to the *Herald-Times* newsroom. Journalists also heard complaints as they made the rounds on their beats. Richard Gilbert, who spent most of his time covering Indiana University, experienced this phenomenon.

Gilbert suspected that some of his university sources were reluctant to complain about his work for fear of offending the president of the university, who enjoyed positive coverage in the *Herald-Times*. Nonetheless, Gilbert did hear complaints on his beat, often from regular sources who would tell him how the president or other officials reacted to his stories. At times, Gilbert said he was even called to meet with the president so that the two could discuss the university and the newspaper's coverage of it.

Like most other reporting in the *Herald-Times* (and in other newspapers in the United States), Gilbert's coverage of the university was not particularly hard-hitting or confrontational. Not long after the study ended, in fact, he left the *Herald-Times* to take a public relations job at the university.

That the university president could successfully summon the *Herald-Times*'s university reporter to his office on campus to discuss the newspaper's coverage suggests that the status of a complainer may affect how a news organization responds to a complaint. Two complaints that arrived at the *Herald-Times* within about three hours of each other one day illustrated the point.

The first caller complained that a name had been misspelled in a photo caption on the front page of the newspaper's Lifestyle section. A debate ensued among several reporters and editors about whether a correction should be published. Strother opposed it.

"I didn't think we should run a correction because it's not our policy to run corrections on misspellings," Strother said. Yet the correction appeared in the newspaper the next day. Strother said the decision was made after the editors realized that it was not possible for readers to determine whether the spelling was correct in the caption or in the accompanying story.[10]

A call that Strother received later in the day produced another correction for the following day's newspaper, but the call was handled differently.

The caller, state representative Mark Kruzan, was upset that the words "president" and "her" had been left out of a quotation of remarks he had made in a speech: "No governor (or president) should want his (or her) legacy to be, 'I didn't raise taxes.'" The story ran on the inside pages of a section of the newspaper, and the quotation appeared near the end of the story.

Despite the facts that the omissions seemed inconsequential and that the offending passage was buried at the bottom of a story that was not prominently displayed, Strother lost no time in dealing with the complaint. He began working on a correction while telephoning the reporter who wrote the story about the correction. Strother said the reporter had lost a portion of the quotation because he had been in a hurry to copy it down. He said he would suggest that the legislator make copies of his speeches available to reporters in the future.

Contrasting how news managers dealt with the caller's complaint about a misspelled name in a photo caption and Kruzan's complaint about an insignificant misquote suggests that Kruzan's relatively high social status made a difference. The journalists were reluctant to correct the misspelling, which had been brought to their attention by an ordinary reader. In contrast, there was no question that they would correct the slight error in the report of Kruzan's speech. Kruzan's complaint was immediately acknowledged to be valid, and editors planned to suggest ways that the legislator could minimize the chances of such mistakes in the future.

The university president's habit of summoning the higher-education reporter to discuss coverage (and the reporter's habit of complying with the summons) also suggests that the newspaper was deferential to high-status sources.

In addition to paying close attention to complaints from such sources, the *Herald-Times* also took seriously those complaints that editors thought might have overtones of a potential libel suit.

It was just such a call that presented the most unusual complaint encountered in this study. The call was channeled directly to editor Zaltsberg. The caller complained about a picture the newspaper had published six months earlier that included his house trailer, which had been located in a trailer park that had been exposed to toxic PCBs. The story had nothing to do with the caller or his trailer; a staff photographer had moved the subjects of the story to the front of the man's trailer for a posed shot.

The caller complained that he had been unable to sell his trailer because of massive publicity about local PCB contamination generally and because of the picture that ran in the *Herald-Times* specifically. Zaltsberg was concerned immediately.

"He [the caller] wanted us to run a correction that said his trailer was not contaminated," Zaltsberg said. "But we had never said that it was. This alerted me to the potential for a lawsuit. You think about not having your p's and q's in place, and even though we had nothing to do with it [the man's failure to sell his trailer], you think, 'This is a poor guy.'"

After some thought, Zaltsberg realized that the potential for a libel lawsuit was slight, but he still thought the newspaper should do something about the situation.

"Does this guy have a [valid] complaint?" Zaltsberg said. "He probably does. We took the picture of these people away from their own trailer. Nobody could tell, and it was innocent enough, but if I were the guy and couldn't sell my trailer, I could see where the guy could logically find a way to blame the newspaper. I can see why he concluded we were to blame, and it's difficult to justify the fact that the story had nothing to do with his trailer."

Zaltsberg's solution was to assign Leonard to write a story about the man's saga without mentioning the newspaper's role in his predicament. Zaltsberg believed that the news story would be legitimate and would represent an effort to "make it up to the guy."

LETTERS OF COMPLAINT

Many of the complaint letters Zaltsberg received were unsigned. He treated them with skepticism. "Of course, I give them less weight than I would somebody who signs the letter," Zaltsberg said. "One of the reasons is that I have no way to respond to them."

The unsigned letters included a complaint that the *Herald-Times* resembled the Indiana University student newspaper too closely, another that an editorial urging readers to enjoy the fall weather ignored all those people who were jobless and homeless, and one that pointed out the newspaper's spelling and grammar errors.

One unsigned letter was particularly revealing about the attitudes of the person lodging the complaint. The writer claimed to be an Indiana University employee who had searched the *Herald-Times* in vain for news about a university vice president who had been seriously injured in an automobile accident. The newspaper had reported that the injured official had been released from a Bloomington hospital but failed to report until two days later the fact that the official had been flown to Indianapolis for treatment.

The writer wrote, "Thanks for bringing the NEWS to concerned IU employees." It was signed, "A longtime customer disgusted with the changes made—particularly the name change [from the *Herald-Telephone* to the *Herald-Times*] and change to a morning newspaper."

The letter suggested that the writer had been upset with the newspaper for some time, but had waited for an event that had personal significance before lodging the complaints.

This phenomenon also was exhibited in an unsigned letter written by a subscriber who was mistakenly sent information designed to solicit another subscription. The mistake prompted the writer to threaten to cancel the subscription. "We do not like the morning paper (neither do our neighbors)," the letter said. "The news is so old by the time we read the paper we just don't need it. We have heard it on TV and radio. Also read it in an evening paper." But the letter did not stop there. The writer criticized the newspaper for giving too much coverage to Bloomington South High School at the expense of other schools.

The comic strip *Doonesbury* produced several complaints about its portrayal of scantily clad women and its satire about a federal flag desecration statute that had recently been adopted. A letter about the comic strip's portrayal of women was signed by its author. The letter troubled Zaltsberg because he was not sure how, or even whether, to respond.

The letter writer, a father with three young children, criticized the newspaper for contributing to the destruction of morals. The letter recalled the days of the man's youth, when comic strips contained material "suitable for young children." The signature was preceded by "Sincerely and May God Bless You."

"I don't really know how to respond to this one," Zaltsberg said. "I'll probably do nothing with it, figuring it was a lost cause." And that's what happened: Zaltsberg did not respond to the father who complained about *Doonesbury*.

"From the public relations side, it would be good to answer every letter," Zaltsberg said. "I just don't have time, so I pick and choose where I think a letter from me will make a difference in thinking. You could argue that a response from me will make a difference. As a result, I'm not totally comfortable with the fact I don't write back to every person."

Writers who intended their letters to be published in the letters to the editor columns received better treatment, however. Every writer who intended his or her letter for publication received notification from Zaltsberg either that the letter had been accepted for publication or that it needed some adjustment.

"I tell them why their letter is not suitable," Zaltsberg said. "It may be too long or involve litigation. So there is one standard for people who write for the letters to the editor column and another standard for unsolicited complaints."

DISCUSSION

This chapter focused on how a typical American daily newspaper dealt with reader complaints. The evidence, gathered in interviews with, and on-site observations of people who handle complaints, suggests that complaint-handling was a fairly haphazard process.

The "Call the Editor" program failed to generate very many calls. The newspaper did not publicize the program in any serious fashion, and the time set aside for calls may well have been inconvenient for readers. Although a "Call the Editor" program offers complainers direct access to the top decision-maker at a news organization, the *Herald-Times* did very little to encourage readers to call.

Despite the apparent good intentions of all concerned, the system of responding to day-to-day telephone complaints (i.e., those not related to the "Call the Editor" program) at the *Herald-Times* let many of them slip through the cracks. The system in place at the *Herald-Times* worked when everyone was near his or her telephone. However, when Strother was away from his desk, or when a reporter was out of the newsroom for an extended period, it was clear that some callers were unable to reach anyone in the newsroom who could respond to their complaints or criticisms.

On the rare occasions when a reader wrote a thoughtful, signed letter of complaint, the *Herald-Times* did not always respond. Although many letter writers did not sign their names, thus making responses impossible, in general the *Herald-Times* did not place a high priority on being accountable—explaining its behavior to readers who complained. An exception was made for readers of high status, such as the university president, who could summon a reporter to his office for a discussion of how the newspaper covered the university, and the state representative, whose complaint was met with a quick correction (and a suggestion for how he could help reporters do their jobs better the next time).

Complainers with high status, who often have extensive experience dealing with the media and skill in articulating complaints, were able to get the newspaper to respond. Other kinds of complainers, though, had difficulty doing so.

It is not surprising that the *Herald-Times* provided meaningful accountability principally to the powerful. The news media in general are solicitous of the powerful.[11] In addition, the typical American newspaper is not flooded with complaints. They are but one of many items to be handled during a busy news day, and they are all too easy to overlook because they deal with yesterday's news rather than with the immediate preoccupation of any newsroom: putting together tomorrow's newspaper.[12]

The effects of this attitude of seemingly benign neglect are difficult to discern. Poor handling of complaints has been linked to an increased likelihood that a complainer will sue a news organization for libel.[13] Less dramatically, a newspaper's relative lack of interest in the ordinary complainer may give those who complain the feeling that the newspaper is simply another powerful community institution that talks more about being accountable than it delivers. Over the long term, newspapers may pay a heavy cost in terms of loss of trust and credibility for their failure to provide accountability to all of their readers.

For these reasons, newspaper managers should recognize that newspapers are powerful, authoritative institutions in their respective communities and that it is in their self-interest, as well as in the interest of their readers, to devise effective means of providing accountability.

NOTES

1. David Pritchard, "The Role of Press Councils in a System of Media Accountability: The Case of Quebec," *Canadian Journal of Communication* 16 (February 1991): 73–93.

2. Randall P. Bezanson, Gilbert Cranberg, and John Soloski, *Libel Law and the Press: Myth and Reality* (New York: The Free Press, 1987), pp. 29–53.

3. The Iowa Libel Research Project found that only about a hundred libel cases are decided annually in the United States. That is an average of about two libel cases per state per year. Bezanson, Gilbert, and Soloski, pp. 29–53, 77, and 168–169.

4. David Pritchard, "A New Paradigm for Legal Research in Mass Communication," *Communications and the Law* 8 (August 1986): 51–67.

5. Richard V. Ericson, Patricia M. Baranek, and Janet B. L. Chan, *Negotiating Control: A Study of News Sources* (Toronto: University of Toronto Press, 1989), pp. 309–376.

6. Marc Galanter, "Reading the Landscape of Disputes: What We Know and Don't Know (and Think We Know) About Our Allegedly Contentious and Litigious Society," *UCLA Law Review* 31 (1983): 4–71.

7. William L. F. Felstiner, Richard L. Abel, and Austin Sarat, "The Emergence and Transformation of Disputes: Naming, Blaming, Claiming . . . ," *Law & Society Review* 15 (1980–1981): 631–654. For some examples of studies of consumer complaints in a business context, see Arthur Best and Alan Andreasen, "Consumer Response to Unsatisfactory Purchases: A Survey of Perceiving Defects, Voicing Complaints, and Obtaining Redress," *Law & Society Review* 11 (1977): 701–742; and Eric Freedman, "Dear Mr. Nader: A Study of Consumer Complaint Letters," in Laura Nader, ed., *No Access to Law* (New York: Academic Press, 1980), pp. 113–170.

8. See John A. Hannigan, "The Newspaper Ombudsman and Newspaper Complaints: An Empirical Assessment," *Law & Society Review* 11 (1977): 679–699; Frank S. Palen, "Media Ombudsmen: A Critical Review," *Law & Society Review* 13 (1979): 799–850; and Michael Mattice, "Media in the Middle: A Study of the Mass Media Complaint Managers," in Nader, *No Access to Law,* pp. 485–522.

9. Donald Black, *Sociological Justice* (New York: Oxford University Press, 1989), pp. 8–13. For other discussions of these issues, see Dan Coates and Steven Penrod,

"Social Psychology and the Emergence of Disputes," *Law & Society Review* 15 (1980–81): 655–680; and Jeffrey Fitzgerald and Richard Dickins, "Disputing in Legal and Nonlegal Contexts: Some Questions for Sociologists of Law," *Law & Society Review* 15 (1980–81): 683–706.

10. The *Herald-Times*'s normal policy was to publish corrections on page 2. Generally, reporters write corrections of their own stories when the newspaper becomes aware of errors. The newspaper does not penalize journalists who make mistakes that require correction.

11. Gaye Tuchman, *Making News* (New York: The Free Press, 1978); Mark Fishman, *Manufacturing the News* (Austin: University of Texas Press, 1980).

12. Bezanson, Cranberg, and Soloski, *Libel Law and the Press.*

13. Ibid.

5

A News Ombudsman as an Agent of Accountability

NEIL NEMETH

IN CHAPTER 4, NEIL NEMETH EXAMINED HOW A TYPICAL AMERI-
CAN NEWSPAPER RESPONDS TO COMPLAINTS (OR TO CLAIMS, IN
THE NAMING-BLAMING-CLAIMING TERMINOLOGY OF THE ACCOUNT-
ABILITY PROCESS). NEMETH FOUND THAT THE TYPICAL NEWS-
PAPER'S METHOD OF DEALING WITH CLAIMS TYPICALLY WAS HAP-
HAZARD. ONLY THE COMPLAINTS OF THE POWERFUL WERE SURE
TO MERIT SERIOUS ATTENTION.

IN CHAPTER 5 NEMETH TURNS HIS ATTENTION TO A LESS
TYPICAL NEWSPAPER, THE *LOUISVILLE (KENTUCKY) COURIER-
JOURNAL*. UNLIKE THE NEWSPAPER DESCRIBED IN CHAPTER 4,
THE *COURIER-JOURNAL* HAS A WELL-ESTABLISHED SYSTEM FOR
DEALING WITH COMPLAINTS. IN FACT, IT WAS THE FIRST NEWS-
PAPER IN ALL OF NORTH AMERICA TO CREATE THE POSITION OF
OMBUDSMAN SPECIFICALLY FOR THE PURPOSE OF RECEIVING AND
RESPONDING TO COMPLAINTS.

THE OMBUDSMAN POSITION HAD SURVIVED THE TEST OF TIME,
IF NOTHING ELSE. IT HAD BEEN IN PLACE FOR TWENTY-FIVE YEARS
WHEN NEMETH CONDUCTED HIS RESEARCH, WHICH INCLUDED
FOUR WEEKS OF OBSERVATION, INTERVIEWS WITH READERS WHO
COMPLAINED, AND A SURVEY OF *COURIER-JOURNAL* REPORTERS
AND EDITORS. NEMETH CONCLUDED THAT A NEWS OMBUDSMAN
CAN BE AN EFFECTIVE MECHANISM OF MEDIA ACCOUNTABILITY.

NEMETH RECEIVED HIS PH.D. FROM INDIANA UNIVERSITY. THE
RESEARCH REPORTED IN CHAPTER 5 IS BASED ON A PORTION OF
HIS DOCTORAL DISSERTATION.

In 1809, the Swedish parliament created an administrative position to hear
citizens' charges of unfair and capricious decisions made by the executive
branch of the government.[1] The person who held the position was called the
"ombudsman." In 1967, a U.S. newspaper adapted the concept to its own needs,
and within a few years more than thirty North American newspapers had ombudsmen.

This chapter explores the history and workings of the news ombudsman at the *Louisville (Kentucky) Courier-Journal,* the first North American newspaper to create an ombudsman position.[2] The chapter pays special attention to the ombudsman's role as an agent of media accountability.

Although the *Courier-Journal* did not create the ombudsman position until 1967, a sense that the American news media needed to be more accountable to the public had been around for some time before then. The widely publicized report of the Commission on the Freedom of the Press concluded in 1947 that the press must be accountable if it wanted to remain free.[3] The commission did not specifically propose that newspapers employ ombudsmen, but it did suggest that the media should engage in vigorous mutual criticism as a means of providing accountability.

The commission's call for accountability went largely unheeded until A. H. Raskin, an assistant editorial page editor of the *New York Times,* proposed that each major newspaper create a "department of internal criticism."[4] Raskin, concerned that increasing concentration of media ownership by large corporations was leading to poorer journalism, believed it was vital that newspapers make themselves accountable to the public.[5]

One of Raskin's readers was Norman Isaacs, executive editor of Louisville's jointly owned daily newspapers, the *Courier-Journal* and the *Louisville Times.* Isaacs and the owner of the newspapers, Barry Bingham, Sr., had been interested for several years in creating a press council in the Louisville area, but their efforts had been frustrated by a lack of interest from other media organizations and local public officials.[6] When Isaacs read Raskin's article, he thought he had found a way to make the newspapers accountable to the public.

"When I read that," Isaacs recalled, "I said, 'That's it.'"[7]

Within the month, Isaacs had named John Herchenroeder, a veteran of forty-one years on the *Courier-Journal* staff and city editor for the previous twenty-five years, as the first news ombudsman in North America.[8] Isaacs felt that newspapers had been unwilling to admit their mistakes; he saw the news ombudsman as a way for newspapers to do something about them.

"I had always felt twenty years before [the news ombudsman was created] that saying we were sorry was an anathema to newspapers," Isaacs said. "It [creating the news ombudsman] was simply based on the ethical conviction that journalism was out of sync with society."[9]

So it was expected that the first news ombudsman in North America would do something about mistakes that appeared in the *Courier-Journal.* In time, Herchenroeder compiled the complaints he received and circulated the compilation on a daily basis inside the newspaper offices. He did not write a regular column about his findings for publication because he felt the nature of the complaints would not interest the public.[10]

Herchenroeder acted mostly as a complaint manager for the *Courier-Journal.* He tried to satisfy unhappy readers without publicly criticizing the

newspaper. However, as other news organizations studied the Louisville ombudsman, some decided that ombudsmen also should write reports to readers
about complaints and, if need be, about their newspaper's shortcomings. Soon
after the *Washington Post* in 1970 became the second U.S. newspaper to create
a news ombudsman, for example, it integrated public media criticism into the
position.

As newspapers and the public gained more experience with ombudsmen,
however, doubts were raised about the impartiality of ombudsmen appointed
by and paid by the very news organizations they were expected to critique. Ben
Bagdikian, the second ombudsman at the *Washington Post,* left the position
over a conflict with management over where his loyalties lay—with the news
organization or with the public.[11] The same dilemma caused the *St. Petersburg
Times* to discontinue its ombudsman position in 1980 following management's
disagreement over the ombudsman's public criticism of the newspaper's decision to assign only black reporters to cover race riots in Miami.[12] Despite a
few such controversies, more than thirty daily newspapers in North America
created ombudsman positions in the 1970s, and most still had them in the late
1990s. The ombudsmen created their own association, the Organization of
News Ombudsmen, best known by its acronym: ONO.[13]

After more than thirty years of experience with ombudsmen, however, the
debate over the ombudsman's basic role remained unresolved: Should ombudsmen focus principally on resolving individual complaints privately, or
should they focus more on offering public media criticism, including criticism
of the news organization that employs them? At the *Courier-Journal,* the focus
of the first four ombudsmen was principally on the complaint-management
function.

The four people who had filled the ombudsman's chair at the *Courier-
Journal* between 1967 and the mid-1990s all had been senior editors with more
than twenty years of experience at the Louisville newspapers. Being the ombudsman tended to be their last job at the newspaper; the first three left the job
through retirement, and the fourth, who was in place at the time of this study,
seemed likely to do the same.

Because there was no real precedent for the position when John Herchenroeder became the first ombudsman in 1967, there were few clear expectations
about what he would do. One thing, however, was clear: that the ombudsman
would investigate complaints about the newspaper's performance. Beyond that
simple goal, the editors of the *Courier-Journal* and the *Louisville Times* had
few specific ideas of what the news ombudsman should do. As a result, Herchenroeder had a great deal of latitude in defining the job, partly as a result of
his seniority at the newspaper and partly because before he became news ombudsman he was already handling many complaints in his role as city editor.

Isaacs and former publisher Barry Bingham, Jr., both said years later that
they believed that the news ombudsman should have written a public column

from the beginning.[14] But neither was willing to force the issue with Herchenroeder,[15] who was not interested in writing the column because he felt the public would be bored with the nature of the complaints.[16]

By 1974, Bingham Jr. was determined that the Louisville newspapers needed public criticism of their activities. He hired Robert Schulman, a veteran newspaper and broadcast journalist, to write regular columns of media criticism in the *Louisville Times* and the Sunday *Courier-Journal*. Schulman acknowledged that ombudsman Herchenroeder initially was less than pleased with Schulman's media criticism. Nonetheless, the relationship between the two was good, and Herchenroeder even provided some of the information for Schulman's columns.[17] Schulman continued as media critic until 1981, when he left to become managing editor of the Public Broadcasting Service series *Inside Story*.[18] The position of media critic was eliminated as part of budget reductions at the Louisville newspapers, though Bingham Jr. said later that the nature of the position made the media critic so unpopular with employees that he could not have found anyone interested in the position anyway.[19]

Herchenroeder was ombudsman for twelve years until his retirement in 1979, when he was replaced by Frank Hartley. Hartley had worked for forty-one years at the Louisville newspapers in a variety of newsroom positions.[20] Though he served only two years as ombudsman, Hartley's tenure was marked by two significant controversies: a National News Council decision upholding a complaint by a Louisville doctor about a *Courier-Journal* series on physicians' fees, and an investigation into charges by the General Electric Co. that the newspaper's coverage of the company had been unfair.[21]

After suffering a heart attack, Hartley retired in 1981. He was replaced by Robert Crumpler, who had worked for the Louisville newspapers for twenty-eight years.[22] Crumpler not only handled telephone complaints, but also wrote a regular in-house writing critique, *Crumpets*.[23]

There were two major sources of complaints during Crumpler's service as ombudsman: misspelled words and the decision by Gannett Co., which had bought the Louisville newspapers in 1986, to close the *Times* in February 1987.[24] After seven years as news ombudsman, Crumpler retired in 1988. His replacement was Stan Slusher, 56, a veteran of twenty-two years with the Louisville newspapers.[25]

Slusher wrote an occasional column during his first years as ombudsman, explaining to readers such matters as the use of syndicated columns and the rationale for the *Courier-Journal*'s coverage of abortion.[26] Slusher did not have to deal with the biggest *Courier-Journal* controversy of the late 1980s, however. Editor David Hawpe took it upon himself to explain the circumstances of a flawed investigative series on sports that required ten corrections and led to the resignation of a reporter.[27]

Slusher's most memorable controversy in his first few years as ombudsman was related to a mass murder in Louisville that grabbed national headlines.

The mass murder, which occurred only a few hundred feet from the *Courier-Journal* offices at the Standard Gravure Corp., claimed the lives of eight persons and injured twelve more.[28] On the front page of the next day's paper, the *Courier-Journal* published a photograph of the body of one of the victims.

The newspaper received more than five hundred telephone and written comments from the public about the photo, with more than 80 percent of the comments critical of the newspaper's decision.[29] As a result, Slusher felt compelled to write a column explaining the newspaper's rationale. The column defended the decision to publish the picture as the only way to demonstrate the magnitude of the tragedy.[30] The victim's family sued the *Courier-Journal* for invasion of privacy by publishing the picture, but the lawsuit was unsuccessful.[31]

During Slusher's tenure, the ombudsman's duties were expanded to include responsibilities for processing staff members' explanations for errors that found their way into the newspaper.[32] Editor Hawpe also directed Slusher to begin writing a regular column,[33] which was published every other Sunday.[34] The move represented the first major changes in the *Courier-Journal*'s ombudsman's responsibilities since the position was created in 1967. Previously, the ombudsman's principal duties had been to handle reader complaints and write a summary of the complaints for the benefit of newspaper staff members.

Complaints from readers continued to be a major component of the ombudsman's work at the *Courier-Journal,* of course. So that I could learn more about the complaints and the complainants, the *Courier-Journal* allowed me to keep a log of phone complaints received by the ombudsman[35] during nineteen days in the fall of 1990. I also telephoned and interviewed thirty-two of the complainants.

During the nineteen days, the ombudsman received 308 calls or complaints—about 16 a day. The most frequent kind of call (121 calls, or about 39 percent of the total) criticized the newspaper's emphasis or the play of a particular story: the major focus was second-guessing editorial decisions. The next most frequent kind of call (79 calls, or about 26 percent of the total) was simply a request for information—not a complaint at all. Other noncomplainers included the 25 people (8 percent of the total) who called with story suggestions and the seven callers (2 percent of the total) who offered praise for the newspaper. About two people a day (38, or 12 percent of the total calls) had circulation problems, something outside the news ombudsman's area of responsibility. He referred such calls to the circulation department.[36] Twenty-seven calls (about 9 percent of the total) brought general or miscellaneous comments.

Only 11 complaints (about 4 percent of the total) were from people who were upset about news stories that either quoted them or were about them. It seemed clear that most complaints from people upset about what the newspaper had written about them went to someone other than the ombudsman. Most likely, such complaints were directed either to an editor in the newsroom or to the reporter who wrote the offending story. The ombudsman would be unlikely to receive such complaints, because the newsroom is "where the power lies,"[37] including the power to produce a correction or apology. In addition, regular news sources may be more comfortable lodging complaints with a reporter they know than with an ombudsman they have never met.

That said, some of the calls to the ombudsman led to published corrections. The *Courier-Journal* published corrections on the front page of the local section each day. During the nineteen days of observation, the *Courier-Journal* published 61 corrections. Of those, the ombudsman had a role in 11 (18 percent). A similar pattern held true for corrections published in the Neighborhoods section, which ran each Wednesday. Seven corrections were published during the study period; the news ombudsman had input into two of them.

The *Courier-Journal* had an advertising ombudsman as well as a news ombudsman. The advertising ombudsman served as a watchdog for advertising that may be deemed tasteless, libelous, or obscene, comparing advertising received against the newspaper's guidebook.[38] The advertising ombudsman received fewer calls from the public than did the news ombudsman because questions or complaints about ads generally are made directly to the advertisers themselves.

The *Courier-Journal* also had a Reader's Service Department, which consisted of two employees assigned to provide information to people who are interested in anything from trivia to obtaining copies of *Courier-Journal* articles. Sometimes, however, readers directed complaints to the Reader's Service Department, according to Annette Norris, a researcher there. "People are angry when the lottery numbers aren't in the paper," Norris said. "Name errors and obituaries that are wrong cause problems, too. Sometimes callers get angry when they don't agree with the articles."[39] On such occasions, Norris forwarded the complainants' calls to news ombudsman Stan Slusher.

Overall, the news ombudsman at the *Courier-Journal* functioned as an information conduit, funneling explanations about the newspaper's editorial decisions to members of the public. Only rarely did the ombudsman handle complaints from readers who had taken offense at something the newspaper did that affected them personally. Far more often, the ombudsman represented a convenient sounding board for readers who wanted to air views about the newspaper's news emphasis, correct a factual error, or complain about general news coverage.

The people who called the news ombudsman seemed to be somewhat different demographically from the typical *Courier-Journal* subscriber. Interviews with thirty-two people who called the ombudsman showed them to be slightly older than the average subscriber (50 years old compared to 46), somewhat better educated (59 percent had college degrees, compared to 33 percent of the subscribers), and less likely to have been a resident of Louisville for at least twenty years (59 percent compared to 76 percent). Most of the people who called the ombudsman were either very satisfied (50 percent) or somewhat satisfied (34 percent) with the experience of contacting the news ombudsman. Only about 13 percent of the complainants said they were somewhat or very unsatisfied.

A news ombudsman can provide two clear services to callers: a handy means for lodging complaints and the prospect of a quick resolution of the problem they have voiced. Complainants received personal service for their grievances against the newspaper. This function is significant and may be the major advantage of the ombudsman concept for both the news organization and the complainant. The news ombudsman can provide quick answers and fair treatment because complainants have someone who is in a prime position to hear their grievances and do something about them.

The people most likely to call the ombudsman were those who had limited experience in dealing with a newspaper and those who simply wanted someone to talk to about the newspaper's performance or, more generally, about public issues. Sources who were used to dealing with a specific reporter lodged their complaints with that reporter, if they lodged them at all. Rather than becoming a repository for all of the complaints about a news organization's performance, then, the news ombudsman provided an added channel for readers to make their views about the newspaper's performance known. However, because news sources tended to lodge their complaints directly with the newsroom or the reporter, the news ombudsman's role in resolving disputes between sources and the newspaper appeared to be limited.

Despite the fact that the ombudsman receives relatively few complaints from news sources (or perhaps *because* of that fact), the eighty-five *Courier-Journal* journalists who responded to a questionnaire about the ombudsman expressed mostly positive viewpoints. About 92 percent of the staff members agreed that the news ombudsman was necessary as a representative of the readers, while only about 6 percent said that the ombudsman was not necessary because the newspaper had editors. About 84 percent disagreed with the statement that the presence of an ombudsman tended to demoralize employees.

Courier-Journal staff members were split on whether the news ombudsman was capable of being independent of the newspaper. About 23 percent agreed with the statement that the ombudsman was incapable of real independence, but 45 percent disagreed. The other 32 percent were neutral: they neither agreed nor disagreed with the statement. The *Courier-Journal* journalists also were split over the question of whether the presence of the ombudsman causes staff members to work more carefully. Forty percent agreed that staff members work more carefully because of the presence of the ombudsman, but 25 percent disagreed, with the remaining 34 percent neither agreeing nor disagreeing.

Slightly more than a third of the respondents (35 percent) believed that the ombudsman's primary function was one of public relations for the newspaper.

However, more than half of the staff members (54 percent) disagreed with that contention, with the other 11 percent being neutral.

In an effort to determine which kinds of journalist tended to have more favorable views about the ombudsman, multivariate analysis was used to try to predict staff members' responses to questions about (1) whether they considered the ombudsman useful to themselves as individual journalists, and (2) whether the presence of the ombudsman caused them to work more carefully. For each of the two questions, multiple regression was used to determine the relative predictive ability of respondents' gender, education, years of experience at the newspaper, and whether the ombudsman had evaluated a respondent's work.

Years of experience was the only significant predictor of whether a staff member considered the ombudsman personally useful. The more experience respondents had, the more likely they were to consider the ombudsman useful. Respondents' gender, years of education, and direct experience with having the ombudsman review their work did not predict responses to the question.

As for the question about whether the presence of the ombudsman caused a respondent to work more carefully, only one factor was a significant predictor: whether the ombudsman had evaluated the respondent's work. Respondents' gender, years of education, and years of experience in journalism did not predict responses to this question.

At first glance, causing journalists to work more carefully seems to represent a positive influence of the news ombudsman. In fact, the result is somewhat ambiguous. The data do not reveal how respondents interpreted the phrase "working carefully." If "working carefully" means taking greater pains to avoid errors or to be more thorough, then it is a good thing. If, however, "working carefully" means that journalists avoid taking on stories about controversy (which may be more likely than other stories to lead to a complaint to the ombudsman) or avoiding complicated stories (where the risk of error is greater than in simpler stories), then "working carefully" may not be such a good thing. The possible "chilling effect" of news ombudsmen—that the mere presence of an ombudsman may subtly censor complex and controversial stories—merits additional study.[40]

A final issue pertains to the news ombudsman's principal role and loyalty. Ettema and Glasser's survey of ombudsmen found that many perceived that they had two jobs: one, to act in a public relations capacity for their newspaper; and two, to hold the newspaper publicly accountable for its behavior.[41]

The public relations role of ombudsmen is an issue that arouses considerable emotion. After he published the Ettema and Glasser article in 1987, *Journalism Quarterly* editor Guido H. Stempel III received angry complaints from several news ombudsmen who protested the contention that they were involved in public relations activities.[42] Stempel believed the reaction was a

result of the tendency among newspeople to associate the term "public relations" with the stereotype of corporate communications specialists who would
do anything to avoid revealing information harmful to their organization.[43]

Nonetheless, because handling complaints unavoidably requires dealing with the public, the ombudsman who successfully handles complaints and
solves problems provides a public relations benefit to the news organization.
The news ombudsman's job is to resolve complaints made by members of the
public, and any ombudsman who does that job successfully is bound to improve
the news organization's image. The improved public stature of the organization
is simply a by-product of making a good-faith effort to resolve complaints.

While it is clear that ombudsmen have a public relations function, it is
less clear that they act as agents of media accountability. Media accountability
can be defined as "the process by which news organizations or journalists are
obliged to render an account of their activities to recognized constituencies
such as audience members, news sources, advertisers, professional colleagues,
or government regulatory bodies."[44]

The news organization that employs an ombudsman to act exclusively as
a complaint manager provides one form of accountability—accountability to
an individual complainant without attendant publicity. This kind of individual
accountability will likely reflect the news organization's perspective and values because the ombudsman who provides the accounting typically will have
worked within the organization for many years. Such an outcome can be satisfactory for the complainant so long as the ombudsman is sufficiently detached
from the daily administrative and production responsibilities of the newspaper
to render an accurate explanation and an honest remedy.

Resolving individual complaints is, of course, an activity that is related
to the public relations function of the ombudsman. Perhaps a more important
kind of accountability is that which results from the regular public airing of
concerns about the news organization's performance. This is the kind of public
accountability envisioned by Ettema and Glasser.[45] The news ombudsman who
provides public accountability must do more than simply manage complaints;
he or she also must be able to provide an accountability that is both public and
comprehensive.

An accountability that is public must include a regular channel for communicating with all of a newspaper's readers, not just with individual complainants. An accountability that is comprehensive needs to focus on whether
the cumulative actions of the news organization are fair, just, and proper, not
simply on whether an individual action was proper. The most obvious vehicle
for providing public accountability would be for the news ombudsman to write
a regular public column, which would provide readers with an account of the
newspaper's activities and do so with an eye toward the wider issues of fairness and taste. Historically, the *Courier-Journal*'s news ombudsman has pro-

vided a form of internal accountability by circulating a report of the day's complaints, but did not provide public accountability by writing a regular column until the early 1990s.

There is a certain tension between the public relations and public accountability functions of news ombudsmen. On one hand, a news ombudsman who solves complainants' problems in an effective and efficient manner provides a public relations benefit to the news organization as an inevitable by-product of his or her work. On the other hand, public accountability requires something more than the effective and efficient handling of individual complaints: it requires public communication that may well be critical of the news organization's performance. Different ombudsmen may balance these tasks in different ways. It seems likely that the ombudsman whose principal focus is handling individual complaints has limited ability to provide public accountability, while the ombudsman who provides public accountability through a regular published column will have limited time for handling complaints.

Despite the tensions that are inherent in the job, the news ombudsman may be an effective method of providing media accountability. When implemented by a news organization that desires to hear public comment and complaints about its performance, the ombudsman can be an agent of internal accountability (if the principal focus is on resolving complaints and communicating through an internal report) or external accountability (if the principal focus is a regular public column), or perhaps even both. The ombudsman is by no means a perfect means of accountability; the fact that ombudsmen are employees of their news organization will always raise doubts about their independence. But none of the alternative means of media accountability—government regulation of press content, lawsuits for libel and invasion of privacy, press criticism, journalism education, enforceable ethics codes, press councils—is perfect.

Media organizations cannot be forced to hire news ombudsmen. But the news organizations that do employ a news ombudsman have taken a voluntary, if imperfect, step toward providing accountability. In a society that places a premium on the value of having a free and unregulated press, a news organization's decision to provide a voluntary form of accountability with a news ombudsman may be all that can be expected.

NOTES

1. For a discussion of the historical development of the ombudsmen, see Walter Gellhorn, *Ombudsmen and Others: Citizens' Protectors in Nine Countries* (Cambridge: Harvard University Press, 1966), and Donald C. Rowat, *The Ombudsman Plan: The Worldwide Spread of an Idea* (Toronto: McClellan and Stewart, 1973).

2. Data for the research presented in this chapter came from four weeks of

observation of the news ombudsman's activities at the *Courier-Journal* in the fall of 1990. In addition, I obtained the names of people who had telephoned the ombudsman and called them to determine their views about the ombudsman's work. I also surveyed members of the *Courier-Journal* news staff to ascertain their reactions to the ombudsman, and conducted numerous interviews. For a complete description of the context and methods of the study, see Neil Nemeth, "The Role of the Newspaper Ombudsman in Media Accountability: The Case of the *Courier-Journal*," unpublished Ph.D. dissertation, Indiana University, 1991.

3. Commission on the Freedom of the Press, *A Free and Responsible Press* (Chicago: University of Chicago Press, 1947), p. 94.

4. A. H. Raskin, "What's Wrong with American Newspapers?" *The New York Times Magazine,* June 11, 1967. Even before Raskin's article appeared, Ben H. Bagdikian had suggested that newspaper owners include a "community ombudsman" on their boards of directors. See Ben H. Bagdikian, "The American Newspaper Is Neither Record, Mirror, Journal, Ledger, Bulletin, Telegram, Examiner, Register, Chronicle, Gazette, Observer, Monitor, Transcript nor Herald of the Day's Events," *Esquire,* March 1967, p. 142. Bagdikian later suggested that other newspapers follow the *Courier-Journal*'s example and employ news ombudsmen. See Ben H. Bagdikian, "Right of Access: A Modest Proposal," *Columbia Journalism Review,* Spring 1969, p. 13.

5. Raskin, "What's Wrong with American Newspapers?"

6. Norman E. Isaacs, "Why We Lack a National Press Council," in Alfred E. Balk and James Boylan, eds., *Our Troubled Press: Ten Years of the* Columbia Journalism Review (Boston: Little, Brown and Company, 1971), p. 349.

7. Norman Isaacs, telephone interview, November 26, 1990.

8. "Ombudsman Named by C-J and Times," *Louisville Courier-Journal,* July 16, 1967.

9. Isaacs interview.

10. John Herchenroeder, personal interview, October 9, 1990.

11. Ben H. Bagdikian, "Bagdikian's Post-mortem: Keep Up Criticism," *The Bulletin of the American Society of Newspaper Editors,* October 1972, pp. 11–13.

12. Cassandra Tate, "What Do Ombudsmen Do?" *Columbia Journalism Review,* May/June 1984, pp. 40–41.

13. See Organization of News Ombudsmen, *Editors for the Public: What Are News Ombudsmen and Why Should the Media Have Them?,* pamphlet, January 1990.

14. Isaacs interview; personal interview with Barry Bingham, Jr., October 10, 1990.

15. Isaacs interview; Bingham Jr. interview.

16. Isaacs interview.

17. Bingham Jr. interview.

18. "News-Media Critic Schulman Resigns to Take Job with PBS," *Louisville Times,* February 24, 1981.

19. Bingham Jr. interview.

20. "Frank Hartley Is Named *Times, Courier-Journal* News Ombudsman," *Louisville Times,* September 28, 1979.

21. For information about the National News Council case, see Robert L. Peirce, "Doctors' Fees Vary Greatly in Louisville Area," *Louisville Courier-Journal,* October

14, 1979; "Complaint against C-J justified, Council Says," *Louisville Courier-Journal,* March 7, 1980; Bob Schulman, "Small Effort, Big Dividends," *Louisville Times,* March 13, 1980; and Paul Janensch, "Unqualified Acceptance of News Council Ruling: A Lesson's Been Learned," *Louisville Courier-Journal,* March 23, 1980. For information about the news ombudsman's investigation of the complaints lodged against the *Courier-Journal* by the General Electric Co., see Paul Janensch, "A Report to GE: 'Positive' and 'Negative' News," *Courier-Journal,* October 19, 1980.

22. Leonard Pardue, "No Complaints: Bob Crumpler, News Ombudsman, Is Loyal Friend, Defender of Readers," *Louisville Times,* July 8, 1981.

23. Personal interview with Bob Crumpler, October 9, 1990.

24. Crumpler interview.

25. Everett J. Mitchell II, "News Veteran Named *Courier-Journal* Ombudsman," *Louisville Courier-Journal,* March 29, 1988.

26. See Stan Slusher, "Ann Landers' Vacation and Various Other Aggravations," *Louisville Courier-Journal,* August 27, 1989; and Stan Slusher, "How the C-J Covers Abortion," *Louisville Courier-Journal,* November 12, 1989.

27. David V. Hawpe, "A Report to Our Readers from David Hawpe, Editor of *The Courier-Journal,*" *Louisville Courier-Journal,* October 9, 1988.

28. See Jim Adams, "Tormented Man Driven by His Secret Excesses," *Louisville Courier-Journal,* September 15, 1989; Cary B. Willis and Gerald A. Ryan, "Families of Wounded Workers Grapple with Fear," *Louisville Courier-Journal,* September 15, 1989; Rob Cunningham, "EMS Workers Recall Harrowing Scene of Rampage," *Louisville Courier-Journal,* September 16, 1989; Deborah Yetter, "The Day After; Employees Struggle to Deal with Emotions," *Louisville Courier-Journal,* September 16, 1989.

29. Personal interview with Stan Slusher, November 2, 1990.

30. Stan Slusher, "Slaying Photo Upset Many—but Reality Can Be Cruel," *Louisville Courier-Journal,* September 17, 1989.

31. Cary B. Willis, "Suit Against C-J for Photograph of Slain Man Will Be Dismissed," *Louisville Courier-Journal,* February 14, 1990; Andrew Wolfson, "Court Backs C-J on Printing Photo of Shooting Victim," *Louisville Courier-Journal,* April 13, 1991; Leslie Scanlong, "High Court Won't Review Ruling on Photo in C-J," *Louisville Courier-Journal,* November 16, 1991; and Andrew Wolfson, "U.S. High Court Refuses to Hear Suit Against C-J," *Louisville Courier-Journal,* April 28, 1992.

32. See David Hawpe and Irene Nolan, "Corrections and Clarification Policy— October 1989," *Courier-Journal* memorandum, October 17, 1989.

33. Personal interview with David Hawpe, November 5, 1990.

34. Personal interview with Stan Slusher, August 9, 1993.

35. Almost all complaints and comments come via phone. The ombudsman received only two letters of complaint during the nineteen days of observation.

36. For about ten years, the circulation department had an ombudsman who handled that department's complaints. When the circulation ombudsman retired in 1987, the position was eliminated, though an ombudsman phone line remained in the department and was staffed in 1990 by circulation supervisors on a rotating basis.

37. Richard V. Ericson, Patricia M. Baranek, and Janet B. L. Chan, *Negotiating Control: A Study of News Sources* (Toronto: University of Toronto Press, 1989), pp. 328–330.

38. Personal interview with Kim Becker, October 11, 1990.

39. Personal interview with Annette Norris, October 23, 1990.

40. For other views of how newspaper journalists react to ombudsmen, see David R. Nelsen and Kenneth Starck, "The Newspaper Ombudsman as Viewed by the Rest of the Staff," *Journalism Quarterly* 51 (1974): 453–457, and David Pritchard, "The Impact of Newspaper Ombudsmen on Journalists' Attitudes," *Journalism Quarterly* 70 (1993): 77–86.

41. James S. Ettema and Theodore L. Glasser, "Public Accountability or Public Relations? Newspaper Ombudsmen Define Their Role," *Journalism Quarterly* 64 (1987): 3–12.

42. Personal interview with Guido Stempel III, April 6, 1991.

43. Stempel interview.

44. David Pritchard, "The Role of Press Councils in a System of Media Accountability: The Case of Quebec," *Canadian Journal of Communication* 16 (1991): 73–93.

45. Ettema and Glasser did not define what they mean by "public accountability," but their article makes it clear that the public accountability role for the news ombudsman includes press criticism. See Ettema and Glasser, "Public Accountability or Public Relations?" pp. 11–12.

6

Media Criticism as Professional Self-Regulation

KRISTIE BUNTON

MORE THAN FIFTY YEARS AGO, THE HUTCHINS COMMISSION'S FAMOUS REPORT, *A FREE AND RESPONSIBLE PRESS,* URGED THE AMERICAN PRESS TO PRACTICE "VIGOROUS, MUTUAL CRITICISM" AS A MEANS OF HOLDING EACH OTHER ACCOUNTABLE (AND, OF COURSE, OF STAVING OFF REGULATION BY GOVERNMENT). UNFORTUNATELY, THE NEWS MEDIA HAVE NEVER SHOWN MUCH TASTE FOR "VIGOROUS, MUTUAL CRITICISM," BUT INDIVIDUALS—OFTEN JOURNALISTS—WRITING IN JOURNALISM REVIEWS HAVE ON OCCASION BEEN QUITE VIGOROUS IN THEIR CRITICISM OF THE PRESS.

IN THE LATE 1960S AND EARLY 1970S LOCAL JOURNALISM REVIEWS, OFTEN FOUNDED BY ACTIVIST JOURNALISTS, SPROUTED IN MORE THAN A DOZEN AMERICAN CITIES. FEW OF THEM SURVIVED VERY LONG, AND IN THE 1990S ONLY ONE LOCAL JOURNALISM REVIEW WAS STILL PUBLISHING.

IN CHAPTER 6 KRISTIE BUNTON FOCUSES ON THE SOLE SURVIVOR, THE VENERABLE *ST. LOUIS JOURNALISM REVIEW.* BUNTON DEFINES THE KINDS OF CONTENT A JOURNALISM REVIEW WOULD HAVE TO PUBLISH TO FULFILL THE ACCOUNTABILITY MISSION FORESEEN BY THE HUTCHINS COMMISSION. HER ANALYSIS OF THE CONTENT OF THE *ST. LOUIS JOURNALISM REVIEW* CONCLUDES THAT THE REVIEW FAILS TO LIVE UP TO ITS POTENTIAL AS A VEHICLE FOR MEANINGFUL PROFESSIONAL SELF-REGULATION.

THE CHAPTER ALSO CONTAINS THE RESULTS OF A SURVEY WHICH SHOW THAT THE REVIEW HAD MINIMAL INFLUENCE ON ST. LOUIS JOURNALISTS' WORK. GIVEN THE LACK OF SELF-REGULATORY CONTENT IN THE REVIEW, ITS LACK OF INFLUENCE WAS NOT SURPRISING.

BUNTON RECEIVED HER PH.D. AT INDIANA UNIVERSITY; THE CHAPTER IS BASED ON PORTIONS OF HER DOCTORAL DISSERTATION. AT THIS WRITING, SHE IS ON THE FACULTY OF THE DEPARTMENT OF JOURNALISM AND MASS COMMUNICATION AT THE UNIVERSITY OF ST. THOMAS IN ST. PAUL, MINNESOTA.

In general, journalists in the United States have an almost visceral opposition to having to answer for their work to government, or indeed to anyone outside of their own news organizations.[1] They cherish the First Amendment to the U.S. Constitution, which they see as insulating them from external control.

That American journalists have considerable legal freedom to gather and disseminate information, however, does not mean that all journalists use the freedom wisely or well. Because of journalism's special social and political role in a system of representative government, how journalists use their freedom is a valid subject for vigorous public debate. Inevitably, such a debate inspires proposals for creating mechanisms by which government could hold journalists to account for their behavior.

It is in such contexts that various means of self-regulation can seem attractive. They are intended to improve the quality of journalism while at the same time maintaining journalism's ideological opposition to external control.

A particularly interesting form of self-regulation is the journalism review, of which there are several in the United States. Journalism reviews differ from the media criticism sometimes featured in the general-circulation press not only because the reviews focus exclusively on journalism, but also because their target audience is composed principally of journalists.

Journalism reviews thus are intended to be a means by which the journalistic profession regulates itself. To the extent that the reviews succeed in that mission, they help improve the quality of journalism while at the same time preempting any need for external regulation. Accordingly, it is crucial to ascertain whether journalism reviews succeed in their self-regulatory mission. Unfortunately, almost no studies of the question have been conducted.

This chapter identifies three kinds of content that a journalism review must publish if it is to function as an effective means of professional self-regulation. The chapter then examines the extent to which the *St. Louis Journalism Review,* the principal local journalism review in the United States, publishes such content. Finally, the chapter reports the results of a survey of St. Louis journalists to determine what influence, if any, the *St. Louis Journalism Review* has on the practice of journalism.

PROFESSIONS AND SELF-REGULATION

Professional self-regulation is important because of the essential function claimed in society today by traditional professions, such as medicine and law, and emerging professions, such as business, social work, public administration, and journalism.[2] Individuals rely on the professions to help control the health, legal, financial, and political matters that occupy daily lives. Even more important, citizens expect the professions to guard basic values such as knowledge, civil liberties, freedom of information, and economic prosperity.[3]

The professions assert exclusive authority to regulate their fields.[4] The traditional idea of self-regulation assumes that the professions' members will create and enforce norms of professional conduct,[5] a process that excludes the public, and sometimes the state, from decisions about what is appropriate professional behavior. Griffith noted that

> a properly functioning profession conforms to a sort of mini-social contract. Under its terms considerable autonomous control over entry into and standards of work in the profession is left to the group collectively. But this is taken to reflect a presumption that the associated professionals will see to it that the group's professional expertise will be made available to, and be used in the best interests of, those who need it, and not merely in the personal interests of the professionals themselves.[6]

Some segments of the public, however, assert that the professions have not lived up to this "mini–social contract" because they fail to identify and punish the failures of professionals to meet public expectations.[7] The professions have responded to such complaints by invoking more self-regulation. Specifically, the major professions have revised their codes of ethics, have devoted more attention to discussions of ethics in their professional journals, and have required ethics courses in their professional schools.[8]

JOURNALISM AS A PROFESSION

Occupations generally are defined as professions when they require specialized intellectual training that is used to serve important societal interests.[9] Professions also can be defined by members who are licensed or credentialed to practice the profession, who organize into professional associations, and who enjoy some degree of autonomy in their work.[10]

Journalism frequently is categorized as an evolving profession,[11] although whether it is a profession at all has been the subject of much study and debate.[12] Reluctance to characterize journalism as a profession may stem from a strict association of professionalization with government-supervised licensing and control, which the First Amendment ideology of journalism will not tolerate. But while journalism may lack the licensing and the strong professional culture of the traditional professions,[13] it nevertheless has acquired a professional outlook with its specialized schools of training, large professional associations, and codes of ethics. Journalism also has acquired a professional outlook in a normative sense; its emphasis on freedom of the press typifies the kind of "distinctive set of ideals" and "characteristic moral ethos and outlook" necessary to be a profession in terms of ethics, or specific moral choices.[14]

This journalistic outlook sometimes becomes a "knee-jerk defensiveness" among journalists who find "in the spirit, not the letter, of the First Amendment a rule prohibiting anyone from calling the press to account even in a nonlegal way."[15] This ideal of independence particularly lends itself to professional self-regulation because the rationale for self-regulation rests on the autonomy most professions assert is essential.[16] Indeed, "every profession has a professional ideology which explains why professional autonomy is not desired out of self-interest, but is a requirement for offering the best possible service in the public interest."[17]

Many professionals have believed their autonomy is so great as to strongly differentiate their roles from those of ordinary workers, giving their professions the authority to establish and enforce their own unique norms.[18] In effect, professional self-regulation is "a collegial form of social control"[19] with lasting ramifications for the public the professions pledge to serve.

But self-regulation is not infallible. Lawyers and doctors, for example, whose systems of self-regulation are among the most highly codified and legally enforceable, rarely report violations of professional norms by their peers.[20] In designing systems of self-regulation, many professions place primary emphasis on their own interests, rather than those of their clients and the public, and often discriminate against the lower economic strata of their own ranks.[21] One result of the fallibility of professional self-regulation has been public criticism focusing on the perceived "costliness and inaccessibility, the self-serving character and dubious usefulness of a good deal of the 'service' provided by professions."[22]

MEDIA CRITICISM

Journalism often has been accused of a variety of alleged sins, and the notion of using self-criticism to respond to threats of external control is not new. Journalism historian Marion Tuttle Marzolf argues that criticism was important in the development of the modern press, which she dates from the late nineteenth century.[23] Between then and about the time of the Hutchins Commission's 1947 report, *A Free and Responsible Press,* media criticism acted as what Marzolf calls a "civilizing agent." The critics, primarily journalistic insiders who included such well-known names as *Nation* editor E. L. Godkin, muckraking author Upton Sinclair, and *New Republic* co-founder Walter Lippmann, played the part of "a conscience, nagging the press to live up to higher standards, ideals, moral behavior."[24]

The Hutchins Commission report, which is known for promulgating a social responsibility theory for the American press, encouraged the press to practice "vigorous, mutual criticism"[25] as one of several ways to ensure that the press remained free of state regulation.[26] Scholars since that time have continued to laud media criticism as a way for the profession to regulate its increasing "power and remoteness," which "breed indifference or hostility" among audiences,[27] and to stave off would-be external regulators.

In more recent times, media criticism published in journalism reviews has been heralded as an effective self-regulatory mechanism for a profession averse to external control. Wrote Edmund Lambeth: "The goal of media criticism, of perfecting mechanisms of accountability, is to furnish the functional equivalent of licensing without any resort whatsoever to the formal power of government or some supposedly equal, informal power of licensing by an organization of professionals."[28]

As noted earlier, however, there is not much evidence about the influence of journalism reviews on the practice of journalism. The influence is asserted, but rarely demonstrated. The few studies of journalism reviews have focused almost exclusively on the tone of the criticism they publish, not on evaluating the extent to which journalism reviews publish content that could lead to meaningful self-regulation.[29] When journalism reviews are discussed in scholarly and trade journals or in books used primarily as texts for media-ethics courses, writers tend to concentrate on the history and function of journalism reviews, also assuming the reviews' self-regulatory impact.[30] Sometimes authors simply assert that readership of a review is a measure of its impact.[31]

This chapter offers evidence rather than assertion.[32] After a brief history of journalism reviews, the chapter explores the extent to which the *St. Louis Journalism Review* publishes articles of the kind that could lead to improved journalism. Finally, it reports the results of a survey of St. Louis journalists to assess how, and whether, the review influences their thinking.

THE EMERGENCE OF JOURNALISM REVIEWS

In the 1960s and 1970s, several local journalism reviews, intended by journalists to be self-regulatory mechanisms, were launched in part as a result of the movements that were questioning mainstream institutions, including the press. The *Columbia Journalism Review,* which remains the leading review today,[33] was established in 1961 at the Columbia University School of Journalism, but most of the subsequently established reviews—"small, critical, activist publications," one scholar called them[34]—were begun by groups of working journalists.[35] The 1968 founding of the *Chicago Journalism Review* was followed by the establishment of at least a dozen other local reviews.[36]

While two national reviews (*Columbia Journalism Review* and *American Journalism Review,* which changed its name from *Washington Journalism Review* in 1993) survive today, the only local review that has published continuously since its founding is the *St. Louis Journalism Review,* which published its first issue in October/November 1970. The review's initial editorial declared that the purpose of the review would be to offer a regular "professional critique of the successes and failures of the local news media in informing the public."[37]

Many of the local reviews died because they lacked the means to survive after their newness wore off,[38] but the St. Louis publication succeeded in staying alive. Strictly speaking, however, the *St. Louis Journalism Review* may not have been economically viable. From its inception, the review's survival depended largely on the subsidy Charles Klotzer, its editor-publisher, diverted to it from his typesetting business.[39] Before publishing the review, Klotzer founded and published a now-defunct "reformist" literary and political magazine that had among its investors leading Missouri and Illinois citizens.[40] Klotzer was instrumental in pulling together the group of reporters who founded the *St. Louis Journalism Review,* and in 1983 he folded his literary and political magazine into the journalism review. He published the review for twenty-five years before giving it to Webster University, effective at the beginning of 1996.[41]

Perhaps because of its longevity, the *St. Louis Journalism Review* has been praised by authors who assume, rather than demonstrate, its influence on St. Louis journalists. A leading journalism reference guide, for example, lists the review as one of journalism's "core" publications and calls it "a lofty-thinking, intelligently written, and occasionally muckraking example of regional journalism watchdogism."[42]

SELF-REGULATORY CONTENT

The *St. Louis Journalism Review* can be considered an effective means of self-regulation only if it has a clear influence on the practices and standards journalists consider acceptable to use in producing the news that is the basis of journalism's social contract with the public.

The logical starting point of the investigation is in the pages of the review itself, for they must contain something by which journalists could be influenced before influence can occur. Does the *St. Louis Journalism Review* publish material that could stimulate reflection about journalistic norms? Only such content fits into the theoretical context of professional self-regulation.

The necessary stimuli for self-regulatory influence include three types of journalism-review content: (1) content that explains the way journalists cover the news; (2) content that criticizes the way journalists cover the news; and (3) content that proposes change in the way in which news is covered. A journalism review that includes articles of these kinds "holds up the new to past standards, judges the results, and introduces new developments and insights."[43]

Explanatory content accepts and reinforces existing journalistic norms. By explaining how a particular news story was covered—who decided which material would be included in the story, for example—a journalism review helps readers learn existing journalistic standards and practices. An explanation published by a journalism review is intended to be read principally by journalists, who may internalize the standards explained in the article and may use them in the future. In this way, explanatory content helps socialize journalists to the profession and its norms. Clearly, self-regulation is impossible if those who are to be regulated do not understand professional norms.

Critical content is a traditional form of self-regulation. In essence, critical articles in a journalism review aim to point out violations of accepted professional norms, in the hope that identifying transgressors will prevent future transgressions. Critical content accepts existing norms without question. Journalistic behavior is measured against the existing standards, whose validity is not questioned by critical content.

The final type of self-regulatory content proposes reform: change in news practices and standards. By challenging accepted norms, reform content is aimed more consciously at improving journalism than are explanatory and critical content. Explanatory and critical content clearly are necessary for socially responsible self-regulation—professionals must understand not only their profession's norms, but also why certain practices violate those norms—but they are not sufficient. To explanatory and critical content must be added reform content that questions whether existing norms satisfy journalism's social obligations. By proposing changes in professional norms, reform content offers journalists a way to adapt to changing conditions in society.

CONTENT OF THE REVIEW

To determine the extent to which the *St. Louis Journalism Review* publishes explanatory, critical, and reform content, 38 issues from 1988 to 1991 were examined.[44] Articles that contained self-regulatory content were classified according to which of the three self-regulatory functions was their main theme. Table 1 shows the results of the classification.

As table 1 makes clear, the *St. Louis Journalism Review* provided rela-

Table 1   Categorization of Content in 55 Articles in the *St. Louis Journalism Review*, 1988–91, by Self-Regulatory Themes

Principal Self-Regulatory Theme	Secondary Self-Regulatory Theme(s)	Total
Explanatory	None	26
Critical	None	10
Critical	Explanatory	8
Reform	None	1
Reform	Critical	4
Reform	Critical, explanatory	6
Total number of articles		55

tively little content that might contribute to self-regulation as it has been defined in this chapter. Fewer than two articles per issue—55 articles in 38 issues—contained such content, and only one-fifth of those 55 articles proposed the change in professional norms that this study suggests is necessary for true self-regulation.

About half the self-regulatory content in the review was limited to explanations of why St. Louis journalists covered news in a particular way. For example, after the Reverend Jesse Jackson and other activists began pushing for public use of the term "African American" instead of "black," the *St. Louis Journalism Review* surveyed media managers to explain which of the city's media had made it their policy to use "African American" and which were continuing to use "black."[45]

The best explanatory articles were the review's systematic comparisons of news practices across competing media outlets. For example, one comparison considered the amount of time each of the city's television stations devoted to local, national, world and business news, weather, sports, and trivia items in their local newscasts.[46]

Although such analyses are a step in the right direction in that they provide a chance to step back from day-to-day news coverage and look at broader trends, the review generally failed to move beyond explanation to question journalistic values. The review's comparison of the local television stations confirmed that more time in local newscasts is spent on trivial items than on business or world news, but the article neither questioned why trivia pervaded newscasts nor proposed how the emphasis on trivia could be changed.

About a third of the 55 articles went beyond explanation to criticize the way in which news was covered by St. Louis journalists. Unfortunately, the critical articles typically failed to be truly incisive.

A case in point was the review's vague criticism of the local news coverage of a $1 million lawsuit filed against the St. Louis Blues hockey team and one of its players by the parents of a teenage girl who allegedly was raped several times over a year-long period by the player.[47] Near the beginning of its examination of the case, the review criticized local media coverage:

> for all the words devoted to covering the lurid saga, including some of the most convoluted legal proceedings in recent memory, few, if any, were aware of all the facts or happenings. The event-driven coverage omitted crucial details that might have altered considerably the public's understanding and opinion of the events themselves.[48]

This kind of criticism accepts established journalistic norms. The article in question implicitly adopted the stance that if only St. Louis journalists had done a better job of untangling the events, coverage of the lawsuit would have been defensible, and the public would have had a much better understanding of the events. The review's article showed how coverage of the lawsuit had been superficial (i.e., in violation of existing norms), and how it could have been better (i.e., consistent with existing norms). The article did not, however, address broader questions about how gender, class, and occupational stereotypes may influence how journalists cover disputes.

Eleven of the 55 articles proposed change in the way news is covered in St. Louis. Interestingly, most of them were written by academics, rather than the publication's customary freelance writers. For instance, former University of Missouri–Columbia journalism faculty member Robert L. Terrell challenged Missouri journalists to investigate the disproportionately large numbers of black prisoners in the state's prisons and to question "the endemic political, cultural and economic circumstances responsible for black crime."[49] Arthur Silverblatt, associate professor of media communications at St. Louis's Webster University, decried local television newscasts' preoccupation with entertainment and proposed ways for newscasts to concentrate on covering substantive issues that should be the focus of public debate.[50] University of Missouri–St. Louis history professor Charles Korr analyzed local news coverage of the flight of the city's professional football team, the St. Louis Cardinals, to Arizona. He chided reporters for framing the team's exodus as a sports event instead of as a "matter of civic policy and economic self interest," and suggested future coverage of attempts to court or keep professional sports franchises in St. Louis should question the hidden economic, social, and political costs of such efforts. Korr wrote:

> Sports issues that affect the public, rather than just fans, cannot be discussed in the normal sports page fashion. . . . The press should offer its readers a cold-blooded cost analysis about the multi-million-dollar relationship between professional sports and government so that they can appraise the issues in depth.[51]

Such reform content went beyond criticizing presumed violations of existing professional norms to suggesting changes in those norms. A journalism review can serve as a stimulus for true professional self-regulation only if it frequently publishes articles that feature reform content.

As is suggested by the relatively small number of articles that explained, criticized, or suggested changes in the way local journalists cover the news, much of the content of the *St. Louis Journalism Review* had little to do with self-regulation. Instead, a great deal of the publication's content typified what sociologist Herbert J. Gans calls "supportive" criticism, which he argues perpetuates established journalistic values, including the claim that professional autonomy is essential.[52]

Large amounts of space in the *St. Louis Journalism Review* were devoted to columns announcing the hirings and firings of news, advertising, and public-relations practitioners in the St. Louis area, as well as to articles chronicling the inadequacies of media-organization managers, who often were portrayed as non-journalists with a lack of appreciation for the autonomy journalists believe they require. In the issues of the review examined for this study, for example, several articles were devoted to cuts in funding and air time for news at television station KTVI, which the review seemed to blame on managers,[53] and to contract negotiations between the St. Louis Newspaper Guild and the city's media employers, particularly the daily *St. Louis Post-Dispatch*.[54]

The review's emphasis on personnel matters also was demonstrated through a seemingly undying fascination with the less-than-Midas touch of Jeffrey M. Gluck, who after buying and shutting down the already foundering *St. Louis Globe-Democrat* bought or started and then closed a number of magazines across the nation. Gluck was the primary or secondary subject of at least ten briefs or articles in the thirty-eight issues of the review examined for this study, including promotions on three covers and three articles that occupied at least one complete page of the review.[55]

In its fascination with personalities—whether Gluck or the *St. Louis Sun*'s successful effort to win columnist Kevin Horrigan away from the *Post-Dispatch*[56] or a retrospective on the career of longtime local television personality Betsy Bruce[57]—the review acted more as an insider magazine for St. Louis news junkies than as a review of journalistic performance. Sometimes, in quoting its own contributors or members of its board of editorial advisers, the review even acted as an insider magazine for its own insiders.[58]

The review also devoted large amounts of space to reprints of articles and briefs from publications outside St. Louis that did not comment directly on journalism in St. Louis. For instance, between November 1986 and November 1988, the review allocated an average of a page and a half each issue to reprinting, in its entirety, a book examining the World Anti-Communist League. For three months in 1991, the review devoted more than ten pages to reprinting a book chapter about corporate control of media.[59]

Although the *St. Louis Journalism Review* showed itself to be a useful publication, and certainly more of an attempt to criticize journalistic practices than can be found in most communities, it published relatively few articles that could contribute to socially responsible professional self-regulation, as defined in this chapter. In addition, the self-regulatory content it did publish most often stopped at explaining why news was covered in a specific manner by St. Louis journalists. Relatively few articles critiqued the way in which news was covered or proposed changes in journalistic norms.

JOURNALISTS AND THE *REVIEW*

The previous section's examination of the *St. Louis Journalism Review*'s content found that it published an average of fewer than two self-regulatory articles per issue from the beginning of 1988 through mid-1991. This section reports how St. Louis journalists reacted to the *Review*.

A two-page questionnaire was mailed to 227 St. Louis journalists in July 1991; 138 of them (61 percent) returned completed questionnaires.[60] The respondents were asked to provide information about their journalism backgrounds, the sources of their values about journalism ethics, their use of national and local journalism reviews, and their opinions about what kinds of articles journalism reviews should publish.

Forty-two percent of respondents (57) were employed by the *St. Louis Post-Dispatch,* the daily newspaper owned by the Pulitzer Publishing Company. Twenty-three percent (32) were employed by the city's major broadcast stations, including the historically dominant all-news and talk radio station, KMOX, and the three network-affiliate television stations, KMOV, KSDK, and KTVI. Thirty-five percent (47) were employed by other organizations, including small broadcast stations and community, suburban, and trade newspapers, or were freelance journalists. Two respondents did not indicate where they worked.

Almost three-quarters (101, or 74 percent) of the journalists who returned completed questionnaires were male. The respondents had an average 16 years of experience in St. Louis journalism, with a range of from one to 50 years of experience, and their average age was 45, with a range from 24 to 86 years of age.[61]

Table 2   Levels of Readership and Discussion of Three Journalism Reviews

Readership

	St. Louis JR (n=136)	Columbia JR (n=135)	Washington JR (n=134)
Read almost every issue	61.0%	14.8%	6.7%
Read fairly often	18.4%	17.8%	14.2%
Rarely read	14.7%	31.3%	30.6%
Never read	5.9%	36.3%	48.5%

Discussion

	St. Louis JR (n=136)	Columbia JR (n=133)	Washington JR (n=133)
Discuss almost every issue	11.8%	0.8%	0.8%
Discuss fairly often	47.8%	14.3%	6.0%
Rarely discuss	31.6%	36.8%	27.8%
Never discuss	8.8%	48.1%	65.4%

Table 2 shows the extent to which respondents read and discussed journalism reviews. The *St. Louis Journalism Review* ranked far ahead of the two national journalism reviews in terms of reading and discussion by St. Louis journalists. A majority of respondents (61 percent) said they read almost every issue of the *St. Louis Journalism Review.*[62] Readership and discussion of national journalism reviews were much lower. About 15 percent of the respondents said they read every issue of the *Columbia Journalism Review,* and only about 7 percent said they read almost every issue of the *Washington Journalism Review.* The findings for level of discussion were similar, with almost 60 percent saying they discussed the *St. Louis Journalism Review* at least fairly often, compared to 15 percent who discussed the *Columbia Journalism Review* at least fairly often, and 7 percent who discussed the *Washington Journalism Review* at least fairly often.

Respondents also were asked whether their journalistic work had been the subject of analysis by the *St. Louis Journalism Review.* Roughly a quarter (26 percent) said the review had analyzed their work.

To gain an idea of the *St. Louis Journalism Review*'s influence relative to other sources of ideas about journalism, respondents were asked to rate the extent to which the review and nine other sources affected their ideas about what constitutes high-quality journalism in St. Louis.[63] Table 3 summarizes the responses.

The responses suggest that day-to-day newsroom practices and interpersonal relationships had a greater influence on St. Louis journalists' ideas about high-quality journalism than did mechanisms of professional self-regulation such as journalism reviews, media criticism, or press ombudspeople. Specif-

Table 3   Influences on St. Louis Journalists' Ideas About What Constitutes Good Journalism in St. Louis

Source of Influence	Average Rating*	Valid Responses
Day-to-day newsroom practices	2.21	129
Other St. Louis journalists	1.82	134
Immediate supervisor	1.69	124
St. Louis friends/acquaintances	1.51	131
Publishers/general managers	1.41	131
St. Louis Journalism Review	1.04	136
National journalism reviews	.96	133
Post-Dispatch reader advocate	.93	133
Local media critic or columnist	.75	120

*The scale ranged from 0 to 3, with 0 indicating that a respondent considered the source to be not at all influential, 1 that it was a little influential, 2 that it was somewhat influential, and 3 that it was extremely influential.

ically, day-to-day newsroom practices were the highest-rated source of influence, with about half of the respondents (49 percent) saying that such practices were extremely influential.

"Other St. Louis journalists" were the second most influential source of ideas about what constitutes high-quality journalism in St. Louis, followed by immediate supervisors, local friends and acquaintances, and publishers or general managers.

The four lowest-rated sources of influence were mechanisms of professional self-regulation. The *St. Louis Journalism Review* was the highest-rated of the four, followed closely by national journalism reviews and the *Post-Dispatch*'s ombudsperson. Local media critics finished at the bottom of the list.

Although respondents overall did not rate the *St. Louis Journalism Review* highly as a source of ideas about what constitutes high-quality journalism in St. Louis, it was possible that certain kinds of respondents would rate it highly. However, statistical analyses showed that not to be the case.[64] Men were no more likely than women, more experienced journalists were no more likely than less experienced journalists, and respondents from one kind of news organization were no more likely than respondents from another kind to consider the *Review* influential.

Whether respondents' work had been analyzed in the pages of the *Review* also made no meaningful difference in their overall rating of its influence. However, most of the 34 journalists who said their work had been analyzed by the *Review* described the experience as negative, most frequently saying that the *Review* criticized their work without seeking their side of the story or that the *Review*'s coverage of their work was biased or inaccurate.

Respondents who read the *St. Louis Journalism Review* more often were more likely to consider it influential. Even avid readers, however, did not rate the publication overly influential. It seems safe, therefore, to conclude that exposure to a journalism review is not a measure of its influence, although some authors have equated the two.

Respondents also were asked to agree or disagree with the proposition that journalism reviews should publish each of the three kinds of self-regulatory content—explanatory, critical, and reform—outlined earlier. By and large, the respondents agreed that journalism reviews in general should include explanatory content (92 percent agreed), critical content (95 percent), and reform content (88 percent).

When asked the same question about the *St. Louis Journalism Review,* however, the responses changed somewhat. A little more than half of the respondents (59 percent) said that the *St. Louis Journalism Review* should explain news coverage. Support for critical content in the *Review* was very strong (94 percent), but respondents split over whether it should propose change in news coverage: 53 percent said it should, while 47 percent said it should not.

These results suggest that local journalists may have had different expectations of national and local journalism reviews. Although they were strongly in favor of both kinds of journalism reviews enforcing existing professional norms via critical content, local journalists were split about whether the local review should challenge the norms that exist in St. Louis. There was strong support for national reviews challenging national norms, however.

Similarly, St. Louis journalists wanted national reviews to explain why journalists cover news they way they do, but they were split on whether the local review should explain why local journalists do what they do. Perhaps many respondents felt no need for such explanations because they believed they already know why St. Louis news organizations do what they do.

Why St. Louis journalists were not enthusiastic about the prospect of the *Review* explaining or proposing change in news coverage was not clear. It is commonly thought that journalists are thin-skinned people who do not welcome any kind of criticism, and if that is true, St. Louis journalists probably were no different than any other journalists. Perhaps St. Louis journalists did not believe that the *Review* and its contributors were qualified to analyze news coverage; a few respondents to the survey commented that they believed the *Review* and its contributors were "too academic" or "lack[ed] an understanding of the realities of journalism."

CONCLUSIONS AND DISCUSSION

This study's examination of the content of the *St. Louis Journalism Review,* as well as the analysis of questionnaires returned by St. Louis journalists, leads to the inescapable conclusion that the *Review* does not provide meaningful professional self-regulation of the kind envisioned by advocates of journalism reviews.

The review publishes relatively few articles that could lead St. Louis journalists to question existing news practices in their community. The 38 issues examined for this study contained only 18 articles whose dominant theme was critical—i.e., that suggested that coverage had failed to live up to established standards. Even fewer articles, only 11, had reform as the dominant theme. Such articles are the keys to effective self-regulation because they question the appropriateness of the established standards, instead of simply examining whether coverage met or failed to meet the standards.

Given that the *St. Louis Journalism Review* published so little self-regulatory content, it was not surprising to find that it lacked influence with St. Louis journalists. A journalism review can be a meaningful agent of professional self-regulation only if it publishes a sufficient amount of self-regulatory content.

Why, then, did the *St. Louis Journalism Review* not publish more critical and reform content? One possible explanation might have been the publication's local ties. Simply put, the *Review* and its writers may have been too close to local news organizations. Some of the *Review*'s frequent contributors had been employees of St. Louis news organizations, for instance. Such connections to local journalists and news organizations may have constrained journalism review contributors. This might also explain why articles by faculty from area colleges and universities were more biting than those of the freelance writers who may have depended for other work on the very media they were writing about for the *Review*. Faculty members can seek shelter inside the academy after castigating journalists; freelancers cannot.[65]

The review's failure to provide much in the way of self-regulatory content also could be explained by the ideological preferences of its longtime editor-publisher, Charles Klotzer, which were reflected in his choice of topics to which space would be devoted. If Klotzer determined, for example, that a book about the World Anti-Communist League was of such importance that readers should be offered its contents, he alone could decide to devote space month after month to reprinting it. Such content was hardly likely, however, to cause St. Louis journalists to reevaluate their ideas about what constituted high-quality journalism in St. Louis.

Klotzer had a strong interest in issues of human rights and social reform; his regular column in the review reflected these concerns. One reason for the relative lack of self-regulatory content in the *St. Louis Journalism Review* may have been that Klotzer's principal goals for the review were not to thwart external regulation of the press by providing self-regulation. Many scholars and journalists may focus on media criticism as a means to preempt external regulation and/or achieve better journalism, but Klotzer seemed to regard media criticism as a means necessary to achieve his larger goal: social reform. The journalism review must critique media because they are crucial agents in effecting that social reform, in Klotzer's view.[66] He wrote the following about his motivation for publishing the *St. Louis Journalism Review*:

> The media control what we know, and here is a source of influence and reform. Reporters are the final link in the publishing process. Thus, collaborating with reporters to establish a watchdog over the media would not only establish peer review of the print and broadcasting industry, but would also propel social consciousness and responsibility into the heart of decision-making. . . . In retrospect, it is obvious that watching the media from a professional point of view was only one aspect of the media reform movement. The second and equally strong motivation was to reform the social process in which the media play such an influential role.[67]

An example illustrated the difference in the views of Klotzer and other media critics. Klotzer said he "didn't understand all the excitement" in the national journalism reviews when *Washington Post* reporter Janet Cooke was forced to return a Pulitzer Prize after it was revealed that she had manufactured a character for a story about heroin abuse. While most critics focused on Cooke's breach of accepted journalistic norms, Klotzer disagreed with their view of the incident. "I couldn't see the significance of the issue," he said. "It was puny. It was like somebody getting a speeding ticket. She speeded to get to a greater good. The bigger picture—heroin use—was more important, but missed."[68]

Certainly this philosophy affected the choices Klotzer made about what was published in the review, and explained why he often published articles that did not comment directly on journalistic practices. Although such choices were without doubt Klotzer's right, perhaps they made the publication more an alternative voice in the St. Louis market than a journalism review in the commonly accepted sense of the term. Some critics of the review, who by virtue of their own St. Louis journalism connections were not without bias, went so far as to suggest that Klotzer's ideology prevented the journalism review from being influential among journalists.[69]

If the *St. Louis Journalism Review* is to function more effectively as a critic and agent of reform—setting aside the issue of whether it desires to function as a mechanism of professional self-regulation—it should focus rigorously, and almost exclusively, on journalistic practices in the St. Louis area. Many journalists interested in criticism and explanation of national and international news coverage, after all, find this information in the national reviews and trade magazines.[70]

Unfortunately, however, the local review too often failed to focus on St. Louis. For example, in analyzing coverage of the Persian Gulf war, the *Review* reprinted a list of "misstatements" by national newspaper and broadcast network reporters instead of attempting to analyze the performance of the St. Louis broadcast crews and newspaper correspondents who went to the Middle East to cover the war.[71] Closer devotion to local news coverage might make the review more relevant to St. Louis journalists.

The *St. Louis Journalism Review*'s failure to provide much critical or reform content raises questions about the ability of local journalism reviews to provide meaningful professional self-regulation. A new model may be necessary, at least for local reviews. Effective criticism might come from the fringes of journalism, such as the alternative press.

In St. Louis, for example, the weekly alternative newspaper *Riverfront Times* regularly published media criticism. On several occasions during the period under study, the *St. Louis Journalism Review* appeared to base its articles on criticisms *Riverfront Times* had aimed at the *Post-Dispatch*. For example, the alternative newspaper made a practice of pointing out the *Post-Dispatch*'s neglect in investigating misuse of public funds by the Veiled Prophet Fair, a St. Louis festival that had its roots in white upper-class society circles and that had as one of its sponsors the mainstream daily.[72]

If not from the fringes of journalism, then perhaps effective local criticism must come from outside journalistic circles—"from intellectuals, scholars, writers and ordinary citizens that are outside the apparatus" of the profession.[73] In other words, rather than insisting on the pure self-regulatory role for local journalism reviews—journalists criticizing the work of other journalists—it may be more fruitful to redefine the role to be played by a local review. A local review might contribute more to the cause of socially responsible journalism by providing outside criticism than by publishing the work of journalistic insiders. As this study showed, the most useful criticism published by the *St. Louis Journalism Review* was that written by critics outside the journalistic profession. A journalism review such as this could, if it desired to, cultivate critics from outside the world of St. Louis journalism, actively seeking and publishing more of their work.

The result of this redefined role could be a local journalism review that provided more explanatory, critical, and reform content. Although it could be argued that criticism by outsiders falls outside a strict definition of professional self-regulation, it is clear that a journalism review can have a meliorative effect only if it publishes explanatory, critical, and reform content.

NOTES

1. Randall P. Bezanson, Gilbert Cranberg, and John Soloski, *Libel Law and the Press: Myth and Reality* (New York: The Free Press, 1987), pp. 40–48.

2. Bruce Jennings, Daniel Callahan, and Susan M. Wolf, "The Professions: Public Interest and Common Good," *Hastings Center Report Special Supplement,* February 1987, pp. 3–10.

3. Ibid.

4. Michael D. Bayles, *Professional Ethics,* 2nd ed. (Belmont, Calif.: Wadsworth, 1989), p. 4.

5. Ibid., p. 190.

6. William B. Griffith, "Ethics and the Academic Professional: Some Open Problems and a New Approach," *Business & Professional Ethics Journal* 1 (Spring 1982): 75–95, p. 75.

7. Ibid.

8. Albert Flores, "What Kind of Person Should a Professional Be?" in Albert Flores, ed., *Professional Ideals* (Belmont, Calif.: Wadsworth, 1988), p. 1.

9. Alan H. Goldman, *The Moral Foundations of Professional Ethics* (Totowa, N.J.: Rowman and Littlefield, 1980), p. 18.

10. Bayles, *Professional Ethics,* pp. 8–9.

11. See, for example, Flores, "What Kind of Person," or Jennings, Callahan, and Wolf, "The Professions."

12. Beam cites more than thirty studies that have focused on questions of professionalization in journalism. Randal A. Beam, "Journalism Professionalism as an Organizational-Level Concept," *Journalism Monographs,* no. 121 (June 1990), 1–2.

13. David H. Weaver and G. Cleveland Wilhoit, *The American Journalist: A Portrait of U.S. News People and Their Work,* 2nd ed. (Bloomington: Indiana University Press, 1991), p. 143.

14. Jennings, Callahan and Wolf, "The Professions," p. 5.

15. Richard P. Cunningham, "Journalism: Toward an Accountable Profession," *Hastings Center Report Special Supplement,* February 1987, p. 16.

16. Flores, "What Kind of Person," p. 3.

17. Arlene Kaplan Daniels, "How Free Should Professions Be?" in Eliot Freidson, ed., *The Professions and Their Prospects* (Beverly Hills, Calif.: Sage, 1973), p. 39.

18. Goldman, *Moral Foundations,* p. 18.

19. Beam, "Journalism Professionalism," p. 2.

20. Bayles, *Professional Ethics,* p. 193.

21. Ibid., p. 192.

22. Griffith, "Ethics and the Academic Professional," p. 75.

23. Marion Tuttle Marzolf, *Civilizing Voices: American Press Criticism 1880–1950* (New York: Longman, 1991).

24. Ibid., p. 5.

25. Commission on Freedom of the Press, *A Free and Responsible Press* (Chicago: University of Chicago Press, 1947), p. 94.

26. Marzolf, *Civilizing Voices,* p. 169.

27. James W. Carey, "Journalism and Criticism: The Case of an Undeveloped Profession," *The Review of Politics* 36 (April 1974): 227–249, p. 241.

28. Edmund B. Lambeth, *Committed Journalism: An Ethic for the Profession,* 2nd ed. (Bloomington: Indiana University Press, 1991), p. 108.

29. One study, for example, compared a national journalism review and a national journalism organization's magazine for criticism that reflected the perspectives of traditional, interpretive, or activist journalism. See Hugh M. Culbertson and Lujuan Thompson, "A Comparison of *The Quill* and *Columbia Journalism Review* Relative to Three Critical Perspectives," *Mass Comm Review* 11 (1–2) (Winter/Spring 1984): 12–21. Another study analyzed the *Columbia Journalism Review* to assess the tone of one column's criticism. See Lianne Fridriksson, "A Content Analysis of the Darts and Laurels Column in *Columbia Journalism Review,*" *Mass Comm Review* 11 (3) (Fall 1985): 2–7. A graduate student outlined twelve themes of criticism based on an analysis of three critical publications. See Anita Hare, "Since the 'Sixties': Themes and Issues in Contemporary Press Criticism" (unpublished M.A. thesis, University of South Carolina, 1989).

30. Examples of media ethics books include H. Eugene Goodwin, *Groping for Ethics in Journalism,* 2nd ed. (Ames: Iowa State University Press, 1987); John L. Hulteng, *The Messenger's Motives: Ethical Problems of the News Media,* 2nd ed. (Englewood Cliffs, N.J.: Prentice-Hall, 1985); Lambeth, *Committed Journalism*; and Philip Meyer, *Ethical Journalism: A Guide for Students, Practitioners, and Consumers* (New York: Longman, 1987).

31. See, for instance, Reese Cleghorn, "Introduction: Journalists in Conflict," in Richard T. Kaplar, ed., *Beyond the Courtroom: Alternatives for Resolving Press Disputes* (Washington, D.C.: The Media Institute, 1991), pp. 1–13.

32. Evidence-based studies of means of press self-regulation other than journalism reviews have cast doubt upon the influence of such mechanisms. See, e.g., David

Pritchard, "The Role of Press Councils in a System of Media Accountability: The Case of Quebec," *Canadian Journal of Communication* 16 (1991): 73–93; Patricia L. Dooley, "The National News Council and the Professionalization of American Journalism," paper presented to the Association for Education in Journalism and Mass Communication, Boston, Massachusetts, August 1991; David Pritchard and Madelyn Peroni Morgan, "Impact of Ethics Codes on Judgments by Journalists: A Natural Experiment," *Journalism Quarterly* 66 (1989): 934–941; and David Pritchard, "The Impact of Newspaper Ombudsmen on Journalists' Attitudes," *Journalism Quarterly* 70 (1993): 77–86.

33. Jo A. Cates, *Journalism: A Guide to the Reference Literature* (Englewood, Colo.: Libraries Unlimited, 1990), p. 133.

34. Lambeth, *Committed Journalism*, p. 94.

35. Everette E. Dennis and William L. Rivers, *Other Voices: The New Journalism in America* (San Francisco: Canfield Press, 1974), p. 96.

36. "Between 1968 and 1973, journalism reviews were established in Baltimore (*Buncombe*), Denver (*The Unsatisfied Man*), Holyoke (*Thorn*), Honolulu (*Hawaii Journalism Review*), Houston (*Houston Journalism Review*), Long Beach (*Southern California Journalism Review*), New York City (*[More]*), Philadelphia (*Philadelphia Journalism Review*), Portland (*Oregon Journalism Review*), Providence (*Journalists Newsletter*), San Francisco (*San Francisco Bay Area Journalism Review*), St. Louis (*St. Louis Journalism Review*), and St. Paul (*Twin Cities Journalism Review*)." Lee Brown, *The Reluctant Reformation: On Criticizing the Press in America* (New York: David McKay Company, 1974), p. 57.

37. "St. Louis Ripe for Journalism Review," *St. Louis Journalism Review,* October/November 1970, p. 2.

38. Cleghorn, "Journalists in Conflict," p. 11.

39. Charles L. Klotzer, "The History and Promise of *St. Louis Journalism Review*," paper presented to Media Accountability and Responsibility Systems conference in Paris on April 19, 1991, p. 5.

40. Patricia Bardon Cadigan, "Pleading the First: For Charles Klotzer, Freedom of the Press Is a Life-Long Mission," *St. Louis People,* August 1990, p. 24.

41. "Journalism Review Gets New Owner," *Editor & Publisher*, September 23, 1995, p. 37.

42. Cates, *Journalism*, p. 142.

43. Marzolf, *Civilizing Voices*, p. 202.

44. The thirty-eight issues represented the publication's entire run from January 1988 through July/August 1991. Only articles dealing with news practices in St. Louis were examined for this study, which focused more on the values reflected in the review's pages than on a purely quantitative analysis. Articles were classified according to the nature of their self-regulatory content: explanatory, critical, or reform.

45. Karl Ross, "Most St. Louis Media Keep On Using 'Black,'" *St. Louis Journalism Review*, September 1989, pp. 1, 16.

46. Staci D. Kramer, "What You Think You Will See Isn't Always What You Get," *St. Louis Journalism Review,* February 1988, pp. 10–11.

47. Staci D. Kramer, "The Gilmour-Schwartz-Westfall Media Feast: Mishandled, Misinterpreted, Misunderstood," *St. Louis Journalism Review*, February 1989, pp. 1, 10–11, 21.

48. Ibid., p. 1.

49. Robert L. Terrell, "'As Outlaws They Glory in Crime, in Anti-Mainstream Behavior,'" *St. Louis Journalism Review*, August 1990, pp. 16–17.

50. Arthur Silverblatt, "Some Suggestions to Improve Local Television Newscasts," *St. Louis Journalism Review*, April 1990, p. 16.

51. Charles Korr, "'Losing' the Cardinals May Not Be a Loss After All," *St. Louis Journalism Review*, February 1988, p. 5.

52. Herbert J. Gans, *Deciding What's News: A Study of CBS Evening News, NBC Nightly News, Newsweek and Time* (New York: Vintage Books, 1980), p. 267.

53. *St. Louis Journalism Review* articles focusing on KTVI included "Channel 2 Brings Back 6 P.M. News," January 1991, p. 4; Staci D. Kramer, "Channel 2 Loses Its Zip," January 1988, p. 5; Kramer, "Credibility Gap at Ch. 2," February 1988, p. 3; Kramer, "Channels," February 1988, p. 6; Kramer, "Veteran Marsh Rediscovered," December 1988, pp. 10–12; and "From the Frontline," December 1988, p. 12.

54. Labor negotiation articles in the *Review* included Dawn Grodsky, "Former Staffer Sues Suburban Journals for Overtime Pay," January 1991, p. 6; Kramer, "Post Lays Down Gauntlet in Labor Negotiations," July/August 1989, pp. 1, 19; Kramer, "Post Fights Back on All Fronts," September 1989, pp. 1, 7; Ed Bishop, "Guild Rejects Two-Tier Post Proposal," October 1989, p. 5; Kramer, "Future of News Guild at Stake in Contract Face Off [*sic*]," February 1990, pp. 1, 10–11; Bishop, "KSDK-TV Guild Signs Contract," February 1990, p. 1; Kramer, "So Far No Deal at Post," March 1990, pp. 1, 10–11; Kramer, "Six Down; Five to Go," April 1990, pp. 1, 12, 15; and Charles L. Klotzer, "Post-Guild Negotiations Enter the 1990s, Hard Bargaining Ahead," June 1990, pp. 1, 6–7.

55. *Review* articles solely about or connected to Gluck included Lynn Venhaus, "Five-Year Wait Over for Globe Staffers," January 1991, p. 5; "Unlike Veritas, at Least Gluck Was Worth Suing," January 1988, p. 3; "SR Sold Again," January 1988, p. 3; "Chutzpah a la Gluck," July 1988, p. 3; Kramer, "Gluck Is Back in the News, 'Builds Up' New Magazine Chain," November 1988, pp. 10–11; "Gluck Rides Again," April 1989, p. 3; "Gluck Rides Again," May 1989, p. 3; Bishop, "'Missouri' Life after Death," October 1989, p. 3; Daniel J. Fiduccia, "Jeff Gluck's West Coast Adventures," November 1989, pp. 1, 10–11; "Former Globers Again Hope for a Green Christmas," August 1990, pp. 1, 8; and Rick Casey, "Chapter 22: The Gluck Saga," August 1990, p. 11.

56. Horrigan's jump to the *Sun* was the cover photograph and an inside two-page article in Kramer, "St. Louis Sun Scoops Up Horrigan," *St. Louis Journalism Review,* July/August 1989, pp. 8–9; and his adventures at the short-lived paper occupied almost a page in Kevin Horrigan, "The Clock Ran Out . . . but What a Time We Had," *St. Louis Journalism Review,* May 1990, p. 9.

57. Bruce was the subject of a cover promotion and a page and a half of inside coverage in Kramer, "The New Betsy Bruce," *St. Louis Journalism Review*, October 1989, pp. 6–7; and Kramer, "18-Year Veteran Broke Ground for Women," *St. Louis Journalism Review*, October 1989, p. 6.

58. For example, Ed Bishop, "Weather Forecasting Provides Rating Edge to TV Stations," April 1991, p. 1, turned to the *Review*'s own television critic for opinions about local weather coverage, and Richard Newman, "St. Louis No Longer a News Hub but Still a Barometer for National Issues," July/August 1991, pp. 9, 19, turned to

frequent *St. Louis Journalism Review* contributor and former associate editor Staci D. Kramer, who freelances regionally and nationally, instead of to freelancers without connections to the *Review.*

59. The reprinted book was Scott Anderson and Jon Lee Anderson, *Inside the League: The True Story of How Terrorists, Nazis, and Latin American Death Squads Have Infiltrated the World Anti-Communist League* (New York: Dodd, Mead and Company, 1986). The reprinted chapter was "The Media Cartel: Corporate Control of the News" in Martin A. Lee and Norman Solomon, *Unreliable Sources: A Guide to Detecting Bias in News Media* (New York: Carol Publishing Group, 1990).

60. Of the 227 potential respondents, the names of 131 (58 percent) came from the circulation records of the *St. Louis Journalism Review.* The review staff sorted those records to provide names only of subscribers employed in media-related positions in the St. Louis area. The names of the other 96 potential respondents (42 percent) came from two weeks of attention to major St. Louis news media. The names of reporters, photographers, and columnists from all sections of the *St. Louis Post-Dispatch* were included in the mailing. The names of on-air journalists on the nightly newscasts of St. Louis's three network-affiliate television stations also were included.

61. A few respondents whose names were drawn from the circulation records of the *St. Louis Journalism Review* had retired. They were considered to be affiliated with the last St. Louis news organization for which they had worked.

62. Of course, given that more than half (58 percent) of the list of potential respondents was drawn from the subscription list of the *St. Louis Journalism Review,* it comes as no surprise that readership and discussion of the publication were high.

63. The list of influences was modeled on that used by Weaver and Wilhoit in their survey of American journalists. See Weaver and Wilhoit, *American Journalist.*

64. To examine the effect of various factors on respondents' rating of the *St. Louis Journalism Review,* a multiple regression analysis featuring five predictor variables was used. The predictors were whether the review had analyzed a respondent's work, respondent's sex, the type of news organization the respondent worked for (the *Post-Dispatch,* major broadcast station, or other), respondent's amount of experience in journalism, and the extent to which the respondent read the review. The only factor that was a meaningful predictor of respondents' rating of the influence of the review was the extent to which they read it (beta = .49). Overall, the analysis accounted for 18 percent of the variance in respondents' rating of the influence of the *St. Louis Journalism Review.*

65. *St. Louis Journalism Review* editor-publisher Charles Klotzer, however, points out that faculty members also may be dependent on ties to the journalistic world "for placing students, for becoming paid consultants, for job switching, etc." Personal correspondence, October 2, 1991.

66. Charles L. Klotzer, personal interview, St. Louis, Missouri, August 15, 1991.

67. Klotzer, "The History and Promise of *St. Louis Journalism Review,*" p. 1.

68. Klotzer, interview.

69. Richard Byrne, *Riverfront Times* media columnist, and Lawrence Fiquette, *Post-Dispatch* reader's advocate, personal interviews, St. Louis, Missouri, August, 15 1991.

70. Weaver and Wilhoit's survey of journalists found that "at least 'sometimes'"

63 percent of all journalists read *Editor & Publisher,* 56 percent read *Columbia Journalism Review,* 50 percent read *Quill,* and 43 percent read *Washington Journalism Review.*

71. Bob Zelnick, "Misstatements," March 1991, p. 13.

72. Staci D. Kramer, "V.P. Fair Loses Most Favored Status," June 1988, p. 20.

73. James W. Carey, "Journalism and Criticism," p. 238.

7

Structural Flaws in Press Council Decision-Making

DAVID PRITCHARD

AFTER CHAPTER 5'S STUDY OF A NEWS OMBUDSMAN AND CHAP-
TER 6'S STUDY OF A JOURNALISM REVIEW, CHAPTER 7 FOCUSES ON
YET ANOTHER MEANS OF MEDIA SELF-REGULATION, THE PRESS
COUNCIL.

DAVID PRITCHARD SPENT LONG HOURS DIGGING THROUGH
FILES AT THE OFFICES OF THE QUEBEC PRESS COUNCIL TO GATHER
DATA FOR THIS ANALYSIS OF THE COUNCIL'S DECISION-MAKING IN
POLITICALLY CHARGED CASES RELATING TO NEWS COVERAGE OF
QUEBEC'S 1980 REFERENDUM ON INDEPENDENCE. THE RESEARCH
REVEALS A PATTERN OF INCONSISTENT DECISION-MAKING THAT
TENDED TO FAVOR PARTIES THAT HELPED FUND THE COUNCIL. THE
RESULTS CAST DOUBT UPON THE ABILITY OF A SELF-REGULATORY
MECHANISM SUCH AS A PRESS COUNCIL TO BE AN INDEPENDENT,
IMPARTIAL AGENT OF MEDIA ACCOUNTABILITY.

THE RESEARCH WAS FUNDED BY A FELLOWSHIP FROM THE
CANADA–UNITED STATES FULBRIGHT PROGRAM, WITH ADDITION-
AL AID FROM THE DEPARTMENT OF EXTERNAL AFFAIRS OF CANADA
AND LE MINISTÈRE DES AFFAIRES INTERNATIONALES DU QUÉBEC.
IT SHOULD BE STRESSED THAT THE ANALYSES AND INTERPRETA-
TIONS REPORTED IN THIS CHAPTER ARE THOSE OF THE AUTHOR
ALONE. PORTIONS OF THIS RESEARCH WERE PUBLISHED EARLIER
IN *QUÉBEC STUDIES*, A PUBLICATION OF THE AMERICAN COUNCIL
FOR QUEBEC STUDIES.

In most Canadian provinces and one American state, citizens or groups
whose accountability demands have not been satisfied by the news organization to which they complained may take their claims to a press council.

The several North American press councils all are established and financed
by the news industry for the purposes of receiving and resolving complaints
about news media performance. Press councils have no legal power. Their
authority depends upon public confidence in their fairness and impartiality.

This chapter looks at the performance of the Quebec Press Council during a time of political tension. Periods of social and political tension are useful natural laboratories for studying institutions because the conditions of stress that accompany such periods tend to highlight flaws in the structures and/or operations of those institutions.

The period of political tension covered by this chapter occurred during the first half of 1980, when the government of Quebec asked its citizens to vote in favor of a referendum that would have led to the secession of Quebec from Canada. The possible breakup of the country was the gravest political crisis in Canadian history to that point. Controversy over media coverage was an important feature of the campaign, and the Quebec Press Council created a special committee to deal with referendum-related complaints.

This chapter begins with some background on press councils and the QPC, a nonprofit institution created by the Quebec news industry with the active encouragement of the provincial government. The chapter then outlines the QPC's actions during the referendum campaign and examines its performance under conditions of unusual stress, with a special focus on how it ruled in cases involving its financial sponsors. The article closes with a discussion of possible causes for the QPC's lackluster performance during the referendum campaign.

BACKGROUND

Although the first press council was established in 1916 in Sweden, the best-known press council—and the one upon which most other councils, including the Quebec Press Council, were modeled—is the British Press Council (called the Press Complaints Commission since 1990).

The British council was created in 1953. American scholars were attracted to the idea, which seemed to be an incarnation of the media accountability ideals expressed in 1947 by the Hutchins Commission. University of Minnesota journalism professor J. Edward Gerald, who strongly supported the idea of news councils,[1] was the first to study the British Press Council. Gerald's enthusiasm for the press council concept was clear. In 1956 he wrote: "The council is significant, from the standpoint of social theory, because it represents a modification of the laissez-faire concept of communication in a democratic society."[2] A few years later Gerald's admiration was undimmed:

> Its [the council's] strength is a nucleus of young and old warriors unashamed to do battle for civilized principles of professional behavior. Theirs is the most honorable and intellectual task of all: To search for and to propagate ethical values. They have not failed the British press or the British public and through the further development of the Council over a period of years the press of Britain has another chance to show the world how to use freedom responsibly and intelligently.[3]

Other American scholars shared Gerald's view.[4] However, a group of Australian journalists who went to Britain to study the press council concluded that the council had not succeeded in reducing sensationalism, distortion, political bias, or tendencies toward press monopoly.[5] The third Royal Commission on the Press in 1977 also was critical: "It is unhappily certain that the Council has so far failed to persuade the knowledgeable public that it deals satisfactorily with complaints against newspapers, notwithstanding that this has come to be seen as its main purpose."[6] In the early 1980s an independent group of scholars came to a similar conclusion:

> The performance of the Press Council has been measured against the yard-sticks provided by its own constitutional objectives. In each respect—the adjudication of public complaints, the maintenance of ethical standards, the defence of press freedom and the combating of monopolistic tendencies—the evidence has dictated the conclusion that the council does not satisfactorily achieve these objectives.[7]

Though solid empirical studies of press council performance are rare, the British Press Council's failure to achieve the goals it set for itself seems more the norm than the exception. Scholars who look beyond the often-rosy statements of press council supporters have questioned the councils' effectiveness. A careful examination of the effects of local press councils in the United States, for example, found little to support claims that the councils improved press responsibility: "Some claims made about the effects of community press councils appear to lack supportive evidence. In other instances, claims appear to have been generalized from what appears to be a consideration of only selected evidence."[8] Studies of the press councils in Australia and Quebec have raised similar doubts.[9]

Although the United States had a news council from 1973 to 1984, the only well-established American press council in the late 1990s was the Minnesota News Council, created in 1971 as the Minnesota Press Council. Professor Gerald, who had become so enamored of the British Press Council, played the key role in the creation of the Minnesota council, and several University of Minnesota graduate students have studied aspects of the council's performance.

The research is somewhat inconclusive. Some of a small sample of weekly newspaper editors reported changing their practices after they were criticized by the Minnesota News Council,[10] but relatively few people who complained to either the MNC or the National News Council thought that the news council decision had a positive long-term effect on the offending news organization's performance.[11] Nonetheless, most of those who had complained would use the council again,[12] though many of them believe news council procedures and rulings are biased in favor of the press.[13]

The main benefit of the Minnesota News Council may be that some disputes that otherwise would ripen into libel suits instead receive adjudication from the news council. One careful study found that "the news council clearly depressed the incidence of media libel cases in Minnesota."[14] A review of the ethical principles contained in the MNC's rulings concluded: "In Minnesota, people unjustly maligned by the press may look to the News Council as a protector of their reputation."[15] The existence of the MNC enabled Minnesota's largest newspaper, the *Star Tribune,* to negotiate a discount on its libel insurance.[16]

Press councils generally are funded by news organizations and foundations, and their members come both from the news media and from the general public. Though they have no legal power to enforce their decisions, press councils receive and adjudicate complaints about press performance. The sole power of press councils is the power of publicity; news organizations are encouraged to publish press council rulings. Press councils exist in about twenty countries, mostly in Europe and in countries whose legal systems have been heavily influenced by the British legal system.[17]

The Quebec Press Council is one of Canada's six regional press councils (the others are the Atlantic Press Council, which covers the provinces of New Brunswick, Newfoundland, Nova Scotia, and Prince Edward Island, and the councils in Ontario, British Columbia, Alberta, and Manitoba). The QPC began operations in 1973; its structure and functioning have not changed significantly since then.

The QPC has three categories of members: journalists (six members), media management (six members), and the public (seven members). Its five-person permanent staff was based in Quebec City until 1997, when it moved to Montreal. The press council rarely comments on press performance outside of the context of a written complaint about a specific incident. When a written complaint arrives, the QPC staff forwards a copy of the complaint to the "defendant"—the party against whom the complaint is directed—asking for comments. Copies of the defendant's response are sent to the complaining party for additional comment. All of the information is presented to a committee composed of two people from each of the QPC's membership categories. The committee considers the facts of the case and then issues a written decision on whether the behavior in question was ethically justifiable. The QPC has no legal power to punish journalists or news organizations; its sole power is the power of publicity. News organizations are encouraged to publish QPC rulings, in hopes that such publicity will educate citizens and journalists about ethical media behavior.

At the time of the 1980 referendum campaign, the QPC defined its core mission as consisting of two principal objectives: (1) "protecting the public's right to free, honest, and complete news in all its forms," and (2) "defending freedom of the press."[18] With specific reference to the media's role in the referendum campaign, the QPC declared that it was important not only that the information transmitted by the news media be factual but that it present the various elements of the debate in their true light.[19]

The referendum was a cornerstone of the political strategy of the Parti Québécois, which favored Quebec's independence from Canada. The PQ gained the right to form the provincial government by winning a strong majority of seats in the provincial legislature in the 1976 provincial elections. The succeeding years were a time of intense debate over the future of Quebec and, by implication, over the future of Canada. Not surprisingly, how the news media reported the debate became a political issue as well. PQ partisans accused major news organizations of having a strong federalist bias; federalists criticized French-language journalists for favoring the separatist option.[20]

Given the intensity of the controversy over press coverage as the referendum neared, it was inevitable that the QPC would receive complaints about news coverage of the campaign. In accepting such complaints and issuing rulings about them, the press council established a record that reveals much about its strengths and weaknesses.

THE REFERENDUM CAMPAIGN

The referendum on May 20, 1980, was one of the most dramatic political events in Canadian history. Although the referendum question merely asked whether the Quebec government should be granted the authority to negotiate "sovereignty-association," people outside Quebec generally perceived that the referendum was about whether Quebec should be independent. As 1979 drew to a close, the campaign began to heat up. Press coverage of the campaign intensified as well.

The QPC received its first referendum-related case in November 1979, when Parti Québécois politician Louis O'Neill filed a complaint about a United Press Canada story. The story was based on a faulty translation of a document about campaign strategy that O'Neill—a member of the provincial legislature who had been Quebec's minister of communications—had circulated among PQ partisans in his district. The story implied that O'Neill's views were at variance with those of Quebec premier (and PQ leader) René Lévesque. The Montreal *Gazette* played the erroneous wire-service story on its front page with the headline "Ex-minister Says PQ Using 'Blackmail, Lies.'"[21]

In January 1980, as the QPC considered O'Neill's complaint against the wire service and the *Gazette,* another referendum-related complaint arrived. A television journalist had said that Lévesque was "un homme à abattre" ("a man to shoot down") during the referendum campaign. A citizen complained that the journalist's words constituted incitement to violence.[22] Later the same month Quebec Minister of Education Jacques-Yvan Morin filed a complaint against four daily newspapers, two radio stations, a television station, and various individuals who worked at the news organizations. As with O'Neill's complaint a couple of months earlier, Morin's had to do with an erroneous story that was transmitted to numerous Quebec media outlets by a wire service.

The French daily *Le Monde* had published an interview in which Morin discussed the political situation in Quebec. *Le Journal de Montréal,* one of Quebec's largest newspapers, had a part-time correspondent in Paris who read the story in *Le Monde,* phoned Montreal, and dictated a story about the views

Morin had expressed in France. Somewhere in the process, a mistake was made: *Le Journal de Montréal* reported that Morin had said that if the federalist side won the referendum there would be a resurgence of political violence in Quebec. Canadian Press, a wire service, rewrote the erroneous story published in *Le Journal de Montréal* and sent it to newspapers and broadcast stations around Canada. The wire-service story led to a variety of expressions of opinion critical of Morin in Quebec media.[23]

After a minor case in March—the local unit of the Parti Québécois in Iberville complained about biased treatment in a weekly newspaper[24]—the press council in early April released its decision on the complaint that former Minister of Communications O'Neill had filed almost five months earlier. The decision, sharply critical not only of the wire-service journalist who made translation errors but also of *The Gazette* for failing to independently verify the facts in the wire-service story, received considerable press attention.[25]

The publicity given to the O'Neill decision raised the press council's profile, and within days two additional major complaints arrived at the QPC's office in Quebec City. On April 8 *The Gazette,* Montreal's only English-language daily newspaper, filed a complaint against *Le Journal de Montréal* and Canadian Press for alleged errors in their stories about *The Gazette*'s strategy for covering the referendum campaign.[26] The same day, the powerful Conseil du patronat du Québec, a business group, filed a complaint against *Le Devoir,* a small but influential Montreal daily.[27] Two days later, a citizen complained that her local weekly paper had misled its readers in a poll about the referendum.[28]

With little more than a month remaining before the May 20 referendum, the QPC had six unresolved complaints about referendum-related coverage and the prospect of more to come. Some of the complaints came from high-profile people or organizations (e.g., Morin, *The Gazette,* le Conseil du patronat). Meanwhile, news coverage of the campaign was becoming more and more of a political issue, with partisans of both sides increasingly claiming that the media were biased against them. In the eyes of some, the future of Canada was at stake.

In such a high-pressure context, prompt and thoughtful action by the press council could have helped resolve tensions about the role of the news media in the referendum campaign. The QPC, however, was ill prepared to take such action.

One problem was the QPC's chronic inability to decide cases quickly. It was taking the press council about six months to gather information, deliberate, and agree on the wording of a decision for a typical complaint.[29] The press council's inefficiency was caused in part by the fact that it had never indexed what it called its "jurisprudence"—the principles that could be derived from the reasoning of previous decisions. The result was that members of the QPC complaints committee were forced to deal with each complaint on an ad hoc basis, without reference to written guidelines that could help ensure coherence and consistency.[30]

In addition to its inefficiency, the press council had a variety of conflicts of interest with parties in the debate over the media's role in the referendum campaign. Always strapped for funds and continually seeking new sources of revenue, the QPC in the late 1970s sought additional contributions from the media and the Quebec government. The result was that during the referendum campaign the QPC was called on to judge the behavior of organizations whose financial contributions it coveted.

The press council was dependent on media organizations and media workers for most of its operating income. Media organizations (75.8 percent) and journalists (9.5 percent) together provided more than 85 percent of the QPC's revenues during the 1979–80 fiscal year, which ended seven weeks before the referendum.[31] The principal contributors were Radio-Canada and les Quotidiens du Québec (Quebec Daily Newspaper Association), an association dominated by large and long-established Montreal newspapers (e.g., *La Presse, The Gazette*). Radio-Québec, an arm of the provincial government, also contributed to the QPC, accounting for about 4 percent of the press council's revenues in 1979–80. The remainder of the QPC's revenues in 1979–80 (14.7 percent) came from the Quebec Press Council Foundation, which had received most of its funds from the provincial government.[32]

Already funded almost exclusively by media interests and the provincial government, the QPC in the late 1970s sought additional contributions from the media and the government. The fast-growing daily tabloids owned by Quebecor (*Le Journal de Montréal, Le Journal de Québec*) were not members of the Quebec Daily Newspaper Association and had never contributed to the press council. Getting funding from Quebecor, either directly or through the newspaper association, had become a prime objective of the QPC.

The press council also hoped for more contributions from the provincial government to the QPC Foundation. The year before the Parti Québécois was elected, the Quebec government gave $100,000 to the foundation, with a pledge of $400,000 more over the succeeding four years. The PQ government gave the foundation the second $100,000 in 1977, but nothing in 1978, 1979, and 1980. The press council's staff regularly sought to obtain the rest of the $500,000 pledge. "Numerous steps are being taken so that the current government of Quebec will come through with the public contribution to the foundation," a QPC report acknowledged at one point. In addition, the Quebec government had funded specific QPC projects, and the press council hoped to attract additional project-specific support from the government.

Such was the state of the press council thirty-two days before the referendum when the head of the federalist campaign, Liberal Party leader Claude Ryan (former editor and publisher of *Le Devoir*) called for the creation of a media oversight committee to monitor press performance in the remaining weeks of the referendum campaign. Claiming that the media favored the pro-independence side, Ryan said it was vital that news organizations cover the campaign impartially. When reporters asked why he did not take his complaints about news coverage to the QPC, Ryan replied that the press council could not deal with complaints quickly enough to resolve them before the referendum, which was less than five weeks away.[33]

The public affront spurred the QPC to action. Three days after Ryan's criticism, the press council announced the formation of a special committee to receive complaints about coverage of the referendum campaign. The special committee would render decisions on complaints within a week of receiving them, the press council promised.[34] The announcement did not explain how the press council, which often had been criticized for the slowness of its decisions, would all of a sudden be able to make coherent decisions within a week's time. Nor did the announcement note the extent of the QPC's financial ties to organizations directly involved in the controversy over press coverage of the referendum campaign.

All in all, it was a situation ripe for ad hoc decision-making, with the risk that the decisions the special committee hoped to make with unusual speed would be unduly sympathetic to the interests of the QPC's actual and potential sponsors.

PATTERNS OF DECISIONS

The analysis that follows is based principally on the trove of documents in the press council's files. A file on a typical case contains the original letter of complaint, a copy of the offending media content, copies of letters between the press council's staff and the parties to each case, internal QPC memoranda discussing issues related to the case, drafts of the QPC's decision in the case, and clippings of newspaper and magazine stories about the decision. The documentary information was supplemented by examination of published QPC reports and by interviews with people who were press council staff members in 1979 and 1980.

The analysis of the referendum-related decisions focused on three questions. First, was the press council able to fulfill its commitment to render decisions within seven days of receiving complaints? Second, did the QPC's decisions consistently favor parties with which the press council had financial ties? Third, how coherent and defensible were the decisions that the press council made under conditions of stress (e.g., intense time pressure, conflict of interest, public scrutiny)?

The answer to the first question is straightforward: in most cases, the press council did not render decisions within seven days of receiving the complaints. The QPC announced the creation of its special committee on April 21. Of the 15 cases[35] either on hand on that date or received before the May 20 referendum, the special committee issued decisions within the promised seven days in only four cases. The committee took between 11 and 27 days to issue decisions in eight other cases. It took the special committee an average of 14.7 days— more than two weeks—to issue decisions.[36] The committee did not rule in three other cases submitted to it. After the referendum, those cases[37] were turned over to the regular complaints committee, which issued decisions months later.

The second question in the analysis asks whether the QPC's decisions consistently favored parties with which the press council had financial ties. To explore the issue, special attention was paid to the nature of the complainant and the defendant in each referendum-related complaint.

Each party to a case was either a "funder" or a "non-funder" of the press council. The QPC would be in a clear situation of conflict of interest when it judged the case of a "funder." Although the press council urges journalists to avoid "not only conflicts of interest, but also any situation that might make them [journalists] appear to be in a conflict of interest or seem to have undue connections with any political, financial, or other interests,"[38] it has no mechanism for dealing with its own conflicts of interest.

I defined the QPC's major groups of funders as people or organizations affiliated either with the Parti Québécois (e.g., PQ members, representatives of the Quebec government) or with the metropolitan media (major broadcast networks, the daily newspapers in Montreal and Quebec City). Non-funders were all other parties.

The press council's conflict of interest with PQ-affiliated parties stemmed from the fact that the Quebec government was both a funder of press council operations (via Radio-Québec, the QPC Foundation, and special projects) and the press council's best hope for a major infusion of new capital at the same time that prominent PQ figures such as O'Neill and Morin were asking the press council to rule in their favor in referendum-related complaints.

The press council's conflict of interest with the metropolitan media was based on two sets of facts. The first had to do with *Le Journal de Montréal* and *Le Journal de Québec*. The two tabloids owned by Quebecor were Quebec's fastest-growing daily newspapers, but they provided no money to the press council. After several years of antagonism, a rapprochement between the Quebecor papers and the press council seemed likely as the referendum neared. Press council staff were hopeful that Quebecor would finally take part in financing the press council.

The second set of facts related to the QPC's conflict of interest with metropolitan media organizations was that such organizations—especially Radio-Canada, *La Presse,* and *The Gazette*—were the press council's most important sources of revenue. In addition, employees of those organizations held a disproportionate number of seats on the press council. In 1979–80, for example, seven of the twelve news industry members of the press council worked either at Radio-Canada (four people), *La Presse* (two people), or *The Gazette* (one person).

The QPC received 20 cases containing 30 distinct complaints about referendum-related matters before the May 20 referendum. Some of the complaints went to the special committee; others did not.[39] During the politically tense period of the referendum campaign and its immediate aftermath, the press council issued decisions on 24 complaints. Two of the complaints were dealt with before the creation of the special committee; the special committee dealt with 22 complaints. The other 6 complaints about referendum-related matters were decided by the QPC's regular complaints committee several months after the referendum.

In 15 of the complaints the QPC handled during the referendum period, funders (defined as a PQ-affiliated party or the metropolitan media) opposed non-funders.[40] The QPC ruled in favor of the funders—the parties with which the QPC had financial ties—in 86 percent (13) of the complaints. The QPC decisions on referendum-related complaints issued months after the referendum show the same pattern. Five complaints decided after the referendum by the QPC's regular complaints committee were disputes between funders and

Table 1 Referendum-Related Cases Opposing QPC Funders and Non-funders

Case names are followed by their QPC case numbers, modified with letters when a plaintiff made multiple complaints. Names of parties affiliated with QPC funders are underlined. The parties the QPC favored in its decisions are indicated by an asterisk (*). Cases in which funders lost are in bold italics.

Funders vs. Non-funders (n=7)

O'Neill* v United Press Canada (79-11-61)
Parti Québécois* v Le Journal de Chambly (80-03-22)
Morin* v La Tribune (80-01-04a)
Morin v CKVL* (80-01-04b)
Morin* v CKGM (80-01-04c)
Morin* v CFCF-TV (80-01-04d)
The Gazette* v La Presse Canadienne (80-04-25)

Non-funders vs. Funders (n=13)

Raymond Carrier v Normand Girard (TVA)* (80-01-02)
Conseil du patronat du Québec* v Le Devoir (80-04-28a)
Conseil du patronat du Québec v Le Devoir* (80-04-28b)
Gabriel Painchaud v Le Journal de Québec* (80-04-32)
Paul Perreault v CBC* (80-04-34)
Marcel Thérien v Radio-Québec* (80-04-36)
Jean-Didier Fessou v Le Regroupement national pour le OUI* (80-05-38)
Madeleine Roy v Radio-Canada* (80-05-40)
Jacques Rivet v Le Devoir* (80-05-41)
Paul Perreault et Claude Letarte v Le Devoir* (80-05-42)
François Leduc v La Presse* (80-05-43a)
François Leduc* v Le Devoir (80-05-43b)
François Leduc v CTV* (80-05-43c)

non-funders. Funders won four of them.[41] Table 1 shows the patterns in the 20 referendum-related complaints opposing QPC funders and non-funders. Funders won 17 of the 20 disputes with non-funders, a success rate of 85 percent.

Although twenty complaints is too small a number to be the basis of a statistically meaningful analysis, the fact that QPC funders won 85 percent of the disputes in which they opposed non-funders raises questions about the QPC's ability to be impartial in cases involving its funders, as this article defines the term.

The third and final issue included in this analysis is whether the press council's referendum-related decisions were logical and consistently applied. At the time of the referendum, the QPC had no statement of principles to guide its decisions in individual cases. It had never adopted an ethics code. It had never organized and compiled the principles that could have been derived from the decisions it had made in several hundred cases since it began operating in 1973. In short, the press council had no set of established ethical principles to guide its decision-making.

The lack of such guidelines may have contributed to problems of logic and consistency in some of the highest-profile cases the QPC dealt with during the referendum period. The central issue in several cases, for example, was whether news organizations had an ethical duty to verify the facts in stories transmitted to them by wire services. When PQ politician Louis O'Neill complained that *The Gazette* had erred by failing to verify the contents of an incorrect wire story, the press council agreed:

> By publishing the article in question, which it acknowledged as being full of serious errors, *The Gazette* did not act with the level of care and professional rigor required by its role as source of public information and by the respect of the public's right to information. . . . In this case *The Gazette* should have exhibited greater vigilance, greater rigor, and greater care in verifying the information contained in the stories of United Press Canada [translation by author].

The press council took a similar view when PQ politician Jacques-Yvan Morin complained about an erroneous *Journal de Montréal* story. Canadian Press rewrote the story and transmitted it. The wire-service story was the basis for a number of criticisms of Morin in Quebec media. The press council was unforgiving. Ruling against *La Tribune,* a daily newspaper in Sherbrooke, and two broadcast stations, the QPC said that the media should have verified the facts in the wire-service story before using it.

In both the O'Neill and the Morin cases, then, the QPC applied the principle that news organizations are ethically obliged to verify the contents of wire-service stories before using them. The principle is fairly absurd. As a practical matter, it is impossible for a news organization to independently verify all of the major facts in wire stories transmitted by reputable news agencies from the four corners of the globe. As the news director of a television station criticized in the Morin case explained: "We feel it unreasonable to expect that any news organization should 'further verify' all reports that are carried on Canadian Press. This would destroy the raison d'être of news agencies."[42] A journalism professor at a Quebec City university was incredulous at the press council's decisions in the O'Neill and Morin decisions: "The Press Council, an organization that ought to be acquainted with the world of news more than anyone, is demonstrating an unforgivable ignorance with respect to wire services."[43]

The press council's principle was all the more unjustified because the news organizations that used the inaccurate wire-service stories about O'Neill and Morin corrected the inaccuracies as soon as possible. Prompt correction of errors reflects a high standard of ethics. Nonetheless, *The Gazette*'s next-day correction of the erroneous United Press Canada story about O'Neill was not sufficient for the press council, just as the prompt corrections of the erroneous Canadian Press story about Morin disseminated by *La Tribune* and CFCF-TV were deemed not to be sufficient.

The press council's message seemed to be that the publication of any inaccurate information is ethically unjustifiable, even when the publisher has acted in good faith (e.g., as when the errors are in a story transmitted by a reputable news agency) and even when the inaccuracies are promptly corrected. The QPC did not apply this principle consistently in the referendum-related cases, however.

In the two cases in which the complainants were important Parti Québécois figures, prompt corrections did not absolve what the press council saw as the news organizations' ethical sins. In two cases in which the complainants were affiliated with the federalist side in the referendum campaign, though, the press council favored news organizations that corrected mistakes they had made.

In the first such case, *The Gazette* complained about mistakes in a Canadian Press story about the strategy of *The Gazette,* a strongly federalist paper, for covering the referendum campaign.[44] In the O'Neill and Morin cases, mistakes had been unpardonable even if they had been corrected. When *The Gazette* complained about clear mistakes, however, the QPC refused to rule against Canadian Press. The QPC ruled:

> The Canadian Press responsibly fulfilled its mission of informing the public by taking the steps necessary to correct its quite involuntary error and by offering its apologies to The Gazette for the embarrassment that its story may have caused the newspaper and its editor.[45]

The second case involved a complaint by the Conseil du patronat du Québec against *Le Devoir* for distorting the views the business group had expressed in a document titled "La question énergétique dans un régime de souveraineté-association." The press council agreed that *Le Devoir* had distorted the news: "The person who wrote the headline of the article in question as well as the reporter distorted . . . the spirit of the position papers released by the Conseil du patronat . . . and misled the public about the scope of its study."[46] Nonetheless, the press council concluded that *Le Devoir* "met the requirements of the public's right to information" by publishing a letter of clarification from the Conseil du patronat four days after the inaccurate article.

Ghislain Dufour, executive vice president of the Conseil du patronat at the time, sent the press council a letter expressing bitter disappointment with the decision. Despite the fact that the press council agreed that *Le Devoir* had misled the public by distorting the Conseil du patronat's message, "the newspaper received the Press Council's blessings for its diligence, its concern for justice, and its manner of satisfying the requirements of the public's right to information!"[47]

Dufour's anger was understandable. The press council had provided no coherent rationale for its decision. And although Dufour did not refer to previous press council cases, the QPC's approval of corrections when *The Gazette* and the Conseil du patronat were victims of error was in stark contrast with its refusal to approve corrections when important Parti Québécois figures were victims of error.

A final case reinforces the point. In March 1980 the local branch of the Parti Québécois in Iberville complained that a weekly paper had published an inaccurate article about a series of resignations. Although the newspaper published an acknowledgment of its error and allowed the complainant to correct the facts, the press council ruled in favor of the PQ organization.[48]

The evidence shows that the press council ruled inconsistently in cases involving good-faith corrections of mistakes in referendum-related cases. Studies of the "coherence" of the QPC's decisions in other time periods show similar inconsistency.[49]

With the referendum-related cases, however, inconsistency was not the same as randomness. The pattern of decisions was not random. Rather, it clearly suggested that the QPC had undue sympathy for parties to which it had financial ties.[50]

DISCUSSION

On May 20, 1980, almost 60 percent of Quebec's voters said "NON." The Quebec government was not given the authority to negotiate sovereignty-association. An independent Quebec no longer seemed just over the horizon, and many journalists and others who favored independence were dispirited.

Anyone who took a close look at the QPC's performance during the referendum campaign would have been dispirited, too. First, the press council promised to render decisions within seven days of receiving complaints, but generally failed to do so. Second, in disputes opposing a party with financial ties to the press council and a party without such ties, the press council favored its funders 85 percent of the time. Third, the principles upon which many decisions were based were neither logical nor consistently applied.

The press council could be reproached for other failings as well. Its refusal to elaborate a set of guidelines for coverage of the referendum campaign not only resulted in inconsistent decisions by the press council, but it deprived the media of guidelines that might well have been useful to journalists. In addition, by continuing its ordinary practice of investigating only those matters about which complaints were made, the press council was reactive rather than proactive during the referendum campaign. The failure to be proactive limited the QPC's effectiveness as an institution of public education and media accountability. In addition, such a stance prevented the press council from taking a broader view of media behavior.

The lack of a broad view can lead to errors. The press council's review of the complaints it had received, for example, led it to conclude that the Quebec media generally did a good job covering the referendum campaign:

> Although it had neither the time nor the resources to conduct a thorough evaluation of the referendum coverage disseminated by different news organizations, the Council was nonetheless able to recognize, by studying the complaints it received, that on the whole the press did its job in an acceptable fashion.[51]

Such a view lacks depth and nuance. Although the press council is not a research institute, it could have offered a more insightful overview merely by monitoring the coverage of major news organizations and by issuing regular commentaries on the quality of information reaching citizens. Despite its expressed satisfaction with the performance of its special committee during the 1980 referendum campaign, the press council chose not to repeat the experience during the 1992 referendum on constitutional reform or the 1995 referendum on independence.

Perhaps it was just as well, because the press council has not solved the problems that the 1980 experience highlighted. The QPC continues to have chronic delays in processing cases.[52] Its revenue still comes overwhelmingly from media sources. It still has not succeeded in compiling its jurisprudence.

The coming years hold the promise of additional periods of political tension in Quebec. The Parti Québécois government was re-elected in 1998. Another referendum on Quebec's future seems quite possible. If the press council is to serve as a meaningful means of media accountability during such important moments in the democratic life of Quebec society, it must address its defects now.

The task is not an impossible one. Each of the major problems that marred the press council's performance during the 1980 referendum campaign—its inability to render decisions quickly, its tendency to rule in favor of its funders, and its inconsistent decisions in cases that presented similar issues—is amenable to solution. Such a solution would need to include at least the following three steps:

First, the press council should adopt a clear set of ethical principles for coverage of the referendum campaign, perhaps drawing on existing decisions related to complaints about coverage of political campaigns. The guidelines should be published and sent to all news organizations in Quebec as well as to any citizen who expresses interest. Clear ethical principles would increase the press council's ability to treat similar cases similarly, and also would temper its tendency to rule in favor of its funders. The principles should deal in a concrete fashion with questions that can be expected to arise in periods of political tension, such as a referendum campaign on sovereignty. For example, what responsibility do news organizations have for errors in wire-service stories? What constitutes an adequate correction of an error? To what extent must news organizations go to achieve balance in their political coverage (or in each political news story)? Do news organizations have an ethical duty to permit citizens (or citizen groups) to have direct access to the audience via letters to the editor or guest commentaries?

Second, because time is of the essence in periods of political tension, the press council should streamline its procedures by making greater use of electronic communication. Instead of requiring that all complaints be made in writing, the press council could accept complaints by phone (or fax or e-mail) and then use electronic means to investigate the validity of complaints quickly. The information-gathering techniques required would not be particularly exotic; journalists conduct telephone interviews and receive documents by fax and e-mail every day.

Third, the press council should actively monitor the performance of major Quebec news organizations during periods of political tension and should on its own initiative investigate problems it perceives, even if no citizen complains about them. Strong public statements by the press council detailing specific ethical lapses and urging the media to follow the press council's ethical guidelines could be an important factor in holding the media to a certain standard of accountability and thus in improving the quality of information offered to the people of Quebec.

NOTES

1. Gerald was "a noted supporter of the news council concept." Louise W. Hermanson, "The National News Council Is Not a Dead Issue," in Richard T. Kaplar, ed., *Beyond the Courtroom: Alternatives for Resolving Press Disputes* (Washington, D.C.:

The Media Institute, 1991), pp. 15–41, quote at p. 23. Gerald was instrumental in the creation in 1971 of the Minnesota Press Council (which changed its name to the Minnesota News Council a decade later). Philip Meyer, *Ethical Journalism* (New York: Longman, 1987), pp. 172–173. See also Louise W. Hermanson, "The Minnesota News Council: A Look at the Beginnings," paper presented to the annual meeting of the Association for Education in Journalism and Mass Communication, Washington, D.C., August 1989.

2. J. Edward Gerald, *The British Press under Government Economic Controls* (Minneapolis: University of Minnesota Press, 1956), p. 165.

3. J. Edward Gerald, "The British Press Council: A Summary and an Evaluation," *Journalism Quarterly* 36 (1959): 295–306, p. 306.

4. See, e.g., Paul B. Snider, *The British Press Council: A Study of Its Role and Performance, 1953–1965* (unpublished Ph.D. thesis, University of Iowa, 1968), and George Murray, *The Press and the Public: The Story of the British Press Council* (Carbondale: Southern Illinois University Press, 1972).

5. Geoffrey Robertson, *People against the Press: An Inquiry into the Press Council* (London: Quartet Books, 1983), p. 5.

6. Quoted in Robertson, *People against the Press,* p. 5

7. Robertson, *People against the Press,* p. 132.

8. L. Erwin Atwood and Kenneth Starck, "Effects of Community Press Councils: Real and Imagined," *Journalism Quarterly* 49 (Summer 1972): 230–238, p. 237.

9. Pat O'Malley, "Regulation, Pseudo-Regulation, and Counter-Regulation: The Operation of the Australian Press Council," *Media, Culture and Society* 9 (1987): 77–95; David Pritchard, "Press Councils as Mechanisms of Media Self-Regulation," in Jacques Zylberberg and François Demers, eds., *L'Amérique et les Amériques/America and the Americas* (Sainte-Foy, Quebec: Les Presses de l'Université Laval, 1992).

10. Fred Johnson, "The Minnesota Press Council: A Study of Its Effectiveness," *Mass Comm Review* (Winter 1976–77), pp. 13–19.

11. Louise Williams Hermanson, "News Councils as Alternative Dispute Resolution" (unpublished Ph.D. thesis, University of Minnesota, 1990), p. 278.

12. Hermanson, "News Councils as Alternative Dispute Resolution," p. 98.

13. Robert W. Schafer, "News Media and Complainant Attitudes toward the Minnesota Press Council," *Journalism Quarterly* 56 (1979): 744–752; Hermanson, "News Councils as Alternative Dispute Resolution," p. 101.

14. F. Dennis Hale and Robert O. Scott, "Impact of the Minnesota News Council on Libel," paper presented to the Association for Education in Journalism and Mass Communication Southeast Colloquium, Orlando, Fla., March 1991, p. 13. See also Ronald Farrar, "News Councils and Libel Actions," *Journalism Quarterly* 63 (1986): 509–516, and Hermanson, "News Councils as Alternative Dispute Resolution."

15. Robert W. Schafer, "The Minnesota Press Council: Developing Standards for Press Ethics," *Journalism Quarterly* 58 (1981): 355–362, p. 362.

16. Farrar, "News Councils and Libel Actions"; Sylvia Paine, "The Minnesota News Council," *Washington Journalism Review* (November 1989), pp. 24–28.

17. David Pritchard, "A quoi servent les conseils de presse et les ombudsmen?" in Jean-Marie Charon and Florian Sauvageau, eds., *L'état des médias* (Montreal: Boréal, 1991).

18. Le Conseil de presse du Québec, *Rapport annuel 1979–80*, p. 7 (translation by the author).

19. *Rapport annuel 1979–80*, p. 29.

20. A 1977 investigation by the Canadian Radio-television and Telecommunications Commission into alleged separatist bias by Radio-Canada found no evidence of bias, though it did reveal differences between the English-language (CBC) and French-language (Radio-Canada) services of the national broadcaster. Arthur Siegel, *A Content Analysis, the Canadian Broadcasting Corporation: Similarities and Differences of French and English News* (Ottawa: Canadian Radio-television and Telecommunications Commission, 1977); Marc Raboy, *Missed Opportunities: The Story of Canada's Broadcasting Policy* (Montreal: McGill–Queen's University Press, 1990). Nonetheless, there is little doubt that French-language Quebec journalists overwhelmingly favored the Parti Québécois. In a 1979 survey of journalists, 79 percent of the respondents said they had voted for the PQ in 1976, and fully 75 percent of the journalists said they still supported the PQ. Pierre Godin, "Qui vous informe," *L'Actualité* (May 1979), pp. 31–40.

21. QPC case 79-11-61.

22. QPC case 80-01-02.

23. QPC case 80-01-04.

24. QPC case 80-03-22.

25. QPC case 79-11-61.

26. QPC case 80-04-25.

27. QPC case 80-04-28.

28. QPC case 80-04-29.

29. Conseil de presse du Québec, *Rapport annuel 1980–81*, p. 18.

30. Pritchard, "Press Councils as Mechanisms of Media Self-Regulation."

31. The media organizations contributing during 1979–80 were l'Association canadienne de la radio et de la télévision de langue française, Les Hebdos régionaux, Les Quotidiens du Québec, la Société Radio-Canada, and Radio-Québec. Money from journalists came from la Fédération professionnelle des journalistes du Québec and from individual journalists who paid a fee to the QPC for its press cards. All of the information about the QPC's 1979–80 finances comes from *Rapport annuel 1980–81*, p. 105.

32. The sources of contributions during the 1980–81 fiscal year were similar to those of 1979–80.

33. Guy Lachapelle and Jean Noiseux, "La presse quotidienne," in *Québec, un pays incertain: Réflexions sur le Québec post-référendaire* (Montreal: Québec/Amérique, 1980); Claude-V. Marsolais, *Le référendum confisqué: Histoire du référendum québécois du 20 mai 1980* (Montreal: VLB Éditeur, 1992).

34. The special committee was chaired by René Pepin, a law professor at l'Université de Sherbrooke. Its other members were Jean-Claude Labrecque, a journalist at Radio-Canada, and Colette Chabot, president and general manager of a small radio station. Chabot was a former employee of Pierre Péladeau, president of the company that published *Le Journal de Montréal* and *Le Journal de Québec*. She would later write an admiring biography of Péladeau. Colette Chabot, *Péladeau* (Montreal: Éditions Libre Expression, 1986).

35. A "case" refers to all of the matters an individual complainant complained about. A single case, then, might be made up of more than one complaint.

36. Cases that were on hand as of the date of the announcement of the creation of the special committee were considered to have been received on that day, April 21.

37. QPC cases 80-04-37, 80-05-43, and 80-05-44.

38. Conseil de presse du Québec, *Les droits et responsabilités de la presse,* 1987, p. 10 (translation by the author).

39. As note 35 indicates, cases sometimes contained more than one complaint. In such cases I treated each complaint as a distinct entity. François Leduc's letter about unbalanced reporting by *La Presse, Le Devoir,* and CTV, for example, was treated as three complaints for purposes of this analysis. When more than one plaintiff alleged the same violation of media ethics, I treated the case as a single complaint. The letters of Paul Perreault and Claude Letarte alleging unbalanced reporting in *Le Devoir,* for example, made virtually identical charges, and thus were treated as a single complaint. Complaints that arrived after the referendum were not included in this analysis.

40. The other nine cases during the referendum period did not involve funder/non-funder disputes. In five cases funders faced off against funders. In four cases non-funders complained against other non-funders.

41. Which party "won" a QPC case was determined by whether the QPC agreed with the principal allegation(s) in a complaint. If so, the complainant "won." If not, the defendant "won."

42. Mike Donegan, letter to QPC general secretary Jean Baillargeon, February 22, 1980. Original in QPC case file 80-01-04.

43. Jacques Guay, "A quoi bon les agences des presse?" *Le 30* (September 1980), p. 22 (translation by the author).

44. Interestingly, the Canadian Press journalist who made the mistake was Jean-François Lisée, who went on to become an award-winning journalist with *L'Actualité* and the author of several penetrating and widely discussed books about Quebec politics. See Jean-François Lisée, *Dans l'oeil de l'aigle: Washington face au Québec* (Montreal: Boréal, 1990), *Le tricheur* (Montreal: Boréal, 1994), and *Le naufrageur* (Montreal: Boréal, 1994).

45. QPC case 80-04-25 (translation by the author).

46. QPC case 80-04-28 (translation by the author).

47. Ghislain Dufour, letter to QPC general secretary Jean Baillargeon, June 3, 1980 (translation by the author). Original in QPC case file 80-04-28.

48. Oddly, this case was not dealt with by the QPC's special committee for referendum-related complaints. Rather, the QPC used its ordinary procedures to handle the case. The file contains no explanation for why the case did not go to the special committee. The complaint arrived at the press council office on March 21, 1980, two months before the referendum, and was not decided until October 23, 1980.

49. Ulric Deschênes, "Légitimation et système normatif: une étude de la jurisprudence du Conseil de presse du Québec," *Communication* 17 (December 1996): 169–187.

50. Beyond the PQ-related cases already examined, the QPC received two other referendum-related complaints involving parties affiliated with the Parti Québécois. Neither involved corrections of erroneous stories. One was a complaint against Radio-

Québec for pro-sovereignty bias in an entertainment program (QPC case 80-04-36). The other was a complaint against the Regroupement national pour le OUI (the separatist campaign committee) for preventing local reporters in Sept-Iles from having access to Premier René Lévesque (QPC case 80-05-38). The press council ruled in favor of the parties affiliated with the PQ in both cases.

51. Jean Ouellette, "Rapport du président du Comité permanent des cas," in *Rapport annual 1979–80* (translation by the author).

52. In early 1994 the QPC announced "Operation Urgence Plaintes," an effort to address the problem of the delays. The success of the effort remains to be demonstrated.

8

Organized Citizen Action
and Media Accountability

PATRICK O'NEILL

CHAPTER 8 MOVES THIS VOLUME FROM THE REALM OF ETHICS AND
MEDIA SELF-REGULATION TO THE REALM OF THE LAW. PATRICK
O'NEILL OFFERS A CASE STUDY OF HOW CITIZEN GROUPS WHOSE
ACCOUNTABILITY CLAIMS HAVE BEEN REJECTED CAN ORGANIZE
TO TAKE LEGAL ACTION, IN THIS CASE ASKING THE FEDERAL COM-
MUNICATIONS COMMISSION TO JUDGE THE FACTS OF THE DISPUTE
IN LIGHT OF APPLICABLE LEGAL STANDARDS.

THE ACCOUNTABILITY PROCESS IN SUCH INSTANCES IS VERY
POLITICAL, ALL THE MORE SO BECAUSE MEDIA ORGANIZATIONS
THAT ARE THE TARGET OF SUCH ATTEMPTS AT ACCOUNTABILITY
TEND TO BRANDISH THE FIRST AMENDMENT AS A SHIELD PROTECT-
ING THEM FROM GOVERNMENT SCRUTINY.

O'NEILL GROUNDS HIS STUDY IN THE LITERATURE OF POLITI-
CAL INTEREST GROUPS, FOR WHOM ACCOUNTABILITY PROCESSES
ARE BUT ONE TOOL AMONG MANY TO USE TO ADVANCE THEIR
GOALS. THE THEORETICAL CONTEXT OF THE INTEREST GROUP IS
USEFUL, AS O'NEILL SHOWS THAT A SEEMING WAVE OF SPONTANE-
OUS EXPRESSION OF CONCERN ABOUT MEDIA CONTENT MAY WELL
BE AN ORGANIZED CAMPAIGN. FEW SCHOLARS BEFORE O'NEILL
HAVE EXPLORED THE INTEREST-GROUP ASPECTS OF MEDIA AC-
COUNTABILITY.

O'NEILL'S STUDY, ORIGINALLY WRITTEN AS A PAPER FOR A
GRADUATE SEMINAR AT INDIANA UNIVERSITY (WHERE HE RE-
CEIVED HIS PH.D.), DRAWS UPON INTERVIEWS, FCC DOCUMENTS,
AND PERSONAL LETTERS OF COMPLAINT TO THE FCC. AN EARLIER
VERSION OF THIS PAPER WAS PRESENTED AT A NATIONAL MEETING
OF THE ASSOCIATION FOR EDUCATION IN JOURNALISM AND MASS
COMMUNICATION. AT THIS WRITING, O'NEILL IS ON THE FACULTY
OF THE MARQUETTE UNIVERSITY COLLEGE OF COMMUNICATION IN
MILWAUKEE, WISCONSIN.

In April 1987, the Federal Communications Commission reprimanded three radio stations for broadcasting sexually explicit material.[1] In so doing, the commission reopened the issue of indecency in broadcasting, an area that it had largely ignored since 1978.

The 1987 action marked the beginning of a new series of battles over this area of law, which remained unsettled a decade later. The FCC's renewed interest in broadcast indecency was even more noteworthy because of the apparent inconsistency between such content regulation and the free-marketplace philosophy that the commission used as its guide for broadcast regulation throughout the 1980s.[2] The crackdown on sexually oriented broadcasting by a regulatory agency that had been so vocal in its opposition to content regulation was clear evidence of the political nature of indecency regulation.

The FCC's legal authority makes it a powerful agent of media accountability, and attempts to persuade the commission to intervene in a media controversy illustrate advanced stages of the media accountability process. Many claimants seek the assistance of the FCC. According to one estimate, the commission has received as many as 20,000 letters in a year protesting indecent broadcasting alone.[3]

In the late 1980s an Indianapolis organization, Decency in Broadcasting, encouraged its members to "flood the Federal Communications Commission with several hundred letters in the next few days" advocating action against a local radio station.[4] The same organization had earlier placed a $5,000 advertisement in the *Washington Post,* reminding the FCC that "hundreds of Hoosiers have written to the Commission" in support of tighter restrictions on supposedly indecent broadcasting.[5]

The station in question, WFBQ-FM in Indianapolis, was eventually fined $10,000 for material aired on its popular morning program, *The Bob and Tom Show.*[6] Because the broadcasts for which the station was punished took place during a period of intense activity by Decency in Broadcasting, the group's anti-indecency campaign offers an opportunity to examine a dimension of political pressure that may have had a bearing on the commission's decision in the WFBQ case.

This study of organized political activity as media accountability is based on an analysis of letters sent to the FCC in 1987 concerning *The Bob and Tom Show.* The study leads to inferences about the concerns of the letter writers and about the immediate results of a campaign intended to encourage letters to the commission.

BROADCAST INDECENCY

Federal law prohibits the broadcasting of "obscene, indecent, or profane language."[7] The category of indecency, as distinguished from obscenity, was recognized by the Supreme Court of the United States in the 1978 *Pacifica* case.[8]

In *Pacifica,* the Court accepted the FCC's definition of indecency as "language that describes, in terms patently offensive as measured by contemporary community standards for the broadcast medium, sexual or excretory activities and organs, at times of the day when there is a reasonable risk that children may be in the audience."[9] The Supreme Court's decision in *Pacifica* established that indecency, unlike obscenity, was constitutionally protected speech, but that the FCC had the authority to "channel" such material to times when children were less likely to be in the audience.[10]

In a clarification issued after the ruling, the FCC announced that it was adopting a narrow interpretation of the decision and would confine its enforcement of the indecency clause primarily to instances involving the "repetitive occurrence" of specific vulgar words.[11] True to its word, the commission did not take another action on indecency grounds for almost ten years.

However, on April 16, 1987, the FCC issued decisions finding three radio stations guilty of broadcasting indecency.[12] One of the programs found to be indecent was *The Howard Stern Show,* one of the more famous examples of a popular morning genre known as "shock radio," "raunch radio," or "morning zoo." Such programs often rely on material with sexual connotations, while avoiding the explicit language that was present in *Pacifica. The Bob and Tom Show* on WFBQ in Indianapolis was such a show.

Although WFBQ was not directly affected by the commission's April 1987 rulings, the commission specifically stated that the federal law prohibiting broadcasting of indecency could be used to support action against program material that relies on double meanings and sexual innuendo.[13]

That stand provided renewed hope for anti-indecency activists, but alarmed many broadcasters. The new standards were challenged as "unconstitutionally vague" by a coalition of citizen groups, broadcasters, and trade and professional organizations.[14] In 1988, the District of Columbia Court of Appeals generally upheld the commission's authority to apply its new and broader interpretation of indecency.[15] Over the next few years, the FCC used the new standards to take action against numerous radio stations, including WFBQ, for indecency.[16]

ANTI-INDECENCY ACTIVISTS

In his extensive study of participation in letter-writing campaigns, James Rosenau identified a set of people whom he called Mobilizables, defined as:

> those who communicate, with some regularity, ideas about public affairs to persons with whom they are closely associated (but not to persons whom they do not know) and who, within a reasonable period after they have been urged to do so by actors seeking to mobilize their support, act in a manner that corresponds with the request to establish first-hand contacts with some aspect of public affairs.[17]

According to Rosenau, most citizen participation is part of an interactive process, involving stimulation by an "activator," who might be an acquaintance, a public official, or an organization.[18] While mobilizability can be identified, its sources are difficult to isolate. Some people are mobilizable only on certain issues and under certain conditions, and the factors that lead to mobilization are complex, involving personality, the identity of the activator, and the salience of the issue.[19]

The specific form of citizen participation under study in this chapter is anti-indecency activism, which is an expression of moral indignation. According to Joseph Gusfield, moral indignation often represents a reaction to a perceived threat to social status or influence.[20] Furthermore, this tendency to defend status is intensified among certain individuals, described as status discrepants, who enjoy high income despite low education and low occupational prestige. Such individuals, it is argued, are more likely to experience stress in the face of change.[21]

Louis Zurcher and George Kirkpatrick, following Gusfield's orientation, focused on status defense in their study of anti-pornography campaigns in two cities.[22] The anti-pornography activists tended to be "middle-class, middle-aged, politically active, religiously active, family-oriented, and conservative."[23] Zurcher and Kirkpatrick concluded that these activists (whom they called "Conporns") identified closely with the mainstream of American life.

> Contrary to expectations, Conporns . . . did not feel a pervasive sense of powerlessness, normlessness, or alienation. Indeed, they felt very much a part of American society, as they defined it, and were basically satisfied with what they perceived to be the dominant societal values and norms. Conporns . . . accurately believed that the norms and values predominant in their communities (and the society at large) for the most part were akin to theirs and that they could effectively counter threats to those norms and values by political, legal, or direct action.

In Zurcher and Kirkpatrick's explanation, activists view the anti-pornography action largely as a symbolic crusade, aimed at countering a challenge to their status by the emergence of alternative lifestyles. Therefore, the "symbolic accomplishments of the crusade are at least as important as the utilitarian accomplishments."[24]

Some scholars discount status defense as an explanation for anti-indecency activism and, with it, the notion that the moral issue in question is actually symbolic. Michael Wood and Michael Hughes, for example, cite a number of studies in which individuals' status was not found to be a significant factor in conservative activism.[25] Their own analysis of attitudes toward pornography also failed to support the status-defense explanation. Instead, Wood and Hughes suggest that conservative activism on behalf of traditional social values, including "decency," can be explained by socialization and cultural values.

> The results of our analysis lead us to believe that no special theories concerned with status frustrations or status deprivations are required to account for the social base of moral-reform movements: popular support for moral reform is explainable in terms of learning experiences and particular cultural environments. Overall, our results point to the importance of principle, beliefs and ideology over class and material interests in the development of support for moral reform.[26]

Regardless of why citizens become activists for a cause, it is clear that letter-writing campaigns are a common component of many political lobbying efforts. In his study of lobbying in Congress, Lester Milbrath observed that a large letter-writing campaign cannot be ignored because members of Congress see it as a "hurricane warning."[27] However, he concluded that letter campaigns can be effective only if they are very large and appear to be spontaneous.[28]

Donald deKieffer, a professional lobbyist, warned that form letters or letters with identical wording are likely not only to be discounted, but also to be answered by a computerized "personal" response.[29] DeKieffer suggested that groups take steps to avoid the appearance of an organized campaign, such as by supplying writers with fact sheets and encouraging them to include personal anecdotes in their letters.[30] Milbrath reported that lobbyists and members of Congress generally rated letter writing low as a form of political communication,[31] largely because politicians are aware that the letter writers do not always reflect the views of the public at large.[32]

Apart from their role in attempting to influence which stand a policymaker takes, letters also may provide justification for a politician's position. U.S. Senator Estes Kefauver once wrote that "it is comforting to be able to tell disgruntled constituents that 'I had twenty letters sustaining my vote to every one I received against it.'"[33]

The letters also may serve other purposes of the organization promoting the letter-writing campaign. Writing may stimulate the interest of the membership, leading to more active participation.[34] In addition, the fact that the letter writer will generally receive a response may encourage further involvement.[35]

Although most studies of letter-writing campaigns have focused on Congress, activists also write to regulatory agencies, such as the Federal Communications Commission, often as a result of an organized campaign. The commission received more than 24,000 complaints about obscene and indecent broadcast programming in 1975, about 20,000 of which were form letters distributed by Morality in Media.[36] In 1987, the FCC answered more than 27,000 of what the FCC staff considers to be "informal complaints," and most of them dealt with indecency.[37]

To enhance citizen participation in the regulatory process, the FCC officially encourages informal complaints.[38] A study by Michael McGregor revealed that the commission's consideration of these letters is "impressive in scope and noble in intent."[39] But the commission does not have an official policy on the importance to be attached to letters from the public.

Barry Cole wrote that "the FCC has learned to process letters, after a fashion, but the agency has never attempted to analyze what the people who write letters are trying to say."[40] McGregor reported that the commission uses letters, rather than opinion polls, as gauges of public support.[41] In its decision implementing a twenty-four-hour ban on indecency, for example, the FCC noted that more than 92,000 responses had been received, with almost 88,000 of them supporting the commission's proposal.[42]

The FCC appears to operate with a great degree of discretionary authority in this area, acting on complaints as it chooses. For example, the commission's 1975 action against Pacifica, which resulted in the 1978 *Pacifica* decision by the Supreme Court, came in response to a single complaint lodged against a station in New York City.[43] In contrast, the commission did not deal with the indecency issue in the mid-1980s until "floods of mail came in about Howard Stern and others," according to Ralph Blumberg, director of investigations for the FCC Enforcement Division.[44]

In the early 1970s, the commission received more than 100,000 letters in support of Action for Children's Television's campaign for reform.[45] According to McGregor, however, there is no evidence that informal complaints have a direct bearing on the commission's actions.[46]

BOB AND TOM AND DECENCY IN BROADCASTING

In March 1983, Bob Kevoian and Tom Griswold came to Indianapolis from Petoskey, Michigan, to host the morning show on WFBQ-FM, an album rock station.[47] Bob and Tom's "morning zoo" format, featuring a stable of regular guests, soon became known for social satire and humor with a steady dose of sexual innuendo. The program rose steadily in the local ratings, finally arriving at the top spot when Arbitron reported a 22.2 morning drive time share for WFBQ in the April–June 1987 rating period.[48] Among 18- to-34-year-olds, WFBQ's target audience, Bob and Tom recorded a 43 share.[49]

Opposition to WFBQ preceded Bob and Tom's arrival. John Price, an attorney from an Indianapolis suburb, attacked the station during an unsuccessful bid for the Republican nomination for a Congressional seat in 1982. At that time, Price objected to WFBQ's slogan: "Kick-Ass Rock and Roll." After losing the primary election, he started an organization called Decency in Broadcasting.[50] Although Decency in Broadcasting has occasionally criticized local television stations, it has focused most of its attention on Bob and Tom.[51]

Before the FCC's indecency rulings in 1987, Decency in Broadcasting had filed several formal complaints against WFBQ. The FCC's usual response was to decline to take action, encouraging Decency in Broadcasting to work directly with the station.[52] The organization also coordinated an advertiser boycott of WFBQ in 1985. Decency in Broadcasting claimed that more than thirty businesses had stopped advertising on the station, but WFBQ's manager stated that the station was maintaining a "sold-out advertising position."[53]

Decency in Broadcasting's efforts were revitalized by the FCC's adoption of tightened Indecency Enforcement Standards in April 1987. The group recorded and transcribed all of Bob and Tom's programs between June 15 and July 10, 1987.[54] According to Price, "We transcribed the bad portions, which were clearly objectionable, and it came down to 336 pages. We distilled that down to 36 pages."[55] Price claimed that Bob and Tom told indecent jokes at the rate of seventeen per hour.[56]

On July 27, 1987, Decency in Broadcasting filed a formal complaint against WFBQ with the FCC. The transcripts were sent along with the complaint.[57] The formal complaint alleged:

> The "Bob and Tom Show" repetitively uses specific sexual or excretory words or phrases and contains material making direct and indirect references to sexual or excretory organs and functions. The material aired on the "Bob and Tom Show" is aired in a pandering and titillating manner and is violative of the Communications Act of 1934.

The complaint continued:

> The hosts of the "Bob and Tom Show," Bob Kevoian and Tom Griswold, include within their broadcast material not only references to sex, sexual activity, sexual organs, excretory organs, beastiality [sic], homosexuality and lesbianism, but also sex with minors and an emphasis upon the use of liquor and illegal drugs. This is particularly offensive to the Petitioning organization and parents in central Indiana, because the program is not a late-evening program but, in fact, airs during a period of time when "there is a reasonable risk that children may be in the audience."

The same day that it filed its complaint with the FCC, Decency in Broadcasting sent out a mailing, which included the thirty-six pages of transcripts of the radio show, to 2,600 of its members and community leaders. The cover letter contended that, contrary to expectations, "the material on the program is actually now much worse than it was prior to the FCC ruling"—the adoption of the stricter Indecency Enforcement Standards in April.[58] Stating that "community pressure can go a long way to bring programs of this nature into conformity with the law," the letter urged members of the community to write to the FCC and to the local newspapers.[59]

ANALYSIS OF LETTERS

Copies of all letters from the public concerning WFBQ sent to the FCC in 1987 were obtained from the Complaints Branch of the FCC's Enforcement Division. In all, 432 personal letters and 117 form letters complained of indecency on *The Bob and Tom Show* in 1987. The 155 personal letters sent in the five-week period following the July 27 mailing by Decency in Broadcasting were analyzed for this study.[60] These letters represented the first waves of Decency in Broadcasting's 1987 campaign.

Fundamentalist clergy played an important role in the campaign. Almost a quarter of the authors (37) identified themselves as members of the clergy. In all of these, the affiliated church was identified, either in the text or on letterhead. All but three of these churches were of denominations generally considered conservative, fundamentalist, or evangelical; the other three were mainline Protestant. In addition, eight other writers phrased their appeals at least partly in religious terms, such as by citing scripture or by encouraging the commissioners to act in accordance with Christian principles.

In addition, clergy were among the quickest to respond to the July 27 mailing. Of the 20 letters dated July 28, July 29, or July 30, 11 were written by clergy. The role played by these religious leaders in generating further letters cannot be determined from this data, although an indication is provided by the fact that two of the seven different form letters identified a religious congregation.

However, it is clear that Decency in Broadcasting was the prime mover in the campaign. There is strong evidence to suggest that nearly all the complaints about WFBQ's programming received by the commission in 1987 were sent in response to appeals by Decency in Broadcasting. The 1987 files contained only two letters sent before July 27. On that day, Decency in Broadcasting sent its letter and *Bob and Tom* transcripts to 2,600 people. The mailing, which provided addresses for the FCC and the two daily newspapers in Indianapolis, encouraged recipients to write to the FCC and the press and to return a response form to Decency in Broadcasting.

Decency in Broadcasting also placed a prominent advertisement on the radio-television page of the widely circulated Sunday, August 9, edition of the *Indianapolis Star:*

Do you favor
RAUNCH RADIO?
If not, let your voice be heard!
Urge the Federal Communications Commission
to enforce the law
and clean up "The Bob and Tom Show"!!!
18 U.S.C. Sec. 1464 prohibits obscene,
indecent or profane broadcast material.

The advertisement also contained the addresses of the FCC and Decency in Broadcasting.[61]

The response to these two appeals is indicated by a breakdown of letters into periods of five days. The letters began arriving at the FCC after Decency in Broadcasting's July 27 mailing, and increased again after the appearance of the August 9 newspaper ad.

Forty-five letters could be linked specifically to the July 27 mailing because they contained extensive quotes from the Decency in Broadcasting letter, references to the accompanying transcripts, or citations to the "Radio Communications Act of 1934," an unusual terminology used three times by Price in the mailing.[62] An additional thirty-six letters sent after the July 27 appeal, but before the August 9 newspaper ad, were presumably responses to Decency in Broadcasting's mailing.

Thirty-two of the letters could be connected directly to the August 9 newspaper advertisement because they "urged" to FCC to "enforce 18 U.S.C. Sec. 1464." This reference to the United States Code was not contained in the material mailed on July 27, and none of the letters including it was sent before August 9.

The combined effect of Decency in Broadcasting's two appeals—the mailing and the newspaper ad—is evidenced by the fact that no letters were received in the period before the mailing, and that response began to fall off noticeably a week after the appearance of the newspaper ad.

People who wrote letters in response to the July 27 mailing tended to include greater detail in their letters than did people who responded to the newspaper ad. For example, those who were responding to the mailing were more likely to identify a specific harm they thought was caused by indecency; they were also more likely to address only content. It is not clear whether this difference is explainable by the greater detail present in the Decency in Broadcasting mailing, which included thirty-six pages of verbatim *Bob and Tom* transcripts, or by the fact that the mailing was directed at a selected population.

All but two of the letters made some reference to the content of *The Bob and Tom Show,* although often this was done in such vague terms as "filth" or "garbage." While it is apparent that the letter writers were offended by content of the program, it is less clear to what extent they believed an actual harm results from the broadcast. Seventy-eight (50 percent) of the letters addressed content only, with no mention of effects. Forty-five (29 percent) mentioned concern over the fact that children are exposed to the program, but without reference to a harm or effect.

Thirty letters (19 percent of the total) specified a harm believed to be caused *by Bob and Tom.* These harms fall into five categories, with some writers naming more than one: lowering the values or morals of children (13), lowering the values of society in general (6), contributing to sex-related problems, such as sex crimes or AIDS (4), damaging the reputation of Indianapolis as a community (10), and the influence of WFBQ's programming on other stations (6).

The concern about community image may have been influenced by a paragraph in the July 27 mailing, in which Price stated that he was "dismayed to learn that the Bob and Tom Show has been including a large portion of material which can only be considered as tasteless and insulting to those thousands of guests who will be in our community for the Pan Am Games." The city's hosting of the games was specifically mentioned by six of the ten letter writers who raised this issue.

Similarly, the references to programming on other stations may have resulted from an article in the *Star* on July 25, reporting the decision by WFBQ's main competitor to broadcast its morning show live from a nudist camp. The article portrayed the stunt as an attempt by the station to recover the top-rated position from WFBQ. Price was quoted in the newspaper story as saying that "this is one of the reasons we're doing what we're doing Monday [the July 27 mailing]."

Most of the references letter writers made to WFBQ's content were in general terms. One hundred writers used pejorative words such as "vulgar" or "offensive," without clearly identifying whether they were referring to sexual content. But the more specific content objections in other letters indicate a far greater concern about sexual material than about other potentially offensive subjects. Forty-eight letters mentioned an objection to sexual content, with 11 of these specifically objecting to material about taboo practices. Five objected to "bathroom" humor. Other objections were to comments degrading to women (2), disrespect for religion (2), and ethnic slurs (1).

In July 1990, three years after Decency in Broadcasting's complaint to the FCC, the commission fined WFBQ's parent company $10,000 for broadcasting indecent material on five occasions in 1987 and 1989.[63] According to the commission, the broadcasts

> contained lewd and vulgar language dwelling on depictions or descriptions of sexual organs and activities. While the passages arguably consist of double entendre and indirect references, the language used in each passage was understandable and clearly capable of a specific sexual meaning and, because of the context, the sexual meaning was inescapable.[64]

The company chose not to appeal, but did not admit wrongdoing. In addition, the station reserved the right to recover the fine in the event that the indecency policy is found unconstitutional.[65]

John Price said he was satisfied with the outcome of Decency in Broadcasting's anti-indecency campaign. According to Price, Bob and Tom were still coming "close to the line" after the FCC action, but he added that they were being more careful in their choice of content. In Price's view, Decency in Broadcasting's campaign accomplished its goal.[66]

DISCUSSION

Organized citizen action against racy media content represents the exercise of media accountability in the service of cultural politics. This study is a useful reminder that media accountability processes are never separate from the broader social context in which the media and their audiences exist.

In addition, the broadcast indecency issue raises difficult First Amendment questions, involving otherwise protected speech in a medium described by the Supreme Court as "pervasive."[67] The constitutional questions become all the more intriguing when the program in question is both popular and controversial. The legal definition of indecency, like that of obscenity, can vary with community standards, but in Indianapolis and elsewhere there are clearly conflicting standards held by large segments of the community.

However, the controversy is not confined to the legal arena. Recognizing the difficulties often present in prosecuting offensive material, the U.S. Attorney General's Commission on Pornography urged pornography opponents to engage in political action, including letter writing, public education, and demonstrations.[68] The efforts of citizen groups such as Decency in Broadcasting reflect this approach by combining legal action before the FCC with other forms of pressure, such as letter-writing campaigns and advertiser boycotts.

In its dealings with the FCC, Decency in Broadcasting adopted a public political strategy, including the placement of an advertisement in the *Washington Post*. Decency in Broadcasting's letter-writing appeals, emphasizing political action more than substantive issues, were apparently intended more to show evidence of public support for FCC action against WFBQ than to provide legal arguments in favor of such a position or evidence of harm caused by *The Bob and Tom Show*.

The specific dimensions of the influence of Decency in Broadcasting's campaign are difficult to determine. On one hand, Decency in Broadcasting's efforts bear most of the marks of the kind of orchestrated campaign that politicians are said to discount. On the other hand, such well-publicized campaigns may provide the necessary political rationale, if not pressure, for the FCC to exercise its broad discretionary power. Furthermore, the FCC, under pressure to do something about radio indecency, may well have targeted stations that were under attack from local organizations such as Decency in Broadcasting.

Studies of the participants in anti-indecency campaigns can be useful in understanding the political dimensions of the indecency issue. The analysis of the letters in this study indicates that, at least in Indianapolis, few complaints to the FCC arise as spontaneous reactions to objectionable content. It seems to take a well-organized appeal for letters to activate a segment of the community.

However, the letters reveal little about the people who were motivated to write the letters, beyond the fact that there was a large representation of conservative religious leaders and that sexual material was more objectionable than other potentially offensive subjects. Nor does the study of unsystematic material such as the content of letters to the FCC lend itself to making inferences about letter writers' attitudes. For example, the fact that only 19 percent of the writers mentioned a specific harm caused by indecent programming does not mean that the remaining 81 percent believed that the programming causes no harm. Similarly, the regulatory outcomes desired and expected by the letter writers were difficult to determine, because most people who suggested FCC action did so in such vague terms as "please clean up our airwaves."

Additional study of both the leaders and the "mobilized," through observation, in-depth interviews, or surveys, would lead to a greater understanding of the participants. Examination of other dimensions of anti-indecency campaigns would shed additional light on the political dynamics of the issue, as well as on the effectiveness of various strategies. Of particular interest is the fact that such grass-roots campaigns are relatively uncommon in the arena of broadcast regulation today. Current policy debates are more typically waged by competing industry interests.

This chapter has shown how a citizens' group can influence policymakers to hold the media accountable. Though valuable for gaining in-depth understanding of processes, the case-study method used here cannot assess the effect of different social and political contexts on the success of grass-roots campaigns for media accountability.[69] Future research should examine other contexts to ascertain the generalizability of the phenomena described in this chapter.

NOTES

1. *Pacifica Foundation*, 2 FCC Recd 2698 (1987); *Regents of the University of California*, 2 FCC Recd 2703 (1987); *Infinity Broadcasting*, 2 FCC Recd 2705 (1987); *Indecency Enforcement Standards*, 2 FCC Recd 2726 (1987).

2. See *Deregulation of Radio*, 84 FCC 2d 968 (1981); *Deregulation of Commercial Television*, 98 FCC 2d 1076 (1984); *Syracuse Peace Council*, 63 RR 2d 541 (1987); Mark S. Fowler and Daniel L. Brenner, "A Marketplace Approach to Broadcast Regulation," *Texas Law Review* 60 (1982): 207–257.

3. Bob Davis, "FCC Limits Shows of Raunchy Nature to After Midnight," *Wall Street Journal*, November 25, 1987.

4. Letter, John Price to Friends of Decency in Broadcasting, February 8, 1988.

5. "Clean Air: This Is Not a Message to the EPA," advertisement, *Washington Post*, November 20, 1987; Steve Hall, "Group Attacks WFBQ in Washington Post Ad," *Indianapolis Star*, November 19, 1987, p. 23A.

6. Letter to Carl J. Wagner, 1990 FCC LEXIS 5819 (1990).

7. 18 U.S.C §1464.

8. *FCC v Pacifica*, 438 U.S. 726 (1978).

9. *Pacifica Foundation*, 56 FCC 2d 94, 98 (1975).

10. 438 U.S. 726, 748–751.

11. *WGBH Educational Foundation*, 43 RR 2d 1436, 1441 (1978).

12. See note 1, above.

13. *Infinity Broadcasting*, 2 FCC Recd 2705, 2706 (1987).

14. "Broadcasters Challenge FCC's Indecency Standard," *Broadcasting*, February 1, 1988, pp. 61–62.

15. *Action for Children's Television v FCC*, 852 F.2d 1332 (D.C. Cir. 1988).

16. "Defining the Line between Regulation and Censorship," *Broadcasting*, April 15, 1991, p. 74.

17. James N. Rosenau, *Citizenship between Elections: An Inquiry into the Mobilizable American* (New York: The Free Press, 1974), p. 106.

18. Ibid., p. xxix.

19. Ibid., pp. 469–486.

20. Joseph R. Gusfield, *Symbolic Crusade: Status Politics and the American Temperance Movement* (Urbana: University of Illinois Press, 1963).

21. Ibid., pp. 16–20.

22. Louis A. Zurcher, Jr., and R. George Kirkpatrick, *Citizens for Decency: Anti-pornography Crusades as Status Defense* (Austin: University of Texas Press, 1976).

23. Ibid., p. 260.

24. Ibid., p. 324.

25. Michael Wood and Michael Hughes, "The Moral Basis of Moral Reform: Status Discontent vs. Culture and Socialization as Explanations of Anti-pornography Social Movement Adherence," *American Sociological Review* 49 (1984): 86–89.

26. Ibid., p. 96.

27. Lester W. Milbrath, *The Washington Lobbyists* (Chicago: Rand McNally and Company, 1963), p. 245.

28. Ibid., pp. 245–249.

29. Donald deKieffer, *How to Lobby Congress: A Guide for the Citizen Lobbyist* (New York: Dodd, Mead and Company, 1981), pp. 59–60.

30. Ibid., pp. 61–65.

31. Milbrath, *Washington Lobbyists*, p. 240.

32. Ibid., p. 247; Rosenau, *Citizenship*, pp. 14–15.

33. Estes Kefauver and Jack Levin, *A Twentieth Century Congress* (New York: Duell, Sloan and Pearce, 1947), pp. 183–184.

34. Milbrath, *Washington Lobbyists*, pp. 248–249.

35. Rosenau, *Citizenship*, p. 136.

36. Barry Cole and Mal Oettinger, *Reluctant Regulators: The FCC and the Broadcast Audience* (Reading, Mass.: Addison-Wesley, 1978), p. 121.

37. Telephone interview with Ralph Blumberg, Director of Investigations, FCC Enforcement Division, February 22, 1988.

38. 47 C.F.R. §1.41 (1990).

39. Michael A. McGregor, "The FCC's Use of Informal Complaints in Rule-Making Proceedings," *Journal of Broadcasting and Electronic Media* 30 (1986): 413–425.

40. Cole, *Reluctant Regulators*, p. 119.

41. McGregor, "The FCC's Use of Informal Complaints," p. 421.

42. *In the Matter of Enforcement of Prohibitions against Broadcast Indecency,* 5 FCC Recd 5297, 5310 n. 6 (1990).

43. *FCC v Pacifica,* 438 U.S. 726 (1978).

44. Ralph Blumberg, telephone interview, February 22, 1988.

45. Erwin G. Krasnow, Lawrence D. Longley, and Herbert A. Terry, *The Politics of Broadcast Regulation* (New York: St. Martin's Press, 1982), p. 59.

46. McGregor, "The FCC's Use of Informal Complaints," p. 423.

47. Scott L. Miley, "Restraint on the Radio," *Indianapolis Star,* September 22, 1985, p. 1B.

48. Bill Koenig, "Bob and Tom Rock WIBC from Radio's Top Morning Spot," *Indianapolis Star,* July 23, 1987, p. 37.

49. Pat Clawson, "Citizens' Group Targets WFBQ," *Radio and Records,* August 21, 1987, p. 9.

50. Richard K. Shull, "It May Be California for Bob, Tom," *Indianapolis News,* May 1, 1987, p. 15; Scott L. Miley, "Restraint on the Radio," *Indianapolis Star,* September 22, 1985, p. 1B.

51. Clawson, "Citizens' Group."

52. *Decency in Broadcasting, Inc.,* 94 FCC 2d 1162 (1983); Richard K. Shull, "Count Them Out," *Indianapolis News,* December 6, 1985, p. 13; Shull, "Bob and Tom under Attack," *Indianapolis News,* January 28, 1987, p. 11; "FCC to Impose Broader Indecency Standard on Air," Indianapolis *Star,* April 17, 1987, p. 37.

53. Lynn Ford, "7 More Firms Cancel 'Bob and Tom' Ads," *Indianapolis Star,* November 20, 1985.

54. *Complaint of Decency in Broadcasting, Inc. v Taft Television and Radio Company, Inc.,* filed with the Federal Communications Commission, July 27, 1987.

55. "Anti-smut Group to File FCC Complaint," *Indianapolis News,* July 28, 1987, p. 34.

56. James G. Newland, Jr., "City Group Complains to FCC About Radio Show," *Indianapolis Star,* July 28, 1987, p. 33.

57. John Price, telephone interview, February 8, 1988.

58. John Price, mass-mailed letter, Decency in Broadcasting, July 27, 1987.

59. Ibid.

60. The unit of analysis was the household. In the single case in which two members of the same household wrote separately, the letters were combined and treated as one. Not all of the letters were dated by the writers. However, all were stamped with a processing date by the FCC. The average difference between the date of the letter and the FCC date was four days. Consequently, undated letters were assigned a date four days before the FCC's date of processing.

61. Advertisement, *Indianapolis Star,* August 9, 1987, p. B12.

62. The statute is almost universally referred to as the Communications Act of 1934.

63. Letter to Carl J. Wagner, 1990 FCC LEXIS 5819 (1990).

64. Ibid.

65. Telephone interview with Christopher Wheat, general manager of WFBQ-FM, May 1, 1991.

66. John Price, telephone interview, April 30, 1991.

67. *FCC v Pacifica,* 438 U.S. 726 (1978).

68. *Report of the Attorney General's Commission on Pornography,* pp. 419–429, 1313–1315.

69. For a theoretical discussion of this issue, see David Pritchard, "Beyond the Meese Commission Report: Understanding the Variable Nature of Pornography Regulation," in Susan Gubar and Joan Hoff, eds., *For Adult Users Only: The Dilemma of Violent Pornography* (Bloomington: Indiana University Press, 1989), pp. 163–177.

9

Ambiguous Standards, Arbitrary Enforcement: Cable Access TV and Controversial Programming

LINDSY PACK

CHAPTER 8 LOOKED AT HOW CITIZENS CAN INFLUENCE GOVERN-
MENT TO ENFORCE LEGAL STANDARDS AS A MEANS OF HOLDING
THE PRODUCER OF A CONTROVERSIAL RADIO SHOW ACCOUNTA-
BLE. IN CHAPTER 9 LINDSY PACK LOOKS AT LEGAL STANDARDS IN
A LESS POLITICALLY CHARGED ATMOSPHERE, A SMALL INDIANA
CITY WHERE THE RELATIONSHIP BETWEEN THE PRODUCERS OF
CONTROVERSIAL PROGRAMMING AND THE PEOPLE RESPONSIBLE
FOR ENFORCING LEGAL STANDARDS IS FAIRLY FRIENDLY AND IN-
FORMAL.

WELCOME TO THE UNSTRUCTURED WORLD OF LOCAL CABLE
ACCESS TELEVISION. THE RESULTS OF PACK'S STUDY SHOW LEGAL
STANDARDS TO BE AMBIGUOUS AND ENFORCED FAIRLY ARBITRAR-
ILY. PRODUCERS OF PROGRAMS HAD ONLY A VAGUE IDEA OF WHAT
THE LEGAL STANDARDS WERE. ALL IN ALL, IT IS NOT A PICTURE
THAT WILL REASSURE PEOPLE WHO FAVOR A LEGAL APPROACH TO
MEDIA ACCOUNTABILITY.

PACK'S RESEARCH INCLUDED OBSERVATION OF AND NUMER-
OUS INTERVIEWS WITH PEOPLE DIRECTLY INVOLVED WITH THE
REGULATION OF CONTROVERSIAL PROGRAMMING, INCLUDING CITI-
ZEN POLICYMAKERS WHO ADOPTED THE RULES, LOCAL GOVERN-
MENT EMPLOYEES WHO WERE RESPONSIBLE FOR ENFORCING THE
RULES, AND PROGRAMMERS WHO SEARCHED FOR THE LIMITS OF
THE RULES.

THE CHAPTER IS A REVISED VERSION OF A PAPER ORIGINALLY
WRITTEN FOR A GRADUATE SEMINAR AT INDIANA UNIVERSITY,
WHERE PACK RECEIVED HIS DOCTORATE. AT THIS WRITING, HE IS
ON THE FACULTY OF THE DEPARTMENT OF COMMUNICATION AND
THEATRE ARTS AT FROSTBURG STATE UNIVERSITY IN MARYLAND.

The concept of "contemporary community standards" is an integral part of
how U.S. law defines obscenity and indecency. The law offers little guidance,

however, on how to determine community standards or on how such standards should be applied. Despite the ambiguity of the law, obscenity and indecency statutes are in force throughout the United States.

This chapter examines the concrete workings of obscenity and indecency law as applied to one medium (cable access television) in one community (Bloomington, Indiana). The chapter focuses on the standards that were applied to controversial programming, who determined the standards, who enforced them and by what authority, and what effect these standards had on citizens who produced programs for the cable access channel.[1] The chapter concludes with some suggestions about how community cable systems could provide adult programming to subscribers who wish to receive it without imposing it on subscribers who do not want such programming.

DEFINING OBSCENITY AND INDECENCY

The problem of defining obscenity and/or indecency is not a new one. Over the years courts, legislatures, and regulatory agencies have made many attempts at defining obscenity and indecency, but no definition that protects free expression has been clear and unambiguous. The definitions used in the United States in the mid-1990s focused on the vague concept of "contemporary community standards."

According to the Supreme Court of the United States, material was obscene, and thus not protected by the freedom-of-expression guarantees of the Constitution, if three criteria were met: (1) "whether the average person applying 'contemporary community standards' would find the work taken as a whole appeals to prurient interest, (2) whether the work depicts or describes, in a patently offensive way, sexual conduct specifically defined by the applicable state law, and (3) whether the work, taken as a whole, lacks serious literary, artistic, political, or scientific value."[2] State and federal statutes make obscenity subject to a variety of criminal and civil penalties.

American law treats indecency as a category distinct from obscenity. Federal law places limits on the right of broadcasters and cablecasters to transmit indecent material; the print media are not subject to any legal prohibitions regarding non-obscene indecency. The Federal Communications Commission has defined indecency as material that "describes, in terms patently offensive as measured by contemporary community standards for the broadcast medium, sexual or excretory activities and organs, at times of the day when there is a reasonable risk that children may be in the audience."[3] The FCC's definition was upheld by the U.S. Supreme Court.[4]

The phrase "contemporary community standards" was the foundation for the definitions of both obscenity and indecency, but no court decision or FCC ruling had attempted to define what the phrase meant. The Supreme Court and the FCC simply seemed to assume that community standards exist and that local prosecutors and policymakers would be able to apply them. This vague approach to definitions of constitutional magnitude seemed inconsistent with courts' traditional intolerance for vagueness. Federal courts, for example, often have invalidated local definitions of obscenity and indecency as being unconstitutionally vague.[5]

The matter was further complicated by the U.S. Supreme Court's determination that obscene material had no First Amendment protection,[6] but that indecent material did.[7] Unfortunately, the Supreme Court had never spelled out the precise extent of indecency's First Amendment protection. The FCC had attempted to channel indecent material to a so-called safe harbor time period (midnight to 6 A.M.).[8] The U.S. Congress was shocked, and passed legislation imposing a total ban on broadcasting indecent material.[9] The courts, however, ruled that the total ban on indecency was unconstitutional.[10] In other words, obscene material had no First Amendment protection. Indecent material had some protection, but the extent of that protection was unclear.

Such was the muddled state of the law policymakers had to work with in the late 1990s. Before taking a close look at how the law was put into practice at one community's cable-access channel, one needs a brief history of cable access regulation and programming, as well as a brief history of cable television in Bloomington.

REGULATING CABLE TV

As cable television systems expanded during the 1960s, the Federal Communications Commission asserted its authority to regulate them. According to the FCC, cable television was "ancillary to" broadcasting, and therefore under the commission's jurisdiction. Cable operators challenged the FCC's action, but the commission's authority was upheld by the U.S. Supreme Court.[11]

The FCC then began issuing rules requiring cable systems to originate programming. This action was also challenged, but once again the Supreme Court upheld the commission's authority.[12] The commission next expanded the rules and required cable systems to make access channels available to the public. These actions were struck down in 1979, when the Supreme Court ruled that the access requirements treated cable operators as common carriers, thus violating the provisions of the Communications Act.[13]

The Supreme Court's ruling did not mean the end of access channels, however. Municipalities began requiring access channels in their cable franchise agreements. While such requirements may have been of dubious legality, cable operators readily agreed to them in order to receive lucrative franchises. The legitimacy of access channels was affirmed in the Cable Communications Policy Act of 1984.[14] In addition, except for banning obscene programming, the act stated that: "[A] cable operator shall not exercise any editorial control over any public, educational, or government use of channel capacity. . . ."[15] The 1984 law also called public access channels "the video equivalent of the speaker's soap box or the electronic parallel to the printed leaflet." Furthermore, the act said, such channels "provide groups and individuals who generally have not had access to the electronic media with the opportunity to become sources of information in the electronic marketplace of ideas."[16]

The Cable Communications Policy Act of 1992 instructed the FCC to formulate rules regulating indecent programming on leased access[17] as well as on public, educational, or governmental access channels. The rules, issued by the FCC in 1993, allowed cable operators to limit all indecent programming to one channel. To receive the channel, a subscriber had to supply a written request and state in the request that he or she was at least eighteen years old.[18] The rules for public, educational, or governmental access channels allowed cable operators to prohibit indecent material and to require certifications from access users that their programming did not contain any indecency.[19] Both sets of rules were challenged by various groups[20] as being overly broad and in violation of the First Amendment. In the spring of 1993, the U.S. Court of Appeals blocked the FCC from enforcing both sets of rules.[21] Consequently, the regulation of indecent programming on access channels was far from settled.

Indecent programming on cable access channels was nothing new; it had been present since the first channels began operation during the early 1970s. One of the earliest access channels was on Manhattan Cable in New York City. Its most famous (or infamous) programs were *The Ugly George Hour of Truth, Sex and Violence,* and *Midnight Blue.* Ugly George (George Peter Urban) roamed the streets of Manhattan with a video camera and asked women to strip while he videotaped them. This material was then edited into an hour-long program that aired Tuesdays, Wednesdays, and Thursdays at 11:30 P.M., attracting a considerable audience.[22] George estimated that about four hundred women agreed to perform in front of his camera.[23] *Midnight Blue* featured a variety of sexually oriented programs such as an interview with an actress who appeared in pornographic movies, a performance by a four-hundred-pound stripper, and a visit to a tropical fish store that featured topless saleswomen.[24]

In 1976, the producer of *Midnight Blue,* Alex Bennett, appeared before a congressional committee that was considering regulation of the cable television industry. Bennett testified that he did not believe his program was violating any community standards. "As far as contemporary community standards is concerned, in Manhattan, there is a hooker on every block, a porn theater in every neighborhood, and we feel that if anything we are trying to curb that to a certain extent by somehow changing the direction of pornography away from a feeling that it is something that you deal with as being dirty." Bennett also strongly defended access channels, "the public access channels in a time of stress in this country could be the only conduit to free speech that we have. We should cherish the public access channel as we cherish any of the constitutional laws that we have protecting our freedoms."[25] This so-called adult oriented programming was only a minor portion of the access programming on Manhattan Cable. Cable officials estimated that it comprised only about six out of six hundred hours of programming offered each month.[26]

During the 1980s controversial programs appeared on access channels on other cable systems. In San Antonio, Texas, *The Worst Show* instructed viewers how to build a bomb. *The Great Satan at Large* in Tucson, Arizona, featured the masked "Sexecutioner" who partially undressed women and fondled their breasts. In Austin, Texas, *Hymns for Heathens* featured a man in a Charles Manson mask who chanted songs about religion and sex in front of a crucifix. *Race and Reason,* produced by the Ku Klux Klan, appeared on cable systems in Lincoln, Nebraska; East Peoria, Illinois; Kansas City, Missouri; Pittsburgh; and Austin.[27]

CABLE TV IN BLOOMINGTON

Cable television came to Bloomington, Indiana, during the mid-1960s. The franchise agreement in effect at the time of the research reported in this chapter required the cable operator to provide two community access channels. Both channels were to operate under the authority of the Monroe County Public Library Board (Bloomington is the county seat and major population center of Monroe County). In addition, the cable operator was required to provide $35,000 yearly for "operation and maintenance of the access facility."[28] The cable operator also donated approximately $70,000 in equipment to the access facility.[29] Bloomington Community Access Television (BCAT), a public entity created in 1974, managed the community access channels. The two channels in operation in 1993 were Channel 3, which presented programming produced or provided by local citizens, and Channel 12, which presented coverage of various public meetings.[30]

The decision to place Bloomington Community Access Television under the authority of the Monroe County Public Library Board meant that BCAT's director reported to an assistant director of the library, who reported to the library's director, who reported to the library board. The seven members of the library board were all appointed: two by the Bloomington City Council, two by the Monroe County Council, and three by area school boards.

In 1985 Michael White was hired as BCAT director. He found that BCAT programming decisions were solely up to him. White was uncomfortable with such unguided discretion; he began working to establish a statement of policy and program guidelines for BCAT.[31] White consulted with Herb Terry, a telecommunications professor at Indiana University in Bloomington, and with John Byers, BCAT operations manager. The three produced both a material review policy and a list of programming guidelines for BCAT that were approved by the Monroe County Public Library Board in 1987. In 1988, White, Terry, and Byers wrote a formal BCAT Statement of Purpose, which also was approved by the board. The role of Terry, a nationally known scholar of media law and regulation, was to provide information about the extent of constitutional protection for speech.[32]

BCAT had no written statement of community standards with respect to obscenity or indecency. The Statement of Purpose and the Programming Guidelines were the only material available. The Statement of Purpose stated that BCAT's purpose was to provide "the citizens of Monroe County, Indiana access to the electronic media for the distribution of information, opinion, and entertainment." The statement declared that BCAT was not a common carrier and would not carry programs that "contain libel, obscenity, child pornography, invasions of privacy, and 'fighting words,' i.e., speech not protected by the First Amendment of the Constitution of the United States of America." Programs were required to have copyright clearances.

Despite these restrictions, programs would not be "rejected because either they or their spokespersons are controversial." Furthermore, BCAT "does not attempt to verify the accuracy or lack of bias in the programming it carries, nor does BCAT attempt to achieve a balance in regards to any issue or political ideology." BCAT's first priority was to carry locally produced programs, but it would also carry "programs produced outside of Monroe County that reflect local concerns."[33]

Most of those principles were reiterated in the Programming Guidelines. "No part of any program shall contain: any solicitation for funds or other property of value, or obscene or defamatory material," the guidelines said. "The producer of each program is exercising her/his First Amendment right to free speech and is solely responsible for the program's content."[34] Producers agreed to "adhere carefully to all applicable federal, state and local regulations concerning limits of public speech and television program content." The guidelines added: "No program which contains any material which would subject the producer or the supplier thereof to prosecution under any applicable local, state or federal law for the production or presentation of obscene material, libel, slander, invasion of privacy or copyright or trademark infringement shall be transmitted over the community access channels. Obscenity, libel, slander, etc., are legal questions which can be determined only after due process by a judge and/or jury."[35]

Producers were required to submit a proposal that explained the purpose of the program they wanted the access channel to transmit. These proposals were made available to the public once the program had been aired. Additional guidelines determined equipment reservation and usage, absolved BCAT for any liability due to program content or technical failure during transmission, and provided conditions for the denial of equipment and facilities.

BCAT director White and his staff attempted to review all programs before they aired. Although the volume of programming involved made the task difficult, the review helped White determine when programs would air. In determining a program schedule, White followed a simple dictate: "The stronger (i.e., more controversial) it is, the later we put it."[36] Any program containing profanity was aired after 9 P.M., and any program containing more controversial material, such as partial nudity, was aired even later.[37]

Because BCAT was a department of the Monroe County Public Library, library policy concerning advance review of questionable material was applied to programs proposed for the cable access channel. If a proposed program contained questionable material, the BCAT director could either reject it on his own authority or request that it be reviewed by three members of the library staff, who acted as a review board. If the director rejected the program, the program's producer also could request the review. The three members of the review board were appointed by one of the library's assistant directors. Although the review board was not required to make a speedy ruling on whether to air a questionable program, the board generally made an effort to meet within two weeks of receiving a request for review.[38]

In a typical program review, each member of the review board watched the program in question on his or her own before the members met as a group to make a written report. The report went to the library director, who sent a copy of the report to the producer. Producers who were unhappy with the report could request a meeting with the library director. Producers were not allowed to meet with the review board. Producers could appeal a review board decision to the Monroe County Public Library Board, and could appear before that board. The library board's decision was considered final. After a library board decision not to air a program, the only recourse left to a producer was to sue the board.[39]

COPING WITH INDECENCY

Over the years, there had been controversies concerning indecent programs on BCAT. *Twinkies,* which used Twinkies as phallic symbols, drew some viewer opposition. White asked the library board to review the program, and the board decided to remove it from BCAT's schedule. Later, after several citizens requested that the program be returned, the board conducted a second review and approved the program. As of mid-1993, *Twinkies* was available and could be requested by cable subscribers.

Another controversy concerned the program *J & B on the Rox.* The program was produced by two Bloomington residents, Joe Nickell (known as "J") and Bart Everson (known as "B"). It aired Tuesdays at 11 P.M. and Thursdays at 10 P.M. The program's stated purpose was to "glorify the responsible use of alcohol." In fact, Nickell and Everson admitted that the statement of purpose was only a "jumping-off point." Nickell and Everson considered the program a means of allowing them to discuss whatever they wanted to: "Our credo has been simply to turn the camera on ourselves and present our own lives in all their ragged splendor."[40]

J & B on the Rox first aired in the fall of 1992; by mid-1993, it was the longest-running regularly scheduled program in BCAT history. Its longevity was a surprise to both producers. "We figured it would last a couple of weeks," Everson said. "We got into it because J had a video camera and we could do it."[41]

Despite their status as regular producers for BCAT, neither Nickell nor Everson was familiar with BCAT's Statement of Purpose or Program Guidelines. When they initially approached Michael White about doing a program, he did not discuss program guidelines with them or provide them with a copy of the written guidelines. However, Nickell and Everson did recall seeing a copy of the guidelines posted at the BCAT offices in the Monroe County Public Library.

By mid-1993, three proposed episodes of *J & B on the Rox* had been reviewed by the library review board. The first episode (entitled "Coprophagia Corner") featured a picture, obtained from a computer bulletin board available to Indiana University staff and students, of a woman defecating into a man's mouth. The episode's purpose, according to Nickell and Everson, was to "engender some kind of discussion about our show and the IU . . . computer system."[42] White recalled that the picture was very detailed: "There was no doubt about what was going on."[43] He thought showing an actual excretory function was probably obscene and asked the library review board for an opinion. The review board was not impressed with the image; some members wanted to dump the entire program series. However, the board reached a decision that was accepted by Nickell and Everson. The episode's audio track, which described the picture, was left intact, but the picture itself was covered by the caption "Censored by the Monroe County Public Library." The review process for "Coprophagia Corner" took four weeks.

The second episode that went through the program review process opened with a scene of a man apparently engaged in furious masturbation. Gradually it was revealed that a large rubber dildo, instead of a real penis, was the object of the man's attention. Eventually the man resorted to hitting the dildo with a crescent wrench in a futile effort to achieve orgasm. White gave the program to the review board, which decided not to air the scene. He then informed Nickell and Everson of the board's decision. They discussed the decision with White and decided that "maybe a judge would say yes, this is obscene,"[44] and agreed not to challenge the rejection of the program.

The questionable material in the third episode was the way the program's title—"J & B's Video Erotica"—was displayed. The program opened by showing a "J" written with a felt-tip pen on the head of Joe's penis and a "B" of the same nature on the head of Bart's penis. Everson said the shot was "definitely not erotic and certainly not sexual. It was just anatomically correct." The producers denied that they hoped to attract attention or grab headlines with the shot. "We didn't think, hey we could videotape our penises and that would cause a lot of controversy and we'd get attention in the media and we'd rile some folks up," Everson said. "Instead we thought, hey, this would be fun to do and we did it, and we had a good time, and we felt really silly."[45]

When Michael White reviewed the episode in January 1993, he asked that the title shot be changed. Nickell and Everson agreed, and the episode aired with the title "J & B's Video Erotica" displayed against a plain background. However, Nickell and Everson asked the library review board for a decision about whether the original title could be aired.

It took the review board three months to reach a decision. In early May, White informed Nickell and Everson that the board would allow the episode to air with its original title only at midnight or later. According to White, the board was concerned that children might be in the audience before midnight. Because Nickell and Everson did not want to move their program from its regular 11 P.M. time slot, and because they believed that an appeal to the full library board would be futile, they gave up their effort to air the episode with its original title shot.

The library review board's three-month delay was legally questionable. In 1965 the U.S. Supreme Court overturned a Maryland law that had authorized a review board to screen films before they could be shown. The Court held that "the exhibitor must be assured, by statute or authoritative judicial construction, that the censor will, within a specified brief period, either issue a license or go to court to restrain showing the film." In addition, "the procedure must also assure a prompt final judicial decision, to minimize the deterrent effect of an interim and possibly erroneous denial of a license."[46] This concept of requiring a swift judicial review of activity protected by the Constitution has been cited by several courts in a variety of cases.[47]

In addition, the review process was conducted orally, and therefore did not follow BCAT guidelines. Nickell and Everson were not asked to submit their request for review in writing, nor were they asked to state their reasons for seeking a review. The decision from the board was relayed to them orally by Michael White; they received nothing in writing from the board.

To the extent that public reaction to a program is an indication of community standards, J & B on the Rox did not seem to be offending community standards. Nickell and Everson solicited viewer comments and displayed their mailing address in each episode. They said they had not received any negative mail. BCAT had received some mail and phone calls opposing the program, but no viewer had filed a written complaint.

Despite their differences of opinion concerning acceptable programming, White, Nickell, and Everson agreed on several issues. One was the importance of public access channels. According to White, Channel 3 provided citizens with the means of expressing their ideas. "The important thing is that you have the opportunity to express whatever idea that is," he said. White considered public access "a way of seeing that's provided in no other medium"; BCAT's role in Bloomington was to provide a "mirror of this community." White hastened to add that "many people see things in the mirror they don't like."[48]

Everson considered public access "the equivalent of the soapbox in the park where someone can get up and say whatever they want and speak their piece."[49] Nickell saw public access as a part of the emerging information age where "censorship is an outmoded concept." He believed people should not stop the flow of information but should "open up avenues of dialogue which allow them to deal with the information which comes to them in a constructive manner. That is the ideal. A lot of people don't think it's realistic; we do."[50]

White, Nickell, and Everson also agreed on the difficulties involved in using the concept of contemporary community standards to determine BCAT programming. To determine acceptable programming standards, White said, "You have to look at things that have already been done, have already been tried and no one made a court case out of it." Some producers asked him for a book of standards and were surprised to learn that no such document existed. White conceded that his job would be easier if such a document existed. For White, determining what was or was not acceptable programming was "a real tough call."[51]

Everson was more emphatic. "There is no such thing" as community standards, he argued. He viewed Bloomington as a diverse community "which has different segments which hold diametrically opposed beliefs. So what do you do, you don't weigh them all in some kind of scale and come out with some kind of average." He considered community standards "a pair of words bandied about in the name of a few people making a decision about what the rest of the community can do and can say."[52]

The three men also agreed on the future need for public access channels in Bloomington. The cable franchise would expire in 1995, and one idea considered for part of the next franchise agreement was to designate a separate channel for adult programming.[53] White had no objection, depending on how the channel was offered to subscribers. He thought the channel should be available to all subscribers. Subscribers who did not want the service could request that the cable company disconnect it. White opposed a system in which subscribers would have to request the service because he believed such a system would result in fewer subscribers receiving the service.

Nickell and Everson agreed with White on how the service should be made available. However, they had reservations about the impact of having a separate channel for adult programming. They thought there would be little programming for such a channel, and they believed this could result in a smaller number of viewers.

DISCUSSION

This study of how obscenity and indecency law were applied to public access channels in Bloomington demonstrates how the conceptual ambiguity endorsed by the U.S. Supreme Court leads to arbitrary decision-making on the local level. In Bloomington, there was no useful list of do's and don'ts for producers of BCAT programs to follow. The nearest things to such a list of standards were BCAT's Statement of Purpose and its written Programming Guidelines, but there was no guarantee that producers were aware of the existence of either document. Producers who did seek guidance from the documents found few clues about what constituted acceptable program material. Both documents were vague and did little more than echo existing federal law. In addition, some producers were not aware of their right to appeal a rejection of one of their programs.

This lamentable situation probably was not unique to Bloomington. Other communities also faced the difficult, if not impossible, task of determining community standards. Perhaps obscenity and indecency cannot be adequately defined; former U.S. Supreme Court Justice Potter Stewart may have done as well as anyone could when he penned his famous concurrence in *Jacobellis v Ohio*. Asserting his view that only "hardcore pornography" could be prohibited, he wrote: "I shall not today attempt further to define the kinds of material I understand to be embraced within that shorthand description; and perhaps I could never succeed in intelligibly doing so. But I know it when I see it. . . ."[54]

Perhaps contemporary community standards also are beyond definition. This chapter's case study makes at least one thing apparent: the absence of clear definitions of legal concepts such as "contemporary community standards" leads to ad hoc policymaking and procedural problems, including undue delays in making decisions. All in all, the situation in Bloomington represented yet another failed attempt to draw the line between permissible and impermissible expression. Nevertheless, throughout the period under study, BCAT continued to offer programming that many subscribers found offensive but that other subscribers found acceptable. No answer had been found to one of the central questions of content regulation: how to satisfy as many audience members as possible, while also protecting the rights of producers who wanted to disseminate questionable material and audience members who wanted to view it.

A possible answer lies not in legal definitions, but rather in the creation of a new access channel for adult programming. All programs the BCAT director found questionable for general airing could be placed on a separate channel available to all subscribers as part of their basic cable service. However, subscribers who did not want to receive such material could have the channel removed from their cable package. The channel could be placed in the highest position on the cable system to minimize the possibility that unwary viewers might "graze" through it as they switched channels. Daily programming could begin after prime-time hours, with the channel being devoted during day-time and prime-time to a bulletin board offering a weekly program schedule for the channel, as well as any other programming information and news provided by the producers.

The review procedures for questionable material also could be improved. The BCAT director could provide all producers with copies of BCAT's Statement of Purpose and Programming Guidelines. The director also could explain review and appeal procedures with each producer. Producers would have the right to appeal the director's decision to place programming on the adult channel. In addition, both the library review board and the Monroe County Public Library Board should be required to rule on appeals expeditiously. The policy void that enabled the three librarians on the review board to take three months to review a few seconds of videotape (the anatomically correct title shot of "J & B's Video Erotica") was unacceptable, and perhaps even unconstitutional. The rationale for the delay was that a member of the board had undergone surgery and was unable to work for several weeks.

The rationale is inadequate. The right of free expression was at issue, and the board should have—and easily could have—met. The board's membership depended on which members of the library staff were available to serve. A replacement for the staff member who was recovering from surgery easily could have been found.

No solution can please everyone. However, changes such as those recommended here would be an improvement over a situation that offered little or no guidance to program producers, provided inadequate safeguards for protecting their First Amendment rights, and offended many cable subscribers who did not wish to have adult programming enter their homes.

NOTES

1. A considerable amount of research has been done on access channels, but none has dealt specifically with the issue of contemporary community standards for public access channels. Several articles dealt with whether requirements for access channels violated the First Amendment. John D. Hollinrake, Jr., "Cable Television: Public Access and the First Amendment," *Communications and the Law* 9 (1987): 3–40, argued that the access channel requirement of the Cable Communications Policy Act of 1984 did not violate the First Amendment rights of cable operators. The opposing argument was presented by Mark J. Bernet in "Quincy Cable and its Effect on the Access Provisions of the 1984 Cable Act" *Notre Dame Law Review* 61 (1986): 426–439, and by Adam R. Spilka in "An Excess of Access: The Cable Communications Policy Act of 1984 and First Amendment Protection of Editorial Discretion," *Cardozo Law Review* 8 (1986): 317–359.

2. *Miller v California,* 413 U.S. 15 (1973).

3. 56 FCC 2d at 98.

4. *FCC v Pacifica,* 438 U.S. 726 (1978).

5. See *Cruz v Ferre,* 755 F.2d 1415 (1985); *HBO v Wilkinson,* 531 F. Supp. 986 (1982); and *Community Television of Utah Inc. v Wilkinson,* 611 F. Supp. 1099 (1985).

6. *Roth v U.S.,* 354 U.S. 476 (1957). Broadcasting obscene material could result in a fine of $10,000 or a jail sentence of two years or both. 47 USC Section 559.

7. *FCC v Pacifica,* 438 U.S. 726 (1978).

8. "FCC Creates Adult Country: Midnight–6 A.M.," *Broadcasting,* November 30, 1987, p. 51.

9. P.L. 100-459, 102 Stat. 2186. A rider calling for a twenty-four-hour ban on indecent programming was attached to the FCC appropriations bill for 1989. "Congress Says 'Safe Harbor' Is Safe No More," *Broadcasting,* October 3, 1988, p. 28. The FCC promptly endorsed the twenty-four-hour ban.

10. *Children's Legal Foundation v Action for Children's TV;* and *FCC v Action for Children's TV, cert. denied,* 60 U.S.L.W. 3599 (March 3, 1992) (Nos. 91-883 & 91-952). See *Broadcasting,* March 9, 1992, p. 35.

11. *United States v Southwestern Cable Co.,* 392 U.S. 157 (1968).

12. *United States v Midwest Video Corp.,* 406 U.S. 649 (1972).

13. *Federal Communications Commission v Midwest Video Corp.,* 440 U.S. 689 (1979).

14. 98 Stat. 2782, Section 611(b).

15. Ibid., Section 611(e).

16. Pub. L. No. 98-549, 1984 U.S.C.C.A.N. at 4667.

17. Under a leased-access arrangement, a producer bought time on a channel from the cable operator and then sold advertising time during programming.

18. "Cable Rereg Gets Under Way at FCC," *Broadcasting,* February 8, 1993, p. 26.

19. "Keeping Up with Cable Rereg," *Broadcasting & Cable,* April 12, 1993, p. 64.

20. Plaintiffs in both cases included the American Civil Liberties Union, People for the American Way, the 90's Channel, Alliance for Community Media, and Alliance for Communications Democracy.

21. "F.C.C. Blocked on TV Curb," *New York Times,* May 8, 1993, p. 18.

22. D. Keith Mayo, "The Cheap Agony of Ugly George," *Playboy,* November 1982, p. 146.

23. "Ugly George Talks about TV," *National Review,* October 14, 1988, p. 57.

24. "The Lewd Tube," *Newsweek,* December 29, 1975, p. 60.

25. U.S. Congress, Senate, Subcommittee on Communications, *Hearing Concerning the Role of Congress in Regulating Cable Television,* 1976, at 265–266.

26. "New York Cables' Answer to Carson: Late-Night Sex," *Broadcasting,* June 9, 1975, p. 49.

27. See "Austin Gets an Eyeful: Sacrilege and the Klan," *Channels,* March/April 1986, p. 43; "Cities Fight Public Access Channel Nudity," *News Media & the Law,* Spring 1990, p. 43; "ACLU Complains about Access Channel Limits," *News Media & the Law,* Fall 1990, p. 34; "Access Channel Program Content Sparks Controversy," *News Media & the Law,* Summer 1991, p. 21; and "Sex, Bombs Spur Furor over Public Access," *News Media & the Law,* Winter 1992, p. 49.

28. Bloomington, Ind. *Herald-Telephone,* August 23, 1985, section 1, p. 1.

29. *Herald-Telephone,* August 23, 1985, section 1, p. 1.

30. In addition to the money received from the cable operator, BCAT also received funds from the city and county governments. These funds were channeled through the budget of the Telecommunications Council, a five-member group appointed by the mayor and city council. The Telecommunications Council's main responsibility was to ensure that the cable operator abided by the franchise agreement. The council did not get involved in programming decisions concerning BCAT. Telecommunications Council member Susan Eastman, personal interview, March 28, 1993.

31. Interview with Michael White, April 8, 1993, hereafter cited as White interview.

32. Interview with Herb Terry, April 9, 1993.

33. Statement of Purpose, approved July 5, 1988.

34. "Access Use," guidelines 2 and 3.

35. "Access Limitations," guidelines 1 and 5.

36. White interview.

37. Ibid.

38. Jan Yeager, assistant to the director, Monroe County Public Library, personal interview, April 15, 1993. Hereafter cited as Yeager interview.

39. Material Review Policy, adopted November 8, 1987, Yeager interview.

40. Interview with Joe Nickell and Bart Everson, April 10, 1993, hereafter cited as J & B interview.

41. Ibid.

42. Ibid.

43. White interview.

44. J & B interview.

45. Ibid.

46. *Freedman v Maryland,* 380 U.S. 51 (1965) at 58–59.

47. Cases involved the procedure nonunion members should follow in objecting to having their wages deducted in order to support union activities, zoning ordinances banning the distribution of adult films, policies prohibiting fixed signs on State House grounds, ordinances covering nude dancing in adult-oriented establishments, laws requiring groups to obtain special permits before they could gather in national forests, and ordinances regulating the placement of newspaper dispensing devices. See *Teachers v Hudson,* 475 U.S. 292 (1986) at 308; *Gascoe Ltd. v Newton T.P., Bucks County,* 669 F. Supp. 1092 (E.D. Pa. 1988) at 1097; *Grass Roots Organizing Workshop (GROW) v Campbell,* 703 F. Supp. 650 (D.S.C. 1989) at 653; *Ellwest Stereo Theater, Inc. v Boner,* 718 F. Supp. 1553 (M.D. Tenn. 1989) at 1580; *U.S. v Rainbow Family,* 695 F. Supp. 294 (E.D. Tex. 1988) at 311; and *Chicago Newspaper Publishers v City of Wheaton,* 697 F. Supp. 1464 (N.D. Ill. 1988) at 1466.

48. White interview.

49. J & B interview.

50. Ibid.

51. White interview.

52. J & B interview.

53. *Bloomington's 1995 Cable Franchise Renewal: Process, Problems, and Participation,* March 1993, p. 16.

54. *Jacobellis v Ohio,* 378 U.S. 184, 197 (1964).

10

Newspapers' Use of Lawyers in the Editorial Process

CRAIG SANDERS

CHAPTER 9 PORTRAYED A SITUATION OF AMBIGUOUS LEGAL STAN-
DARDS AND ARBITRARY ENFORCEMENT OF MEDIA LAW IN AN INDI-
ANA CITY. PERHAPS THINGS WOULD HAVE BEEN BETTER IF ONLY
PEOPLE HAD CONSULTED LAWYERS.

IN CHAPTER 10 CRAIG SANDERS ADDRESSES THE INTER-
ESTING QUESTION OF WHAT HAPPENS WHEN MEDIA PEOPLE IN
INDIANA DO CALL UPON LAWYERS. HE EXAMINES HOW INDIANA
NEWSPAPERS USE LAWYERS TO HELP DEFINE AND RESOLVE NEWS-
RELATED CONFLICTS IN THEIR COMMUNITIES. INTERVIEWS WITH
EDITORS SHOWED THAT NEWSPAPERS IN LARGE COMMUNITIES
CONSULTED LAWYERS MORE OFTEN AND ABOUT A WIDER RANGE OF
LEGAL ISSUES THAN DID NEWSPAPERS IN SMALLER COMMUNITIES.

SANDERS FOUND THAT LAWYERS CAN BE A HINDRANCE AS
WELL AS A HELP TO MEDIA WORK. ALL OF THE EDITORS WERE RE-
LUCTANT TO INVOLVE LAWYERS IN THE DECISION-MAKING PRO-
CESS. EDITORS IN SMALLER COMMUNITIES HAD TWO ADDITIONAL
CONCERNS: THEY BELIEVED THAT THEIR LAWYERS DIDN'T KNOW
MUCH ABOUT PRESS LAW, AND THEY WERE CONCERNED ABOUT
THEIR LAWYERS' POSSIBLE CONFLICTS OF INTEREST.

THIS CHAPTER IS BASED ON A PAPER WRITTEN FOR A GRAD-
UATE SEMINAR AT INDIANA UNIVERSITY, WHERE SANDERS OB-
TAINED HIS PH.D. A SUBSEQUENT VERSION OF THE PAPER WAS
PRESENTED AT A NATIONAL MEETING OF THE ASSOCIATION FOR
EDUCATION IN JOURNALISM AND MASS COMMUNICATION. AT THIS
WRITING, SANDERS IS ON THE FACULTY OF THE DEPARTMENT OF
COMMUNICATIONS AT JOHN CARROLL UNIVERSITY IN CLEVELAND.

Lawsuits for libel or invasion of privacy can be powerful means of media accountability because they force news organizations to provide an account
of the behavior that was offensive enough to cause someone to take legal action.

News organizations rarely emerge unscathed from such lawsuits. Juries are notoriously unsympathetic to media defendants; when lawsuits against the media go to a jury, the news organizations usually lose.[1] Although jury verdicts against news organizations usually are overturned on appeal,[2] even the cost of winning a libel or privacy lawsuit can be quite high.[3]

The high cost of being sued raises the possibility that some news organizations may incorporate legal calculations into their journalistic decisions. This chapter uses the responses from a survey of editors to explore how newspapers in different kinds of communities use lawyers in the editorial process. The results showed that although most of the newspapers had used attorneys, all were reluctant to do so. Smaller newspapers tended to use attorneys differently than larger newspapers.

BACKGROUND

Whether or not the legal climate for the press in the 1990s actually was bad, it is clear that many journalists believed it was bad. In the 1980s and early 1990s the Supreme Court of the United States made several decisions that can be characterized as anti-press.[4] For example, the court ruled in 1985 that a libel plaintiff need not prove fault when a false and defamatory statement is not a "matter of public concern."[5] In addition, some observers suggested that lawsuits were increasingly being used to punish and silence news organizations.[6] In 1988, the high court refused to review a $3.05 million libel award against a Chicago television commentator.[7] A year later, the court declined to overturn a $2.2 million libel award won by a public official against the *Pittsburgh Post-Gazette*.[8]

Although not all of the major press cases in the 1980s went against press interests,[9] the long-term impact of conservative justices appointed by Presidents Reagan and Bush caused concern among newspeople.[10] Lyle Denniston, a widely respected reporter who covers the Supreme Court for the *Baltimore Sun*, observed that the Court "appears to be skeptical, at best, of most of the constitutional claims of the press; it may be downright hostile to any significant expansion of previously declared rights."[11] How journalists' behavior was affected, if at all, by these developments was difficult to assess. Some researchers have suggested that unfavorable court rulings have had little effect on press behavior.[12]

Yet the horror stories from the journalistic front lines persist. The threat of being sued for libel reportedly has had a "chilling effect" on many news organizations, particularly on smaller organizations that lack the financial resources to aggressively defend themselves in court.[13] A study of small Kentucky newspapers found that the threat of a libel lawsuit had "chilled" some.[14] Many managers claimed they did not fear losing in court as much as they feared the cost of litigation.[15] "However painful a successful libel action may be to CBS or the *National Enquirer,* it can be fatal to a small media outlet," law professor Rodney A. Smolla wrote.[16]

Whatever the effect of the legal climate on press behavior, there was some evidence that the increasing complexity of press law and the increasing uncertainty of outcomes in court were leading some news organizations to increase their reliance on lawyers. Kent R. Middleton and Bill F. Chamberlin, authors of a major communications law textbook, suggested that "[l]awyers have become more important to the public communication process as legal issues in communication have demanded more attention."[17] The duties that attorneys could be asked to perform in the editorial process include providing advice about how to respond to such legal documents as a subpoena, handling requests for retractions, reading stories in advance of publication to check for potentially troublesome material, responding to the legal moves of an adversary, explaining the legal consequences of trespassing or obtaining stolen documents in pursuit of a story, assisting in filing of requests for information from government agencies, and helping journalists obtain access to closed records or meetings.[18] Attorneys might also conduct staff seminars on press law and mediate disputes before they escalate into litigation.

Some observers, such as textbook authors Middleton and Chamberlin, assert that journalists should not fear or avoid media lawyers, but rather should use them intelligently.[19] Others, however, see little good resulting from lawyers in newsrooms. For example, Lois G. Forer, a judge who has written about press rights, argues that having attorneys examine stories before publication is costly and largely nonproductive. "When defensive journalism is practiced, readers and viewers are given sanitized print and electronic material, not for their benefit, but to save the authors, publishers and producers the expense of litigation and the possibility of substantial damage awards," she wrote.[20] When lawyers do take part in the editorial process, their welcome is sometimes muted. George Freeman, an attorney for the *New York Times,* observed that when a newspaper's lawyers enter the newsroom, they are often greeted with comments such as, "Uh-oh, here come the lawyers."[21]

Few people have studied the interaction between news organizations and their attorneys. The widespread assumption is that attorneys have tremendous influence on the behavior of news organizations. A lawyer speaking at a conference on the problems of libel law said that attorneys "[u]ndoubtedly . . . influence editors' and publishers' decisions about what they will investigate and report, perhaps even more than liability standards or a medium's previous litigation experience does."[22] But systematic research on the extent and nature of the influence is lacking.

Much of the existing research has been descriptive, often focusing merely on frequency of contact between journalists and news organizations' lawyers. One study found that many Florida daily newspapers had increased their budgets for legal assistance, were relying more on attorneys who were media law specialists, were using multiple sources for legal help, and had increased their frequency of consultation with lawyers.[23] A study of Florida's weekly newspapers found similar results: most respondents were consulting attorneys more frequently than they had ten years earlier.[24] Many of the weekly newspaper editors said that their attorneys did not understand the roles and values of journalists. Some editors said that journalists and the legal profession have conflicting goals. Editors also complained that many local attorneys have a poor grasp of press law, do not keep themselves up to date, and because of their ties to community power structures are ill-suited to offer advice and representation to newspapers.[25] Almost all news organizations consult lawyers for help with editorial problems at least occasionally,[26] with large news organizations consulting lawyers much more often than small ones.[27]

This body of research suggests that although it is common for news organizations to contact attorneys, the contacts tend to be relatively infrequent, particularly in the case of smaller news organizations. That lawyers may seldom be consulted does not necessarily mean that their influence on the editorial process is small, but the influence of lawyers on press behavior is difficult to observe directly. Journalists frequently make decisions about matters that may have legal implications without consulting attorneys or other press law specialists. Accordingly, it is important to know more about the circumstances in which a journalist or news organization is likely to seek the help of an attorney and how contacts with lawyers influence the editorial process.

METHOD

The research reported in this chapter focused on interactions between journalists and lawyers at eight daily newspapers in six Indiana communities. The newspapers represented the spectrum of Indiana's daily press, ranging from small-town papers with circulations of just over 3,000 to well-known metropolitan dailies. Table 1 contains details about the newspapers surveyed.

Table 1 Data on Newspapers in the Study

Newspaper	Community Size	Circulation
Indianapolis Star	large	228,582 (morning)
		411,044 (Sunday)
Indianapolis News	large	101,091 (evening)
Evansville Courier	medium	63,175 (morning)
		116,962 (Sunday)
Evansville Press	medium	35,567 (evening)
Bloomington Herald-Times	medium	28,709 (morning)
		44,205 (Sunday)
Bedford Times-Mail	small	14,766 (evening)
Spencer Evening World	small	3,800 (evening)
Bloomfield Evening World	small	3,395 (evening)

Two of the newspapers were published in Indianapolis, the state's largest community with a population of 1.2 million in its six-county metropolitan region. Three newspapers were based in medium-size cities: two in Evansville (population about 130,000) and one in Bloomington (population about 60,000). The other three newspapers were small-town dailies: one was based in Bedford (population about 14,000), while the other two were based in towns with populations of less than 3,000.

Interviews with the highest-ranking editor at each of the newspapers were based on a questionnaire composed of closed and open-ended questions about the newspaper's use of lawyers. The interviews focused on a variety of issues, including how often an editor's newspaper had consulted a lawyer in the previous year, how often the newspaper was threatened with legal action, what types of lawsuits the newspaper had been involved with in the previous five years, how the newspaper handled threats of legal action against it, and how editors felt about involving lawyers in the editorial process.

FINDINGS

Editors were asked to estimate how many times their newspaper had consulted a lawyer during the previous year. Table 2 shows that newspapers in the largest communities (Indianapolis and Evansville) consulted lawyers far more often than did the newspapers in smaller communities.

The *Evansville Courier,* the *Evansville Press,* and the *Indianapolis Star* reported the most contact with lawyers in the previous year. The *Courier* estimated it contacted its lawyer 30 to 40 times, the *Star* 25 to 30 times, and the *Press* 25 times. By contrast, the *Bloomington Herald-Times* and the *Spencer Evening World* reported fewer than six consultations with a lawyer, and the *Bedford Times-Mail* and the *Bloomfield Evening World* reported no consultations. Editors of the latter two newspapers explained that they had not con-

Table 2 Number of Consultations with a Lawyer in the Past Year

Newspaper	With paper's lawyer	With HSPA* Counsel
Indianapolis Star	25 to 30	16
Indianapolis News	8 to 10	6
Evansville Courier	30 to 40	6 to 10
Evansville Press	25	12
Bloomington Herald-Times	5	10
Bedford Times-Mail	0	3
Spencer Evening World	4	3
Bloomfield Evening World	0	12

*Hoosier State Press Association

tacted a lawyer because they had not been threatened with legal action. *Times-Mail* editor William Schrader said his newspaper receives a threat of legal action nearly every week, though he added that he rarely considers those threats to be serious. All eight editors reported that they had consulted with Richard W. Cardwell, general counsel of the Hoosier State Press Association.

The editors were read a list of ten press law issues and asked if their newspaper had consulted a lawyer about any of those issues. Table 3 shows that the Indianapolis and Evansville newspapers consulted with their lawyers on a wider range of legal issues than did newspapers in the smaller communities. The *Indianapolis Star* consulted with its lawyer on all ten issues. The *Indianapolis News* and *Evansville Press* discussed seven of the issues with their lawyers; the *Evansville Courier* discussed six. The *Bloomington Herald-Times* consulted with its lawyer about clarifying and using the state open meetings law; the *Spencer Evening World* sought clarification of the open meetings law and the state public records law, and assistance with a potentially libelous story.

Editors were asked how often during the previous year someone had contacted their newspaper and threatened to take legal action against the paper

Table 3 Issues Discussed with Newspaper's Own Lawyer in the Past Year

Newspaper	A	B	C	D	E	F	G	H	I	J
Indianapolis Star	y	y	y	y	y	y	y	y	y	y
Indianapolis News	-	y	-	y	y	-	y	y	y	y
Evansville Courier	y	y	-	y	y	-	-	-	-	y
Evansville Press	y	y	-	y	y	-	y	y	-
Bloomington Herald-Times	-	y	-	-	y	-	-	-	-	-
Bedford Times-Mail	-	-	-	-	-	-	-	-	-	-
Spencer Evening World	-	y	-	-	-	-	y	y	-
Bloomfield Evening World	-	-	-	-	-	-	-	-	-	-

A. Prior restraint (3 newspapers)
B. Clarify Indiana public records law (5 newspapers)
C. Clarify Indiana open door (public meetings) law (6 newspapers)
D. Clarify federal Freedom of Information Act (1 newspaper)
E. Use state public records law (4 newspapers)
F. Use state open door law (5 newspapers)
G. Use federal Freedom of Information Act (1 newspaper)
H. Answer pre-publication libel question (4 newspapers)
I. Advice on handling threat of libel suit (4 newspapers)
J. Responding to a libel suit (3 newspapers)

The *Courier* also consulted on whether a reporter could be forced to testify at a murder trial. The *Herald-Times* used its lawyer to fight a subpoena for a photo negative.

Table 4 Number of Threats of Legal Action Received in the Past Year

Newspaper	Pre-publication	Post-publication
Indianapolis Star	10 to 15	5 to 6
Indianapolis News	6	2
Evansville Courier	20 to 25	2 to 3
Evansville Press	50	12
Bloomington Herald-Times	3	0
Bedford Times-Mail	*	*
Spencer Evening World	2	1
Bloomfield Evening World	0	0

*The *Times-Mail* editor's response was: "People every week call you up and say, 'I'll sue you.'"

either in reaction to a published story or in an effort to prevent the publication of a particular piece of information. Table 4 shows that the larger newspapers received substantially more threats of legal action than did the smaller ones. At all newspapers, most of the threats received came before a story was published. *Evansville Press* editor Bill D. Jackson estimated he had received fifty threats during the previous year, the highest number reported.

Editors differed in their perception of the likelihood that a threat of legal action would result in litigation. Editors were asked how many of the threats of legal action were serious. Newspaper size made no difference in the responses. The editors of the *Indianapolis Star* and *Spencer Evening World* said they considered all threats of legal action to be serious; the *Bloomington Herald-Times* editor did not think any of the threats he received had been likely to evolve into litigation. Editors at the *Indianapolis News* and *Bedford Times-Mail* said few threats of legal action were likely to turn into litigation. The *Evansville Press* editor said he considered most threats to be serious, but his counterpart at the *Evansville Courier* considered only some threats to be serious.

The newspapers seldom used lawyers to mediate or to help resolve disputes that had not resulted in legal action. During the previous year, only the *Indianapolis Star* and the *Evansville Press* had used a lawyer in such a fashion. *Press* editor Jackson said his newspaper used a lawyer three or four times during the previous year to help resolve disputes. None of those situations evolved into litigation.

Indianapolis Star managing editor Lawrence S. Connor said that the one case during the previous year in which his newspaper used a lawyer to try to resolve a dispute had ended up in court anyway. The *Star* did not routinely call in a lawyer to help resolve conflicts, but it did so when a conflict reached an

Table 5   How Threats of Legal Action Are Handled

Newspaper	When aggrieved party makes the threat	When attorney for aggrieved party makes the threat
Indianapolis Star	A	A
Indianapolis News	D	D
Evansville Courier	A	A
Evansville Press	D	A
Bloomington Herald-Times	D	A
Bedford Times-Mail	D	C
Spencer Evening World	A	B
Bloomfield Evening World	A	B

A. Handle the situation as best I can, and then contact our newspaper's attorney to let him or her know what happened.

B. Handle the situation as best as I can and then instruct the person making the threat to contact our newspaper's attorney.

C. Tell the person making the threat that I cannot discuss a threat of legal action. I tell the person to contact our newspaper's attorney.

D. Response varies by situation.

impasse and the newspaper wanted to demonstrate its willingness to defend itself. Connor said that in previous years using a lawyer to help resolve disputes has helped his newspaper avoid lawsuits.

Indianapolis News managing editor Frank Caperton said he generally opposed turning over the management of conflicts to lawyers. Caperton called lawyers only after managers at the newspaper had engaged in a "great deal of conversation" with a disputant. Editors of the *Bedford Times-Mail* and the *Bloomfield Evening World* both said that using a lawyer to help resolve a conflict risked needlessly prolonging it. The Bedford editor said lawyers prolong disputes to make money. The Bloomfield editor said using lawyers might discourage disputants from quickly settling their differences.

The editors varied in how they responded to threats of legal action against their newspaper. Table 5 shows that when an individual contacted a newspaper to threaten legal action, four of the newspapers said their initial response was to attempt to work out a solution to the conflict with the aggrieved person. However, the other four newspapers said that their response varied depending on the situation. When lawyers contacted these newspapers to threaten or discuss possible legal action on behalf of a client, most of the newspapers initially attempted to discuss the conflict with the lawyer. But then the editor contacted the newspaper's lawyer. Only the *Bedford Times-Mail* refused to attempt to

Table 6   Number of Lawsuits Involving the Newspapers in the Past 5 Years

Newspaper	As Plaintiff	As Defendant
Indianapolis Star	0 to 10	at least 3
Indianapolis News	2	0
Evansville Courier	2	0
Evansville Press	3 to 4	0
Bloomington Herald-Times	1	0
Bedford Times-Mail	0	0
Spencer Evening World	0	0
Bloomfield Evening World	0	0

discuss conflicts with lawyers representing aggrieved individuals. When lawyers called the Bedford paper, they were immediately instructed to contact the newspaper's lawyer, according to editor Schrader.

Table 6 shows how many lawsuits each newspaper had been involved in, either as defendant or as plaintiff, in the previous five years. The Indianapolis and Evansville newspapers were litigants more often than the smaller newspapers. However, most of the time, the newspapers were plaintiffs. Only the *Indianapolis Star* reported having been a defendant in a lawsuit; it had been sued for libel several times. With the exception of an effort by the *Evansville Press* to overturn a prior restraint order, all of the lawsuits initiated by the Indianapolis and Evansville newspapers were attempts to gain access to public records or meetings of public agencies. The *Bloomington Herald-Times*'s sole lawsuit sought to quash a subpoena for unpublished photographs of an automobile accident.

Seven of the eight newspapers reported having used a lawyer in the editorial process during the previous year. Table 7 shows that lawyers most often were used to read stories before publication for potentially libelous material, and to inform public officials that certain conduct may have been unlawful.

The editors generally opposed involving lawyers in the newsgathering process. *Indianapolis Star* editor Connor commented: "I think it harms your professional status. Journalists should not rely on the legal profession to do their [journalists'] work. It helps to maintain some distance between journalists and the legal profession."

Evansville Courier editor Thomas W. Tuley said lawyers should help in the newsgathering process only as a last resort. *Indianapolis News* editor Caperton said that involving lawyers in the newsgathering process might create a conflict of interest because a lawyer who helped gather information for a story might not be able to be a "dispassionate reader" of the story if he or she were later asked to review it for potential legal problems.

Table 7 Use of Lawyers in the Editorial Process in the Past Five Years

Newspaper	A	B	C	D	E	F
Indianapolis Star	y	y	y	-	y	-
Indianapolis News	y	y	-	-	y	-
Evansville Courier	y	-	-	-	-	-
Evansville Press	y	y	-	-	y	-
Bloomington Herald-Times	-	-	-	-	y	-
Bedford Times-Mail	y	-	-	-	-	-
Spencer Evening World	-	y	-	-	y	-
Bloomfield Evening World	-	-	-	-	-	y

A. Inform public officials that certain conduct was unlawful (5 newspapers).

B. Help file requests or complaints under open records, open door, or federal Freedom of Information laws (4 newspapers).

C. Help conduct searches for information in legal records (1 newspaper).

D. Provide advice on how to search for information in legal records (0 newspaper).

E. Read a story in advance of publication to determine if the story contained potentially libelous material (5 newspapers).

F. Did not use an attorney in the editorial process in any capacity (1 newspaper).

Spencer Evening News managing editor Tom Douglas said that using a lawyer to help gather news might damage his newspaper's credibility in the community. Nevertheless, Douglas said he once considered using a lawyer to help gather information for a story about a judge who was allegedly acting improperly.

The editors' reaction was mixed when they were asked if their newspaper would be willing to put a lawyer in the newsroom to routinely read stories for potential legal problems, and advise reporters and editors on how to avoid legal difficulties. *Evansville Courier* editor Tuley supported the idea, but said his newspaper lacked the money to hire a lawyer for that purpose. *Indianapolis News* editor Caperton said his staff probably would not object so long as the newspaper remained aggressive in its news coverage. In contrast, *Indianapolis Star* editor Connor said his staff would resent having a lawyer become an integral part of the newsroom. "It's just like an outsider coming in. It would be intimidating," he explained. *Bedford Times-Mail* editor Schrader also said his staff would react negatively to a lawyer in the newsroom. Several editors said their staffs might question why the money used to hire a lawyer was not instead being used to hire additional reporters or editors.

For the most part, the editors said they were comfortable with the roles their newspapers' lawyers were playing in the editorial process. *Indianapolis News* editor Caperton spoke for many editors when he said, "Ours is about right. We're comfortable with what they're doing. To have no role [for lawyers] would be foolhardy. On the other hand, we don't expect attorneys to make journalistic judgments for us."

Indianapolis Star editor Connor and *Spencer Evening World* editor Douglas expressed support for the idea of having their newspapers' lawyers play a larger role in advising reporters and editors about how to avoid legal problems. The *Indianapolis Star* and the *Evansville Courier* periodically have lawyers speak about recent developments in press law. Of the eight editors interviewed, only *Bedford Times-Mail* editor Schrader opposed involving an attorney in the editorial process in any capacity. "If attorneys play any role, it's too large of a role," Schrader said.

Editors of the larger newspapers believed their lawyers strongly supported the media's legal rights; editors from all four Indianapolis and Evansville papers held that view. *Evansville Courier* editor Tuley said he had met many lawyers who represented news organizations who passionately supported the legal rights of the press.

However, Bedford editor Schrader, Spencer editor Douglas, and *Bloomfield Evening World* editor William C. Miles expressed doubt that their lawyers were supportive of these legal rights. "No, their approach is entirely different from that of journalists," said Miles. Commented Douglas: "I doubt it. A regular guy [a local lawyer] wouldn't look at it the same way I would."

The attitudes that the editors of the smaller newspapers hold toward their lawyers appear rooted in their beliefs that lawyers practicing in smaller communities know little about press law. The Bloomfield editor said that was why he wouldn't hire a local lawyer. Although *Bloomington Herald-Times* editor Bob Zaltsberg has not had any major disagreements with his newspaper's lawyer regarding press legal rights, he questioned whether any Bloomington lawyer knows much about press law. Zaltsberg added: "The key is to find an attorney who has the same goals [as the newspaper]. We could get an attorney [who] may be extremely conservative . . . and might [recommend against] reporting a story we had every right to report."

Zaltsberg also expressed concern that his newspaper's lawyer could have a conflict of interest. He commented: "An attorney may be biased. He may have a government unit he's representing. That's quite possible, especially here. In a small town, [a newspaper's attorney] could be the school board attorney. Our attorney has represented developers and public agencies."

The Bloomfield editor said lawyers' conflicts of interest are a serious problem for smaller newspapers because a small-town lawyer representing a newspaper probably also represents an individual or an organization the newspaper has written about in its news columns. It may be, then, that one reason why smaller newspapers are less willing to use lawyers in the editorial process is because the editors do not believe that their lawyer will act with the newspaper's best interests in mind at all times.

DISCUSSION

One major finding of this study is that how newspapers use lawyers depends to a great extent on the size of their communities. The newspapers in the largest communities in this study, Indianapolis and Evansville, consulted lawyers more often and about a wider range of legal issues, received more threats of lawsuits, were parties to litigation more often, and were more likely to believe that their lawyers were supportive of the legal rights of the press. Newspapers in the smaller communities—Bedford, Bloomfield, Bloomington, and Spencer —seldom consulted local lawyers, and when they did they discussed a narrower range of issues. Editors in the smaller communities believed that their lawyers know little about press law. The editors in the smaller communities also were concerned about their lawyers' possible conflicts of interest.

These findings are consistent with research showing that people and organizations in smaller communities are less likely than those in urban communities to use the judicial system or resort to a third party as a means of resolving conflict.[28] Researchers have suggested that the network of relationships commonly existing in smaller communities discourages the use of third parties and the courts to settle disputes. Small-town residents typically are more dependent upon each other for their social welfare than is usually the case in urban communities.[29] Disputants in smaller, more homogeneous communities are less likely to resolve conflict by resorting to litigation or third parties for fear of endangering important social ties. The potential gains to be won in court are viewed as not worth the cost of the resulting social disruption.[30] That small-town lawyers and journalists interact in a common network of relationships may tend to mute conflict.[31]

By contrast, people living in larger and more heterogeneous communities may view going to court or resorting to a third party as merely one step in conflict resolution. In such communities, networks of relationships tend to be looser and to overlap less than in small towns. Accordingly, there is less chance that using lawyers and the legal system will damage important social ties.[32]

It is possible, however, to overstate the role of community size. All of the editors, those from the small towns as well as those from the larger cities, expressed reluctance to involve lawyers in the editorial process. In addition to the reasons outlined in the body of this chapter, the editors' reluctance may be rooted in the ideology of journalistic autonomy: that journalists should guard against intrusion by anyone into the editorial process. In this regard, the findings of this study are consistent with research showing that journalists tend to resist scrutiny of their work by outsiders partly because the concept of an outsider serving a regulatory role in regard to press behavior is contrary to the ideology of an independent, unfettered press.[33]

Although all but one editor saw some need to involve lawyers in the editorial process, the editors tended to believe that lawyers should not play a major role in directing editorial operations or making news decisions. The roles editors apparently consider most appropriate for lawyers to perform include managing litigation, providing an assessment of the legal risks of a particular action, reading stories for potentially libelous material, advising the staff about legal issues, and helping educate the staff about press law. Indiana editors would rather not share any decision-making power with lawyers, particularly when it involves journalistic judgment. Thus while lawyers and journalists often are partners, it is a partnership into which journalists enter reluctantly.

This study has suggested that larger news organizations use lawyers more than smaller news organizations do. That finding, however, does not necessarily mean that large news organizations face a proportionately greater number of demands for accountability than do their small counterparts. It is possible, and perhaps even likely, that larger newspapers were more involved with lawyers and with litigation merely because larger communities have fewer social constraints on using the legal system as a means of media accountability. This is not to suggest that residents of the smaller communities are less likely to hold their newspaper accountable for its behavior. It is to suggest that residents of small communities may have other, less formal ways of holding local news organizations accountable.

That the accountability environment is different in big communities than in small communities is demonstrated by the fact that the Indianapolis and Evansville newspapers were more likely than were the smaller papers to demand accountability from public officials by going to court to gain access to public information. None of the smaller newspapers used the legal system as a means to demand accountability of public officials in their communities. Although the newspapers in the large communities do not often go to court to demand that public officials be accountable, their willingness to do so upon occasion makes their threats to do so credible. An important question not addressed in this study is how often the news organizations threaten public officials with legal action in an effort to hold them accountable. Do newspapers in larger communities more often threaten legal action than do newspapers in smaller communities?

The Indianapolis and Evansville newspapers used lawyers more often in the editorial process because they were more often involved in situations where either they or an outsider used or threatened to use the courts to demand accountability. Leaving aside their fears of conflicts of interest and lack of knowledge of press law by their lawyers, the smaller newspapers used lawyers in the editorial process less often because they less frequently faced situations in which the newspaper or an outsider used or threatened to use the legal system to demand accountability.

NOTES

1. Randall P. Bezanson, Gilbert Cranberg, and John Soloski, *Libel Law and the Press: Myth and Reality* (New York: The Free Press, 1987), pp. 142–144.

2. *Libel Law and the Press*, pp. 236–237, 243.

3. Howard Kurtz, "When Does Publishing Mean Perishing?" *The Washington Post Weekly*, December 3–9, 1990, p. 32; Elizabeth K. Hansen and Roy L. Moore, "Chilling the Messenger: Impact of Libel on Community Newspapers," *Newspaper Research Journal* 11 (Spring 1990): 86–99; Everette E. Dennis and Eli M. Noam, eds., *The Cost of Libel: Economic and Policy Implications* (New York: Columbia University Press, 1989).

4. Cases often cited included *Herbert v Lando*, 441 U.S. 153 (1979) [Libel plaintiffs may probe a journalist's state of mind]; *Gannett v DePasquale*, 443 U.S. 368 (1979) [No constitutional right to attend pre-trial hearings]; *Seattle Times v Rhinehart*, 467 U.S. 20 (1984) [Newspaper can be restrained from publishing information acquired during discovery proceedings of a lawsuit to which it is a party]; *Harper & Row, Publishers, Inc. v Nation*, 471 U.S. 539 (1985) [Magazine infringed copyright laws by publishing portions of a stolen copy of President Ford's memoirs]; *Department of Justice v Reporters Committee for Freedom of the Press*, 109 S. Ct. 1468 (1989) [FBI rap sheets on private individuals exempt from disclosure under Freedom of Information Act even if information is public record elsewhere].

5. *Dun & Bradstreet v Greenmoss Builders*, 472 U.S. 749 (1985). Of course, not all recent Supreme Court decisions have been adverse to press rights. See, for example, *Bose Corporation v Consumers Union*, 104 S. Ct. 1949 (1984) [That a writer admits that a remark was false does not prove it was made with knowing falsehood]; *Anderson v Liberty Lobby*, 477 U.S. 242 (1986) [Libel plaintiff can defeat motion for summary judgment only if they can meet their burden of proof with "clear and convincing evidence"]; *Philadelphia Newspapers v Hepps*, 106 S. Ct. 1558 (1986) [Burden of proving falsity in libel case falls on plaintiffs in suits involving private figure plaintiffs]; *Hustler Magazine v Falwell*, 108 S. Ct. 876 (1988) [Rejecting the imposition of an "outrageous conduct" standard in libel actions]; *Florida Star v B.J.F.*, 109 S. Ct. 2603 (1989) [First Amendment bars punishment of a newspaper for publication of lawfully obtained truthful information unless punishment would further a government interest of the "highest order"].

6. Anthony Lewis, *Make No Law: The Sullivan Case and the First Amendment* (New York: Random House, 1991).

7. *Brown & Williamson Tobacco Corp. v Walter Jacobson*, 644 F. Supp. 1240 (N.D. Ill., 1986); aff'd in part, 827 F.2d 1119 (7th Cir. 1987); cert. denied, 485 U.S. 993 (1988).

8. *Disalle v P.B. Publishing Co.*, 544 A.2d 1345 (Pa. Super. 1988); cert. denied 557 A.2d 724 (Pa. 1988); cert. denied, 109 S. Ct. 3216 (1989).

9. See, for example, *Richmond Newspapers, Inc. v Virginia*, 448 U.S. 555 (1980) [Public has limited First Amendment right to attend criminal trials]; *Bose Corporation v Consumers Union*, 466 U.S. 485 (1984) [That a writer admits a remark was false does not prove it was made with knowing falsehood]; *Anderson v Liberty Lobby*, 477 U.S. 242 (1986) [Libel plaintiff must defeat motion for summary judgment with "clear and convincing evidence"]; *Philadelphia Newspapers v Hepps*, 475 U.S. 767 (1986) [Burden of proof to prove falsity in libel case falls on plaintiffs in suits involving private figure plaintiffs]; *Press Enterprise v Riverside County Superior Court*, 478 U.S. 1 (1986) [Finds First Amendment right of public to attend pre-trial proceedings]; *U.S. v Providence Journal*, 485 U.S 693 (1988) [Upholds appeals court decision that newspaper could ignore a transparently unconstitutional prior restraint order]; *Hustler Magazine v Falwell*, 485 U.S. 46 (1988) [Rejects the imposition of an "outrageous conduct" standard in libel actions]; *Florida Star v B.J.F.*, 109 S. Ct. 2603 (1989) [First Amendment bars punishment for publication of lawfully obtained truthful information unless punishment would further a government interest of the "highest order"].

10. Reagan appointed Antonin Scalia, Sandra Day O'Connor, and Anthony M. Kennedy. Bush appointed David H. Souter and Clarence Thomas.

11. Lyle Denniston, "How Souter Has Ruled on Press Issues," *Washington Journalism Review*, September 1990, p. 18.

12. Douglas A. Anderson and Marianne Murdock, "Effects of Communication Law Decisions on Daily Newspaper Editors," *Journalism Quarterly* 58 (1981): 525–528, 534; James Bow and Ben Silver, "Effects of *Herbert v Lando* on Small Newspapers and TV Stations," *Journalism Quarterly* 61 (1984): 414–418.

13. Michael Massing, "The Libel Chill: How Cold Is It Out There?" *Columbia Journalism Review*, May/June 1985, p. 31; Rodney A. Smolla, *Suing the Press* (New York: Oxford University Press, 1986); M. L. Stein, "The Chilling Effect: Lawyers Say the Increase of Libel Suits Has Had an Effect on Both the Media and the Insurance Companies," *Editor & Publisher*, July 4, 1987, p. 10.

14. Elizabeth K. Hansen and Roy L. Moore, "Chilling the Messenger: Impact of Libel on Community Newspapers," *Newspaper Research Journal* 11 (Spring 1990): 86–99, p. 94.

15. *The Cost of Libel: Economic and Policy Implications*, a Conference Report of the Gannett Center for Media Studies, 1986, pp. 2–3.

16. Smolla, *Suing the Press*, p. 74.

17. Kent R. Middleton and Bill F. Chamberlin, *The Law of Public Communication* (New York: Longman, 1988), p. 26.

18. Ibid., p. 27.

19. Ibid.

20. Lois G. Forer, *A Chilling Effect* (New York: W. W. Norton and Co., 1987), p. 31.

21. George Freeman, "A Lawyer in the Newsroom," *Times Talk*, August 1985, p. 6.

22. *The Cost of Libel*, p. 9.

23. Jo Anne Smith, "Nature of and Changes in Media-Lawyer Relationships," *Journalism Quarterly* 60 (Winter 1983): 714–717, p. 716.

24. Jack P. Pizzolato, Jr., "Availability and Use of Lawyers and Legal Help on

News-Editorial Matters by Florida's Non-Daily Press," unpublished master's thesis, University of Florida, 1980, pp. vi–vii.

25. Ibid., p. 97.

26. Douglas A. Anderson, Joe W. Milner, and Mary-Lou Galician, "How Editors View Legal Issues and the Rehnquist Court," *Journalism Quarterly* 65 (1988): 294–298; Matthew D. Bunker, "Application of Libel Law Principles by Kansas Editors," *Newspaper Research Journal* 13 (Summer 1992): 13–24; Anderson and Murdock, "Effects of Communication Law Decisions"; Hansen and Moore, "Chilling the Messenger."

27. Bow and Silver, "Effects of *Herbert v Lando*." See also Douglas A. Anderson and Marianne Murdock, "Effects of Communication Law Decisions."

28. David M. Engel, "The Oven Bird's Song: Insiders, Outsiders, and Personal Injuries in an American Community," *Law & Society Review* 18 (1984): 551–582; Donald Landon, "LaSalle Street and Main Street: The Role of Context in Structuring Law Practice," *Law & Society Review* 22 (1988): 213–236; Donald Landon, "Clients, Colleagues, and Community: The Shaping of Zealous Advocacy in Country Law Practice," *American Bar Foundation Research Journal* (1985): 81–111.

29. Laura Nader and Harry F. Todd, Jr., eds., *The Disputing Process—Law in Ten Societies* (New York: Columbia University Press, 1980), p. 21.

30. Sally Engle Merry, "Going to Court: Strategies of Dispute Management in an American Urban Neighborhood," *Law & Society Review* 13 (1979): 891–925, 894–895; Engel, "The Oven Bird's Song," pp. 553–554.

31. Landon, "LaSalle Street and Main Street"; Phillip J. Tichenor, George A. Donohue, and Clarice N. Olien, *Community Conflict and the Press* (Beverly Hills, Calif.: Sage, 1980).

32. Merry, "Going to Court."

33. Pat O'Malley, "Regulating Contradictions: The Australian Press Council and the 'Dispersal of Social Control,'" *Law & Society Review* 21 (1987): 83–108, p. 106.

11

Helping the Press Define Its Rights and Responsibilities

CRAIG SANDERS

CHAPTER 10 SHOWED THAT MANY NEWSPAPERS, ESPECIALLY SMALL ONES, LACK CONFIDENCE IN THEIR LOCAL LAWYERS' EXPERTISE AND LOYALTY TO THE NEWSPAPER. IN SUCH SITUATIONS IT MAY MAKE SENSE FOR A NEWSPAPER TO DRAW UPON THE LEGAL EXPERTISE OF ITS STATE PRESS ASSOCIATION. EVERY STATE HAS A PRESS ASSOCIATION, AND MOST OF THEM OFFER SOME KIND OF LEGAL ADVICE SERVICE.

FOLLOWING UP ON HIS STUDY OF HOW INDIANA NEWSPAPERS USE LOCAL LAWYERS, CRAIG SANDERS IN CHAPTER 11 EXAMINES THE ROLE OF THE HOOSIER STATE PRESS ASSOCIATION IN HELPING NEWSPAPERS RESOLVE THEIR LEGAL PROBLEMS. THE CHAPTER IS BASED UPON A REVIEW OF INTERNAL HSPA DOCUMENTS, INTERVIEWS, AND A SURVEY OF EDITORS AT ALL SEVENTY-THREE INDIANA DAILY NEWSPAPERS. THE RESULTS SHOW HSPA'S GENERAL COUNSEL TO BE A MAJOR INFLUENCE ON HOW NEWSPAPERS INTERPRET THEIR LEGAL RIGHTS AND RESPONSIBILITIES—IN SHORT, ON HOW NEWSPAPERS ACT WHEN ISSUES OF ACCOUNTABILITY ARE INVOLVED.

THE CHAPTER IS BASED ON PORTIONS OF SANDERS'S PH.D. DISSERTATION AT INDIANA UNIVERSITY.

At least once a day Richard W. Cardwell picks up the telephone in his downtown Indianapolis law office and hears another tale of legal woe.

A town board met behind closed doors; can they do that? The police will not release a report about a shooting; can we force them to give it to us? One of our reporters has been subpoenaed; how do we get out of it?

As the general counsel of the Hoosier State Press Association, Cardwell is paid, as he puts it, to "baby-sit the phone" and offer legal counseling to Indiana newspapers that are HSPA members. Somewhere in Indiana on any given business day a newspaper needs advice about the law.

Underlying many of these consultations are demands for accountability of various kinds. Someone may be trying to hold a newspaper accountable for its actions by threatening a lawsuit. Or a newspaper may be trying to hold government accountable by demanding the right to inspect public documents or attend public meetings.

This chapter addresses the role a state press association plays in helping its members define their rights and obligations in such situations. The chapter examines the ways in which Indiana newspapers use the HSPA to help resolve conflicts and disputes. The HSPA's role in conflict resolution is important because most Indiana newspapers call on the HSPA's general counsel for legal information and advice more often than they contact other sources.[1]

BACKGROUND

All state press associations in the United States serve as newspaper industry lobbyists before state legislatures and regulatory agencies, and all provide member newspapers with at least some information about the legal rights of the press.[2]

State press associations are important conduits for information about press law, but they are not necessarily neutral or passive conduits. By nature, a state press association's purpose is to promote the interests of the newspaper industry. Therefore, a state press association can be expected to filter its interpretations of press law in ways that promote or support press rights and interests.

In addition to lobbying and providing information about press law, a substantial minority of state press associations also provide advice about how newspapers should deal with situations in which press law is a factor, either because a newspaper believes its legal rights may have been violated (e.g., a government agency refuses to release documents) or because the newspaper may believe that it risks being sued for libel or invasion of privacy.[3] Among the minority of press associations that provide legal advice, the HSPA is one of the most active. The Indiana association had special prominence at the time of this study because Cardwell, its general counsel, had been an articulate advocate for the legal rights of the press in Indiana for thirty-five years. Perhaps because of Cardwell's prominence, most Indiana newspapers are HSPA members. In 1990, 70 of the state's 73 daily newspapers were HSPA members, as were 107 of Indiana's 158 weekly and semi-weekly newspapers.[4]

The HSPA sometimes used publications and seminars to provide information to its members about press law. Cardwell estimated that he conducted press law seminars at individual Indiana newspapers about three times a year. An HSPA publication that discussed legal issues and summarized court decisions affecting Indiana newspapers was sent to members several times a year.

The HSPA has been providing legal counseling to its members almost from the time of the organization's founding in 1938. Cardwell estimated that about 80 percent of the HSPA's legal counseling was done via telephone, though the fax machine has become increasingly important. Cardwell said he charged a legal fee for legal counseling "if I get into a particular situation in any formalized way," including appearing in court on a newspaper's behalf or writing a retraction in response to a threat of a libel lawsuit. Cardwell acknowledged that drawing the line between assistance that was part of the duties of the general counsel and legal representation for which he charged a fee could be difficult.

Indiana newspaper managers tended to call the HSPA's general counsel when they were unsure about the law or when they had a pressing legal problem. Twenty-two of the seventy-three respondents indicated that the HSPA's general counsel was their first or primary source of legal assistance. Managers said they contacted the HSPA's general counsel for reasons of cost, expediency, Cardwell's knowledge of press law, and the manager's familiarity and previous dealings with Cardwell.

From 1986 to 1989, Cardwell took notes on his telephone contacts with Indiana newspapers.[5] According to the notes, 25 of Indiana's 73 daily newspapers (34 percent) called him 11 or more times during those years, 22 newspapers (30 percent) called 4 to 10 times, and 26 newspapers (36 percent) made three or fewer calls. Larger newspapers tended to call Cardwell more often than did smaller newspapers.

Newspaper managers were asked to provide examples of legal issues about which they had contacted the HSPA. Although respondents could mention as many issues as they wanted, most cited three or fewer issues. The issue most frequently cited was the Indiana open meetings law, mentioned by 55 respondents. Next was libel (27 mentions), followed by the Indiana public records law (24 mentions).

When asked to name the legal issues that newspapers most frequently discussed with him, Cardwell's list was similar to that compiled from the responses of the newspaper managers. Access to public information, including public records, government meetings, and court hearings, topped the list. Libel and invasion of privacy issues ranked second and third, respectively.

Newspapers' interest in securing access to public information—public records, government meetings, court hearings—is directly related to their social role as agents of accountability. They most often contacted Cardwell for help in playing that role. They also contacted Cardwell when there was a possibility that an outsider might use the legal system to attempt to hold the newspaper accountable by means of a lawsuit for libel or invasion of privacy.

Cardwell's response to the calls varied. This study's interviews with Cardwell and the newspaper managers identified four roles that the general counsel played as he responded to calls for help with conflicts and disputes. The roles were Reality Tester, Security Blanket, Authoritative Source, and Blame Taker.

REALITY TESTER

The role that Cardwell played most often was Reality Tester, which can be defined as a third party providing confirmation that an aggrieved person's sense of having been wronged was justified, and that there was some hope of obtaining redress.[6] The Reality Tester role manifested itself in two ways. The first had to do with situations in which a newspaper was the aggrieved party in a dispute. In these cases, managers usually were seeking confirmation that the position they had taken or wanted to take was legally defensible. The second way involved situations in which an outsider was the aggrieved party in a dispute with a newspaper. In these cases, the newspaper hoped to invoke the law to refute an assertion of a legal right by another, such as in a lawsuit alleging libel. In some instances, a newspaper called Cardwell simply to learn what its legal rights were. Some newspapers used the HSPA to determine whether they should contact their local attorney for assistance with a legal problem.

Cardwell said many of the callers already had formed a theory about what the law is in a given case. He explained: "A lot of them see they've got a problem, which is why they called in the first place. They've kind of formed a judgment on what they'd like to do with this thing. They call me for confirmation of that."

This point was echoed by W. Alan Miller, executive editor of the *Marion Chronicle-Tribune,* who said that if Cardwell "tells us we're on solid footing," then the newspaper felt better about asserting a legal right. Likewise, Eric Bernsee, editor of the *Greencastle Banner-Graphic,* commented, "Well, we always use him [Cardwell] in substantiating our stands."

However, not all newspapers had formed correct opinions about how the law affected their particular case. Cardwell said he tried to set them straight: "You have a lot of newspapers that have hellacious understandings of what the laws are with respect to their rights. And I don't know what the percentage of time is that I tell people they're wrong, but it's not infrequent. Better for me to tell them, than for them to find out later."

In some instances, a newspaper had consulted its local attorney, but wanted a second legal opinion. Several managers in smaller communities said they did this out of fear that a local attorney inexperienced in press law would give a narrow or overly conservative reading of a newspaper's legal rights in an important situation.

SECURITY BLANKET

A second role the HSPA general counsel played was that of Security Blanket. The Security Blanket role was similar to that of Reality Tester to the extent that a newspaper was seeking confirmation from the HSPA that the newspaper's legal position was justified. Cardwell acted as a Reality Tester when a newspaper sought reassurance that it had been wronged. He acted as a Security Blanket when a newspaper sought reassurance that what it had done, or what it wanted to do, was legally defensible. For some Indiana newspaper managers, the advice of the HSPA's general counsel provided a reassurance that the managers felt they could not get from any other source. It was almost a blind faith that if Cardwell said the newspaper was on solid legal ground, then it must be so.

Paul Fedorchak, editor of the *Greenfield Daily Reporter,* recalled that when his newspaper inadvertently published the name of a juvenile who had been arrested, he had consulted his company's attorney about the legality of the action, but he did not feel reassured until he also had consulted with Cardwell. "Even though I felt pretty comfortable and he [the company attorney] was 90 percent reassuring to me, I still wanted to hear it from Dick," Fedorchak said.

An important reason managers said they contacted Cardwell was because they believed he usually supported the legal rights of the press. This was particularly the case among newspaper managers from smaller communities, where local attorneys may not be as sympathetic to press rights. Gayle Robbins, managing editor of the *Bloomfield Evening World,* explained:

> Mostly it's just knowing he's up there and we can reach him with a phone call. It's a lot easier knowing he's there than us having to depend on the local attorney, especially in a small town where these things affect everybody. And having an outsider like that available to us is really reassuring.

This theme also was expressed by managers at some larger newspapers. The *Fort Wayne Journal-Gazette* relied almost solely on its local attorney to give legal advice. But editor Craig Klugman said he still felt better knowing that he could call on the HSPA if the local attorney had a possible conflict of interest. Klugman commented: "It's always good to know that he's there. When we ran into one of those conflict-of-interest situations, it was nice for me to be able to tell the managing editor not to worry."

Cardwell said some of the newspapers that contacted him did not do so with the intent of asserting a legal right. The paper simply wanted someone to verify that the newspaper was justified in feeling aggrieved. He noted: "They call up all the time and say, 'Look what they're doing to me.' I say, 'That's wrong.' And they say, 'Thank you—I thought it was wrong.' They feel better about it."

AUTHORITATIVE SOURCE

A third role played by the HSPA's general counsel was that of Authoritative Source. Indiana newspapers used Cardwell as an authoritative source in two ways: (1) as a quoted source in news stories; and (2) as a tactic in negotiating the meaning of the law in a dispute.

When newspapers were denied access to information they thought should be public, they sometimes published a news story or editorial accusing a public official or government agency of violating open meetings or public records laws. Many newspaper managers believed such stories had more credibility if they quoted an authoritative source as saying that the law had been violated. Gary Blackburn, publisher of the *Princeton Daily Clarion,* said his newspaper quoted Cardwell in news stories about local government secrecy because "that then takes it off of our opinion and puts it into 'here's a recognized expert in the field.'" Gary Gerard, managing editor of the *Warsaw Times-Union,* made a similar comment:

> It allows us to go to print with a source, an authority on the codes. Like, for example, we could do a story with an authoritative source stating that "Yes, this was an illegal meeting." Well, then later we can editorialize on that and the public officials involved are cognizant of the fact that they broke the law. And you know, they usually adjust their behavior. And if they don't, they know there's a threat of litigation.

Indianapolis Star managing editor Lawrence S. Connor said the *Star* relied on a local attorney for legal advice about the open meetings and public records laws, but the newspaper quoted Cardwell in news stories about those matters. Connor explained:

> Generally, what it does is support a position we take in the paper. If we are faced with being barred from some meeting and we want to make an issue out of it, it helps to have a man like Cardwell's comments in that story. In that sense, we use him because he supports a position that we think the paper ought to take. That would be more effective than getting our own attorney to comment because you figure, well, that's to be expected. But when you go outside the organization it gives you more credibility.

Newspapers also used Cardwell's opinions during discussions about the law with potential disputants. Cardwell helped the Indiana legislature write portions of the state's access-to-information laws, and his expertise in interpreting those state laws was recognized by many public officials, according to several newspaper managers.

"If you throw in Cardwell's name, the argument's usually over," said Howard Hewitt, managing editor of the *Frankfort Times.* "Most of them [public officials] have heard of him and most of them realize he is the ultimate expert on open door and public records matters in Indiana."

In some cases, newspapers were not looking so much for an authoritative source to quote as for an authoritative source to tell them which statutes or court cases to cite to adversaries. The ability to cite the law gave the newspaper the appearance of knowing more about the law than it actually did. James Morrison, editor of the *Greensburg Daily News,* said the appearance could be important: "A lot of times we might know what the law is, but we don't know what the specific Indiana code [is]. And we can get answers a hell of a lot quicker from someone who can cite the Indiana code number and [we can] at least give [public officials] the impression that we've actually looked up the law."

BLAME TAKER

The final role played by the HSPA's general counsel was Blame Taker. Cardwell said newspaper managers who contacted him sometimes wanted an outsider to blame in the event that a decision was contested or it proved to be unpopular with certain members of the community. Cardwell explained:

> For example, you get a question about whether legally they can accept an ad. Or reject an ad. They've usually made their mind up they don't want this ad. And they're seeking a legal corroboration of their policy decision that's been made. I say, "No, you can't run that," and they say, "Well, good. I didn't want to run that."

Although Cardwell perceived the Blame Taker role, none of the newspaper managers indicated that they had used the HSPA to take the blame for unpopular or distasteful actions. No one suggested that he or she needed an HSPA opinion to help deflect social opprobrium or political retaliation. Nonetheless, Cardwell said he had been called upon to play the role of the "heavy," the Blame Taker.

A BROAD VIEW OF PRESS INTERESTS

Cardwell viewed his role as the HSPA's general counsel in broader terms than as a mere provider of information, advice, and reassurance. He was paid not just to give legal counseling, but also to serve as the guardian of the legal rights of the Indiana newspaper industry. Where an editor might see a legal problem as causing short-term difficulties, Cardwell sometimes could see long-term implications.

Having devoted much of his professional life to fighting in the trenches of the Indiana General Assembly to win rights for newspapers, pointing out to Indiana newspapers what those legal rights are, and defending press rights many times in court, Cardwell got frustrated when Indiana newspapers were reluctant to assert their rights. He explained: "I get frustrated by people who are calling me with these grievous violations of the law that are being committed in their community. They know it is [a violation of the law]. They just call me for corroboration of it. But they won't act. And that is frustrating to me."

The comment illustrates how Cardwell saw his role as HSPA general counsel. When Cardwell examined an issue, problem, or dispute brought to him by an Indiana newspaper, he often gave legal answers and/or provided advice on how to use legal means to resolve the problem, when he believed such means would have been effective. But Indiana newspapers were not always seeking legal solutions to their problems, Cardwell said:

> Take access issues. The law provides that the remedy for violations of the records laws [and] meetings laws is the filing of a lawsuit and gaining of redress through litigation. That is the legal recourse. That is a remedy that most [Indiana newspapers] do not want to pursue. So they want another remedy that is different from and easier than that one. And I can't always provide that.

However, the legal approaches that Cardwell recommended or pursued on behalf of Indiana newspapers often were effective. He cited a case where the *Marion Chronicle-Tribune* had been rebuffed in an effort to obtain an Indiana Department of Transportation report that identified the most dangerous railroad grade crossings in Marion. Cardwell contacted the state attorney general's office, which admitted that a mistake had been made, and the report was released to the newspaper.

But Cardwell said that many disputes over the meaning of a law ended in stalemate. In such cases, Cardwell believed that a newspaper's only viable option was to go to court. He explained: "That's what courts are for, to resolve controversies about what the law is. So, people call me and tell me these things and they say, 'Well, what can I do?' And I say, 'You can file suit.' And they laugh and say, 'Well, what can I really do?' And I say, 'Why do you call me if you're not willing to pursue the remedies that are available to you?' What good can I do? I can't send a death squad in. I can't round up people with guns."

However, there is one step short of litigation that Cardwell could take: he could write a letter on a newspaper's behalf. Cardwell had a standard letter that he often sent to opposing attorneys warning that if they sued, the newspaper would not settle, there would be no easy money, and "we will make you spend a lot of time and effort." Jan Connors, editor of the *Elwood Call-Leader,* said Cardwell's letters on behalf of her newspaper had kept her newspaper from being sued. The *Call-Leader* periodically received letters from an attorney threatening legal action on a client's behalf. The lawyer, who practiced in a larger city near Elwood, generally was representing people, often juveniles, whose names had appeared in court and police news stories. When the attorney threatened legal action, Connors said, the newspaper obtained copies of police and court records and wrote a letter to the HSPA explaining how the story was handled.

"He [Cardwell] writes a letter [to the attorney], quotes whatever statutes, [and writes] 'we have copies of the arrest, ticket, whatever in front of us and you know you're wrong and back off,'" said Connors, adding that the *Call-Leader* had been able to resist the big-city attorney "because we had the strength of Richard Cardwell behind us." She continued:

> It has done away with the intimidation factor. Letters from attorneys, they
> are an intimidation factor. That's what they're designed for. I think without
> this [HSPA] service, we would pay up instead of fighting. I've seen cases like
> that at another paper I worked at where the paper would go ahead and pay
> knowing they were in the right, but it was cheaper because of the deductible
> on the libel insurance. They had like a $2,500 deductible. They could buy out
> for $1,000. I hate that because we are selling out our ethics for that extra
> $1,500.

Connors was one of the few managers who said that lack of financial resources had affected the way her newspaper responded to legal problems.

Cardwell's letters also could be effective when written on behalf of a
newspaper that was the aggrieved party in a dispute. After the *Bloomington
Herald-Times* assigned a new reporter to the police beat, the police department, which disliked the new reporter, withheld police reports from him. The
newspaper became aware of this when it began receiving telephone calls from
people asking why certain police investigations had not been reported. *Herald-
Times* editor Bob Zaltsberg contacted the HSPA. Cardwell wrote a letter to the
police department's attorney stating that the police were violating the public
records law. Zaltsberg subsequently met with the police department's attorney.
Zaltsberg quoted the attorney as stating during the meeting: "The way I read the
law was this way. I understand the point. I've read it again and I can see that
these are things you have to have and we'll comply with the law."

Although relations between the *Herald-Times* and the police department
remained strained, the police began allowing the newspaper greater access to
police reports. Zaltsberg believed that the HSPA's intervention was instrumental in getting the police to be more cooperative with the newspaper. He
said: "A lot of times the difference that his [Cardwell's] assistance makes involves letting us know whether it's feasible to go forward, to push our point, or
whether we'd be wasting our time. It gives me the confidence to know whether
I'm right or not."

Having learned that it had a valid legal claim, the *Herald-Times* was able
to push its point without wasting its time.

DISCUSSION

This study makes clear that a state press association can be quite influential
in helping newspapers define their legal rights. The assistance tended to take
place not in abstract settings such as seminars, but rather in the context of concrete problems that confronted a newspaper. Most of these problems had to do
with accountability in one way or another.

Before contacting the state press association, newspaper managers usually
had made a preliminary determination of what they believed their legal rights

to be. Sometimes, however, newspaper managers and staff had been unable to determine the law, even after reading it themselves. When newspaper personnel were unable to understand the law as it applied to a specific situation involving their newspaper, they often called the HSPA.

Most Indiana newspaper managers believed that Cardwell was eminently effective in getting public officials to accept interpretations of the state's access laws that were favorable to the press. Whether the HSPA's general counsel was actually as influential as the managers suggested is a question that cannot be answered by a study that did not include interviews with public officials. But the important point is that Indiana newspaper managers perceived that Cardwell had been instrumental in tipping the balance in favor of newspapers in disputes regarding access to information.

The managers interviewed for this study tended to focus on how Cardwell had assisted their newspaper in disputes in which the newspaper prevailed or believed that it had prevailed. Managers were less willing to discuss disputes in which their newspaper had not prevailed, had given up, or had given in. Some managers suggested that their newspaper usually prevailed in disputes regarding access to information. That newspaper managers would make such claims was not surprising, given that it is human nature to emphasize one's triumphs rather than one's defeats.

However, it seems unlikely that Indiana newspapers had been as successful in "winning" disputes as the comments of the managers interviewed for this study suggested. Many disputes involving newspapers reach a stalemate, with one side refusing to accede to most or all of the claims of the other. In Indiana, such stalemates seldom resulted in a newspaper either suing or being sued. Richard Cardwell, the HSPA's general counsel, often suggested that newspapers locked in stalemate over access to information should consider going to court to assert their rights. The inability or unwillingness of many Indiana newspapers to take that step frustrated him.

Similarly, despite frequent threats it was rare for Indiana newspapers to be sued. As a result, Cardwell's legal activity on behalf of newspapers did not take place in courtrooms. Rather, it fell into two categories: providing information to newspapers, and sending messages to potential adversaries, either directly (e.g., via a letter) or indirectly (e.g., via a press interview). Cardwell played a variety of roles—Reality Tester, Security Blanket, Authoritative Source, and Blame Taker—and the information he provided was used in a variety of ways by newspaper management to determine what steps to take to resolve or defuse a dispute.

Despite Cardwell's comment that he was sometimes frustrated by the unwillingness of newspapers to assert legal rights in court, his advice often was influential. As noted earlier, in some cases newspapers abandoned legal claims or decided not to make legal claims because the general counsel said the law did not favor the newspaper in a particular dispute. In other cases, Cardwell's advice led newspapers to assert legal claims they might otherwise have abandoned.

When newspapers failed to follow Cardwell's advice, he was reluctant to criticize them publicly. He walked a fine line. Newspapers wanted to know what their rights were, but they did not always—or even often—want to exercise those rights. If Cardwell had criticized individual newspapers, his influence might well have declined.

In general, a state press association's legal counsel can be influential only to the extent that his or her interpretations of press laws and advice about how to handle disputes are considered authoritative by the association's members. In Indiana, newspapers gave great weight to Cardwell's views. Perhaps because of his perceived influence with the state legislature, and certainly because of his long tenure and relatively high profile, Cardwell had become the best known and most respected source of information about press law in the state. Cardwell's influence may not be matched by that of staff members of press associations in other states. Influence and authority do not spring up overnight; Cardwell's status in Indiana was the result of years of lobbying and providing legal advice on behalf of Indiana newspapers.

That the HSPA's general counsel was not a neutral conduit of information about law also needs to be emphasized. When a newspaper asked Cardwell for legal advice, he had a tendency to interpret the law in ways favorable to the press. Although he did not automatically assume that the press had a legal right to do what it wanted to do in every case, the general counsel's job involved trying to fashion legal tools that served the interests of the press.

News organizations often assert that they exist to further democratic ideals, to serve the public's "right to know." Many journalists argue that their efforts to hold public officials accountable, often by trying to gain access to secret documents and meetings, are intended to serve society, rather than to serve only the news organization's self-interest. Perhaps ironically, journalists use the public interest as the basis for their claim that news organizations need special immunities from having to account for their behavior in court; lawsuits alleging libel and invasion of privacy can be powerful means of enforcing accountability.

The Hoosier State Press Association, like every state press association in the United States, represents an interest group. The HSPA is not unlike other organizations that lobby government and try to promote their members' self-interest. When state press association staff members intervene in disputes, dispense legal advice, or lobby the legislature, they do so with the express purpose of furthering the interests of the newspaper industry.

Like any other commercial enterprise, a newspaper exists to make money for its owner. The interests of journalists and newspaper owners do not always nor necessarily represent the interests of the rest of society. Therefore, while state press associations such as the HSPA may promote policies that would benefit society as a whole, such promotion occurs only when the news industry believes that its interests intersect with the interests of society.

NOTES

1. Interviews with Indiana newspaper managers and the HSPA's general counsel yielded the bulk of the data analyzed in this chapter. HSPA general counsel Richard Cardwell was interviewed five times between May 1989 and June 1990. Although the HSPA received calls from advertising and circulation departments as well as from newsrooms, most of the legal problems discussed with the HSPA involved news. Accordingly, I attempted to contact the highest-ranking manager of the editorial department at each of Indiana's seventy-three daily newspapers. Telephone interviews were conducted during April and May 1990; managers at all seventy-three newspapers participated. A questionnaire of open- and closed-ended questions was used to structure the interviews.

2. Craig Sanders, "How State Press Associations Provide Legal Assistance," *Newspaper Research Journal,* 13 (Summer 1992): 25–35.

3. Sanders, "How State Press Associations Provide Legal Assistance."

4. *Indiana Newspaper Directory and Rate Book,* published by the Hoosier State Press Association.

5. The notes contained a summary of who had called and what the caller had discussed with Cardwell. Although the notes were useful in showing the types of legal issues Indiana journalists discussed with the HSPA, their value was limited by two factors. First, there was no way to know what proportion of telephone calls received by the HSPA the notes represented. If a caller had a question that Cardwell could answer with a simple reply, he did not always make a note of the call. Second, the information in the notes was fragmentary. The notes sometimes did not make clear why people had called the HSPA, what Cardwell had told the callers, and how his response had influenced the outcome of a conflict or dispute.

6. Jeffrey Fitzgerald and Richard Dickins, "Disputing in Legal and Nonlegal Contexts: Some Questions for Sociologists of Law," *Law & Society Review* 15 (1981): 681–706, p. 698.

12

What Happens to Libel Cases after They Have Been at the Supreme Court

EDDITH DASHIELL

SOMETIMES UNHAPPY MEDIA CONSUMERS TAKE THEIR CLAIMS TO
COURT. A HANDFUL OF THESE CASES MAKE IT TO THE SUPREME
COURT OF THE UNITED STATES, WHICH ISSUES RULINGS ON THE
CONSTITUTIONAL ISSUES INVOLVED IN THE CASES.

THE STORY OF THOSE CASES, AS DEPICTED IN THE NEWS
MEDIA AND IN MEDIA LAW TEXTBOOKS, GENERALLY ENDS WITH
THE DECISION OF THE SUPREME COURT. THE CASES THEMSELVES,
HOWEVER, TEND TO BE SENT BACK TO LOWER COURTS FOR RESO-
LUTION AFTER THE HIGH COURT HAS RESOLVED THE CONSTITU-
TIONAL ISSUES.

IN CHAPTER 12 EDDITH DASHIELL REVEALS THE LITTLE-
KNOWN STORIES OF WHAT HAPPENS TO LIBEL CASES AFTER THE
SUPREME COURT HAS DEALT WITH THEM. GATHERING INFORMA-
TION NOT ONLY FROM AVAILABLE DOCUMENTS BUT FROM INTER-
VIEWS WITH PLAINTIFFS, DEFENDANTS, AND LAWYERS WHO WERE
INVOLVED IN THE CASES, DASHIELL FINDS THAT SUPPOSEDLY DE-
FINITIVE RULINGS BY THE U.S. SUPREME COURT DO NOT NECES-
SARILY PREDICT THE ULTIMATE OUTCOMES OF THE CASES IN THE
LOWER COURTS.

THIS CHAPTER, WHICH REPORTS RESULTS OF DASHIELL'S
PH.D. DISSERTATION AT INDIANA UNIVERSITY, BREAKS NEW
GROUND BY FOCUSING ON WHAT HAPPENS TO MEDIA-RELATED
CASES AFTER THEY HAVE BEEN THE SUBJECT OF SUPREME COURT
DECISIONS. AT THIS WRITING, DASHIELL IS ON THE FACULTY OF
THE SCHOOL OF JOURNALISM AT OHIO UNIVERSITY IN ATHENS.

Beginning the first Monday in October of each year, the nine justices of
the Supreme Court of the United States don their black robes and begin a new
term. From October through June, the justices make judgments on crucial social and economic issues. The Court, which often finds itself wrestling with the

most vexing controversies in American life, is sometimes known as the "court of last resort" because many Americans perceive it to be the final stop in the judicial process.

Many educators share this perception. In law schools as well as in undergraduate courses focusing on law, the cases discussed tend to be Supreme Court cases, and the discussion tends to end with the Supreme Court's decision. The implicit assumption is that legal disputes come to an end after the Supreme Court has ruled.

The implicit assumption, however, is to a great extent wrong. The Supreme Court is not always the court of last resort. Although many people realize that the Supreme Court often returns cases to lower courts, what happens to such cases after the Supreme Court has dealt with them has never been examined.

This chapter focuses on what happens to libel cases after the Supreme Court has ruled on them. The research is pertinent to media accountability because a lawsuit alleging libel (i.e., harm to reputation) is the principal legal tool that unhappy subjects of news coverage can use against the press. This chapter examines the life histories of the twenty-two media-related libel cases that were the subject of Supreme Court opinions from 1965 through 1990.[1] The chapter is based on interviews with dozens of people who were part of disputes that led to Supreme Court libel cases, on contemporary newspaper accounts of the disputes, on published writings by people either involved in or close to the disputes, and on facts contained in courts' written opinions in the cases.

In some cases, the decision of the Supreme Court went to the heart of the dispute, and the matter was resolved by the High Court without further proceedings in other courts. The landmark *New York Times v. Sullivan* was such a case.[2] More often, though, the Supreme Court's decision merely sets the stage for further activity in the state courts or lower federal courts. Sometimes, for example, the High Court has been asked to determine whether a judge has been justified in dismissing a libel lawsuit without a trial.[3] If the Supreme Court rules that the dismissal was improper, then the case is returned to the lower court for further proceedings.

The search for the post–Supreme Court histories of the disputes in this study revealed some surprises. In several cases, libel plaintiffs who won at the Supreme Court failed to pursue their claims to a final adjudication after the case was returned to the lower courts. Some simply dropped the matter; others were content to settle out of court. Similarly, of the libel plaintiffs who lost at the Supreme Court level and who had the right to pursue their lawsuits after the case was returned to the lower courts, many dropped the matter, while others negotiated out-of-court settlements. In all, most of the twenty-two disputes ended without a clear-cut judicial victory.

The cases can be grouped into four categories (see table 1). One category contains the six cases in which the opinion of the Supreme Court ended the

Table 1 Categories of Outcomes for Media-Related Libel Cases upon Which the U.S. Supreme Court Ruled, 1965–1990

Disputes Resolved by the Supreme Court Decision (6)

Curtis v. Butts (1967).
Associated Press v. Walker (1967).
Rosenbloom v. Metromedia (1971).
Bose v. Consumers Union (1984).
Hustler v. Falwell (1988).
Harte-Hanks v. Connaughton (1989).

Cases Decided in Lower Courts after Supreme Court Decision (4)

Beckley Newspapers Corp. v. Hanks (1967).
Time, Inc. v. Pape (1971).
Gertz v. Welch (1974).
Herbert v. Lando (1979).

Out-of-Court Settlements after Supreme Court Decision (7)

Rosenblatt v. Baer (1966).
Monitor v. Roy (1971).
Calder v. Jones (1984).
Keeton v. Hustler (1984).
Anderson v. Liberty Lobby (1986).
Schiavone Construction Co. v. Fortune (1986).
Milkovich v. The Lorain Journal Co. (1990).

Disputes Not Pursued after Supreme Court Decision (5)

Greenbelt Cooperative Publishing Co. v. Bresler (1970).
Ocala Star Banner v. Damron (1971).
Time, Inc. v. Firestone (1976).
Wolston v. Reader's Digest (1979).
Philadelphia Newspapers v. Hepps (1986).

dispute. A second consists of the four cases in which the Supreme Court returned the dispute to the lower courts, where there was a final judicial resolution. The third and fourth categories consist of the twelve cases in which there was no final judicial resolution. The third category contains the seven cases in which disputants ended the case with out-of-court settlements. The fourth category contains the five cases in which the person who sued the media for libel did not pursue the case after the Supreme Court decision.

Because this chapter focuses on what happened to disputes *after* the Supreme Court of the United States ruled, there will be no further discussion of the six cases in which the Supreme Court's decision ended the dispute.[4] Instead, the chapter will focus on (a) the four disputes that were resolved in lower courts after a Supreme Court decision, (b) the seven disputes that were settled out of court after a Supreme Court decision, and (c) the five disputes that were not pursued after a Supreme Court decision.

CASES DECIDED IN LOWER COURTS

The cases that arrive at the U.S. Supreme Court often involve issues of law or procedure that must be decided before a valid trial may be held. In such cases, it is common for the U.S. Supreme Court to return cases to state courts or lower federal courts for a trial not inconsistent with its ruling. As we have seen, the cases are often dropped or settled out of court after decisions by the U.S. Supreme Court. In some cases, however, new trials are held, and the disputes are resolved judicially. Such was the case in four of the twenty-two disputes examined in this study.

BECKLEY NEWSPAPERS CORP. V. HANKS (1967)

In 1962, Emile Hodel, editor of the *Beckley Post Herald* in West Virginia, published a series of editorials aimed at discrediting Raleigh County court clerk C. Harold Hanks, who was running for re-election.[5] Hanks, believing Hodel's editorial campaign had damaged his political career and his reputation, sued Beckley Newspapers Corporation for libel in West Virginia state courts.[6] A jury returned a verdict in favor of Hanks, and the newspaper was ordered to pay him $5,000.[7] The newspaper's appeals in the state court system were unsuccessful, but the U.S. Supreme Court reversed the decision of the lower court and sent the case back to West Virginia for a new trial.[8] There the circuit court granted the newspaper's motion to dismiss the case.[9] Hanks appealed again, but the West Virginia Supreme Court affirmed the summary judgment decision.[10] Not only did Hanks lose his $5,000 verdict, he also was ordered to pay the newspaper's costs—approximately $25,000.[11]

TIME, INC. V. PAPE (1971)

Frank Pape had been with the Chicago police department for twenty-eight years in 1961, when *Time* magazine published as fact allegations of police brutality that had been made against Pape in a lawsuit.[12] The lawsuit alleging police brutality had been settled out of court, and Pape contended that the charges had been totally false.[13] Pape sued Time, Inc., for libel in federal court. A complicated series of appeals on pretrial matters finally ended up at the U.S. Supreme Court. The High Court ruled that *Time*'s failure to indicate in its story that the brutality charges against Pape had been merely allegations, rather than findings of fact, could not be construed as actual malice on the magazine's part.[14] By reversing and remanding Pape's libel suit against Time, Inc., the

Court "pretty well killed the case" for Pape.[15] The case then went back to the district court for a fourth time, and the court entered an order for Pape to pay Time, Inc., certain court costs.[16] Not only did Pape ultimately lose his libel dispute with Time, Inc., he also had to pay the magazine $5,000 to help defray the expenses incurred by the magazine in defending itself against his lawsuit.[17]

GERTZ V. WELCH (1974)

In 1968 a Chicago family hired attorney Elmer Gertz to file a lawsuit against a Chicago police officer who had been convicted of killing a teenage member of the family. In March 1969, *American Opinion,* an ultra-conservative magazine published by John Birch Society founder Robert Welch, ran an article attacking Gertz's involvement in the lawsuit against the police officer. The lawsuit, according to the article, was part of a Communist plot to take over the Chicago police department.[18] Gertz found out about the article from the wife of one of his law partners,[19] and sued Welch for libel in federal court. The jury awarded Gertz $50,000, but the judge set aside the jury's verdict, saying that Gertz, as a public figure, would have had to prove actual malice, something he had failed to do. Gertz appealed to the U.S. Court of Appeals for the Seventh Circuit, but the appeals court upheld the trial judge. Gertz appealed to the U.S. Supreme Court, which ruled that Gertz was *not* a public figure for purposes of his libel suit against Welch.[20] The Supreme Court sent the case back, and Gertz was granted a new trial.[21] Seven years passed before Gertz's second trial began in April 1981.[22] At the second trial, Gertz won a $400,000 verdict against Welch.[23] Welch's appeals were unsuccessful, and Gertz eventually received a check for almost $500,000—the $400,000 in damages, plus interest.

HERBERT V. LANDO (1979)

Herbert v. Lando was another libel case that had a complex life long after the U.S. Supreme Court rendered its decision in the case. Retired army colonel Anthony Herbert sued *60 Minutes* producer Barry Lando, *60 Minutes* correspondent Mike Wallace, the CBS network, and *Atlantic Monthly* magazine over their 1973 reports that Herbert had lied when he charged that the U.S. Army was guilty of war crimes committed during the Vietnam War.[24] In the years that followed the *60 Minutes* report and the *Atlantic Monthly* article, the libel suit was stalled by the question of just how much Lando could be required to explain about his thoughts as he made his editorial decisions in producing the "The Selling of Colonel Herbert" segment for *60 Minutes*. During the gathering of evidence for trial, Lando refused to answer certain questions about his thought processes, saying that the First Amendment protected the editorial process of his role as news producer.[25]

In early 1977, the federal judge hearing the case ordered Lando to answer the questions pertaining to his editorial process. Lando appealed, and the U.S.

Court of Appeals reversed the district court. Herbert then appealed to the U.S. Supreme Court, which ruled that Lando must answer questions about his "state of mind" at the time he was preparing "The Selling of Colonel Herbert."[26] Although Herbert won a victory at the U.S. Supreme Court, the dispute was far from being resolved.

As a result of the Supreme Court decision, Lando was forced to answer the questions he had refused to answer. After the responses from Lando, Herbert's lawsuit was ready for trial. However, in the fall of 1984—five years after the U.S. Supreme Court's decision in the case—the district judge dismissed nine of Herbert's eleven claims against CBS and *Atlantic Monthly*. All of the claims against the magazine were dismissed; the judge ordered trial on the remaining counts against CBS.[27] Neither side liked the ruling. Herbert wanted all of his claims against CBS and *Atlantic Monthly* reinstated, while CBS wanted the case dismissed entirely. They both appealed the judge's ruling to the U.S. Court of Appeals, where CBS won a major victory. The appeals court dismissed what was left of Herbert's libel suit against Lando and CBS. Herbert vainly appealed to the U.S. Supreme Court, but the High Court refused to hear the appeal, thus bringing an end to the case.[28]

OUT-OF-COURT SETTLEMENTS

Once the U.S. Supreme Court renders its decision, the adversaries may decide that it is in their best interest, legally and/or financially, to settle out of court rather than to continue to do battle in court. Seven of the twenty-two cases examined in this study were resolved with post–Supreme Court out-of-court settlements.

ROSENBLATT V. BAER (1966)
In the 1950s Alfred Rosenblatt was a store owner in Laconia, New Hampshire, who was fulfilling his dream of being an investigative reporter by working as an unpaid columnist for the *Laconia Evening Citizen*.[29] Rosenblatt's column was called "Out of My Head," and many residents of Laconia and surrounding Belknap County did not like the controversy he regularly stirred up. In December 1958, Rosenblatt began a series of articles criticizing the management of the Belknap County Recreation Area and its supervisor since 1950, Frank Baer.[30] Baer's son Robert was assistant manager at the resort. Robert's wife Brenda worked there as a secretary.[31] Rosenblatt's critical columns continued into 1959, including one that called the recreation area "an antique relic run for the benefit of one family and favored few friends."[32] In June 1959, Baer was fired as supervisor. In January 1960, Rosenblatt returned to the subject, heaping praise upon the new administration of the recreation area and strongly implying that Baer had been corrupt.[33]

The column implying corruption had a major effect on the Baer family. Frank Baer's daughter-in-law, Brenda Baer, said: "We got personal reactions from kids on the playground taunting [our] children . . . calling [their] father a crook. It affected the entire family that there might have been that view from neighbors and from friends."[34]

The playground taunting against Frank Baer's grandchildren prompted a series of lawsuits. Frank Baer sued the *Evening Citizen* and Rosenblatt, as did his son and daughter-in-law. Because Frank had a good business relationship with the newspaper, the owners of the *Evening Citizen* settled with him for $2,000 before the case went to trial. In return for the newspaper's payment to Frank, his son and daughter-in-law dropped their lawsuits, leaving Frank Baer's lawsuit against Rosenblatt remaining.[35]

Baer's lawsuit was filed in March 1960; it went to trial in April 1963, with the jury awarding Baer $31,500. Rosenblatt had little money, and appealed the decision to avoid having to pay the damages.[36] The New Hampshire Supreme Court upheld the verdict against Rosenblatt, who then asked the U.S. Supreme Court to hear the case. In February 1966 the U.S. Supreme Court overturned the award of damages to Baer, saying that as a public official, Baer could win damages only if he could prove actual malice.[37] The case was returned to the New Hampshire courts for adjudication on the matter of actual malice.

Despite the favorable decision from the U.S. Supreme Court, Rosenblatt—nearing retirement and discouraged by the cost of pursuing the case—decided to accept his lawyer's advice to settle the case without further legal proceedings. Rosenblatt paid Baer about half of the $31,500 awarded at the trial.[38]

MONITOR V. ROY (1971)

The *Concord Monitor,* a daily newspaper in Concord, New Hampshire, was one of the hundreds of American newspapers in the 1950s and early 1960s that published Drew Pearson's syndicated "Washington Merry-Go-Round" column. On September 10, 1960—three days before New Hampshire's primary to choose a Democratic candidate to run for the U.S. Senate—the *Monitor* published a column by Pearson that referred to the criminal records of several of the candidates, and characterized one, Alphonse Roy, as a "former small-time bootlegger."[39]

Roy did not win the primary. He blamed his defeat on the *Monitor*'s publication of Pearson's column,[40] and sued the owners of the newspaper and the North American Newspaper Alliance, which distributed Pearson's column, for libel. The case went to trial in 1966, with the jury awarding Roy $20,000 in damages.[41]

The newspaper appealed the decision to the New Hampshire Supreme Court. Although Roy died shortly after the trial, his widow kept up the legal fight. In 1969, the state supreme court ruled in favor of Roy. Drew Pearson died soon after the state supreme court's decision, but it was his last wish that the case be appealed and not settled.[42] The appeal to the U.S. Supreme Court was successful; the award against the news organizations was reversed, and the case was sent back to the New Hampshire courts.[43]

Although the news organizations won at the Supreme Court level and had the opportunity to retry the libel case against it, the expense of the litigation process outweighed the desire to fight for freedom of the press. Rather than go through the expense of another trial, Tyler Abell, the stepson of Drew Pearson and the executor of Pearson's estate, decided to settle the case for an undisclosed amount.[44]

CALDER V. JONES (1984)

Shirley Jones was an American sweetheart. Her career included starring roles in film versions of musicals such as *Oklahoma!* and *The Music Man* before she acquired additional fame as one of the stars of the long-running television program, *The Partridge Family.*[45]

In 1977, Jones married Marty Ingels. Two years later, the *National Enquirer*—America's best-selling supermarket tabloid—published a lurid account of the couple's purported marital problems under the headline "Husband's Bizarre Behavior Is Driving Shirley Jones to Drink." The article alleged that Jones was drinking so heavily that she was unable to fulfill her obligations as an actress and entertainer. Jones and Ingels filed a libel suit against Iain Calder, editor of the *Enquirer.*

Jones and Ingels lived in California; the *Enquirer* was based in Florida. Typically, when a citizen of one state sues an individual or business based in another state, the lawsuit is filed in federal court. Jones and Ingels, however, filed their libel suit against the *Enquirer* in California state court. This unusual move led *Enquirer* to ask that the case be dismissed. The tabloid argued that because its principal offices were in Florida, California courts had no jurisdiction over it. The issue was an important one to the *Enquirer.* California state courts were known for their sympathies in favor of libel plaintiffs; if Jones were allowed to sue the *Enquirer* in California state court, then other entertainers who lived in California could use state courts as well. The threat to the *Enquirer* was serious, given that many of its stories focused on Hollywood-based stars.

The California trial court agreed with the *Enquirer* and dismissed the case, but the California Court of Appeals reversed, allowing Jones to sue the *Enquirer* in California state court.[46] *Enquirer* editor Calder appealed to the Supreme Court of the United States, which ruled in favor of Jones,[47] thus permitting the lawsuit to proceed in California state court, Jones's "potentially sympathetic environs of Los Angeles."[48] The *Enquirer* decided not to risk losing in court, and initiated attempts to reach a settlement with Jones.[49] Six weeks after the Supreme Court decision, both sides met in closed-door sessions and settled on an undisclosed cash award for Jones and Ingels, as well as an arrangement for a retraction.[50]

In May 1984, the *Enquirer* published a detailed four-paragraph apology admitting that the 1979 article contained "unfortunate inaccuracies." The tabloid apologized "to the Ingels, to their family and friends, and to their many fans across the country."[51] Not only did the *Enquirer* publish the retraction, but Jones and Ingels were permitted to reprint it in newspapers such as the *New York Times,* the *Los Angeles Times,* and the *Washington Post.*

KEETON V. HUSTLER (1984)

Kathy Keeton, vice president of *Penthouse* magazine and live-in girlfriend of *Penthouse* publisher Robert Guccione, claimed never to have heard of Larry Flynt, publisher of *Hustler* magazine, before they both appeared on a late-night television talk show in early 1975.[52] During the show, Flynt made insulting remarks about Keeton, Guccione, and *Penthouse.* After the show, Flynt tried to attack Keeton physically.[53] Over the next year, *Hustler* published a series of editorials attacking Keeton and Guccione, a centerfold of a nude woman falsely identified as Keeton, and a cartoon implying that Guccione had given Keeton syphilis. Keeton, a resident of New York, sued Flynt for libel in federal court in Ohio, where *Hustler* was headquartered. Her action was dismissed, however, because it had not been filed before Ohio's statute of limitations period expired. In fact, the statute of limitations periods had expired in all states but New Hampshire, which allowed people six years from the date of an alleged tort to file a lawsuit. So Keeton filed suit in federal court in New Hampshire.

Hustler challenged the move; the district court and the First Circuit U.S. Court of Appeals agreed that the case had nothing to do with New Hampshire. Keeton, however, appealed to the U.S. Supreme Court, and there she won.[54] Her lawsuit was allowed to proceed in New Hampshire. A federal jury in New Hampshire awarded Keeton $2 million. *Hustler* appealed the verdict, but while appeals were pending, Keeton and Flynt reached an out-of-court settlement for an undisclosed amount.[55]

ANDERSON V. LIBERTY LOBBY (1986)

After the death of muckraker Drew Pearson in 1969, Jack Anderson inherited the "Washington Merry-Go-Round" column. In addition to the column, Anderson also published a short-lived magazine, *The Investigator.*[56] Anderson continued Pearson's tradition of being a watchdog to Washington politicians, and as a result, Anderson, like Pearson before him, faced a variety of libel suits.

Anderson v. Liberty Lobby involved three articles published in the October 1981 issue of *The Investigator* about Liberty Lobby, a right-wing, not-for-profit organization. The articles were accompanied by two cartoons, one depicting Liberty Lobby's founder, Willis Carto, with a Hitler-like mustache and the second portraying him giving a Nazi salute.[57] Liberty Lobby sued Anderson in federal court for libel, claiming that twenty-nine statements and the two cartoons were false and derogatory.[58]

The district court dismissed the case before trial, finding that as a matter of law Liberty Lobby could not succeed, but the U.S. Court of Appeals reinstated portions of the lawsuit. Anderson then appealed to the U.S. Supreme Court, which vacated the ruling of the appeals court and returned the case to the lower courts.[59] The district court judge instructed both Anderson and Liberty Lobby to submit new briefs on the question of whether the case should be dismissed a second time. The new briefs were filed, but the case lay dormant for a number of years because the district judge's health began to decline. In May 1990, the case was reassigned to a different judge, who threw out most portions of the lawsuit, leaving only one statement and the two cartoons as the basis for Liberty Lobby's libel claim against Anderson.[60] Rather than go to trial, Anderson and Liberty Lobby agreed to an out-of-court settlement in April 1991, ending the ten-year-old dispute.[61]

In the settlement, Anderson and Carto each issued a statement reaffirming their First Amendment rights. Anderson and Liberty Lobby made a joint contribution of $1,000 to the Reporters Committee for Freedom of the Press, but no money changed hands between Anderson and Carto.[62]

SCHIAVONE CONSTRUCTION CO. v. FORTUNE (1986)

There never would have been a dispute between Schiavone Construction Company of Secaucus, New Jersey, and *Fortune* magazine, part of the Time, Inc. media empire, if one of the company's executives had not been named U.S. Secretary of Labor.[63]

In February 1981, the U.S. Senate confirmed Raymond J. Donovan, Schiavone executive vice president, as Secretary of Labor. Shortly after Donovan took office, he was linked to organized crime, and a special prosecutor was appointed to investigate the allegations. While the investigation was under way, *Fortune* published an article discussing the FBI's role in the Senate confirmation of Donovan. The article hinted that Donovan and Schiavone Construction Company were linked with organized crime.[64] Company president Ronald Schiavone sued *Fortune* for libel in federal court in New Jersey. The company also sued *Time* magazine for an article about the firm's alleged links with organized crime.

The libel suit against *Fortune* turned into a legal fight over New Jersey's statute of limitations. Although the lawsuit was filed on May 9, 1983, ten days before the statute of limitations period expired, the notice of the suit was not mailed to *Fortune*'s attorneys until May 20, 1983, one day after New Jersey's one-year deadline to file for libel actions.[65] Schiavone's lawsuit against *Fortune* faced another procedural problem; the original complaint named *Fortune* as the sole defendant and not Time, Inc., the owners of the magazine. The

Fortune name was only a trademark; the law required that the name of the corporate entity be on the lawsuit. An amended complaint naming Time, Inc., as the corporate entity owning *Fortune* was not served until two months later.[66]

The trial court dismissed the libel suit, saying Schiavone failed to meet the statute of limitations deadline. The company appealed, but the appeals court agreed with the trial court. Schiavone Construction appealed to the U.S. Supreme Court, which also agreed that Schiavone had missed the New Jersey deadline.

The U.S. Supreme Court decision did not end the dispute, however. Aware of the Supreme Court's decision in *Keeton v. Flynt*, Schiavone's lawyer filed another libel suit against *Fortune*, but this time in New Hampshire, which had a longer statute of limitations period.[67] Time, Inc., decided to settle with Schiavone rather than fighting the libel suits against *Fortune* and *Time*. Time, Inc., paid Schiavone $500,000 to drop the lawsuits.[68]

MILKOVICH V. THE LORAIN JOURNAL CO. (1990)

In February 1974, the Maple Heights High School wrestling team met its archrival, Mentor High School. Ted Diadiun, at the time a sportswriter for the *Lake County News Herald,* covered the match in person. During the match, an official made a controversial call and a fight broke out.[69] After an investigation of the fight, the Ohio High School Athletic Association (OHSAA) censured Maple Heights wrestling coach Michael Milkovich for his conduct at the match, placed the Maple Heights team on probation, and declared the team ineligible to compete in the state wrestling tournament.[70]

During a court hearing appealing the OHSAA decision, Milkovich and Maple Heights school superintendent Don Scott, who attended the February 1974 match, took the witness stand to tell their version of the events leading up to the fight. In January 1975, a judge ruled in favor of the wrestlers and reversed the team's suspension.[71] The next day sportswriter Diadiun wrote a column criticizing the court's decision to reverse the team's suspension. Headlined "Maple Beat the Law with the 'Big Lie,'" Diadiun's column accused coach Milkovich and superintendent Scott of lying about the fight when they testified in court.[72] Milkovich sued the Lorain Journal Co., owner of the *News Herald,* for libel.[73]

After a complicated series of appeals of pretrial rulings that dismissed his libel suit, Milkovich won a victory at the U.S. Supreme Court, which reversed the state appeals court's ruling that Diadiun's column had been constitutionally protected as the expression of opinion.[74] The U.S. Supreme Court sent the case back to Ohio state courts for trial.

Rather than going to trial on the merits of the case, however, the sixteen-year-old dispute was resolved outside the courtroom. The newspaper realized that settling the case would be cheaper than going back to court. From a legal standpoint, an out-of-court settlement also would leave intact an Ohio Supreme

Court decision in the media's favor. Therefore, rather than risk additional court battles, the *News Herald* paid Milkovich $116,000.[75]

DISPUTES THAT WERE NOT PURSUED

In five of the twenty-two cases examined, libel plaintiffs did not pursue their lawsuits in lower courts after the decision of the U.S. Supreme Court. Essentially, the parties in the cases decided it was not worth the time, money, or effort to continue their disputes any further. The first of these cases involved a small newspaper in Maryland and a real estate developer.

GREENBELT COOPERATIVE PUBLISHING CO. V. BRESLER (1970)

Greenbelt, Maryland, was created in the late 1930s to be a haven from the urban life of Washington, D.C., sixty miles to the southwest. By the 1960s, Greenbelt's open land caught the attention of apartment developers, and Greenbelt slowly began to be surrounded by "groves of apartments rather than trees."[76] One of the developers was Charles Bresler.

In 1965, Bresler owned a large amount of undeveloped land in Greenbelt, and the city was interested in purchasing a parcel of Bresler's property as the site for a new junior-senior high school complex. Bresler told city officials he would sell the land in exchange for the rezoning of another parcel of land he owned so that he could build a high-density apartment complex.[77] If the city refused his offer, Bresler threatened court action to delay the school site acquisition as long as possible.[78]

Bresler's stance was controversial, and was heatedly discussed at many city council meetings. The meetings were reported at length in the news columns and editorials of the *News Review,* a weekly newspaper distributed free to the residents of Greenbelt. At one meeting, according to the *News Review,* some residents characterized Bresler's negotiating position as "blackmail."[79] Bresler filed a $2 million libel suit against the *News Review,* claiming that the newspaper had accused him of the crime of blackmail.[80]

Bresler won at the trial level; the jury awarded him $17,500 in damages.[81] With community donations of more than $30,000 and the law firm of Rogers and Wells representing the newspaper free of charge, the *News Review* was able to appeal the verdict, but lost in the state appeals court. The newspaper's appeal to the U.S. Supreme Court was successful, however. The Supreme Court reversed the appeals court decision and sent the case back to the state courts.[82] By the time of the U.S. Supreme Court opinion, Bresler—a longtime political ally of Vice President (and former Maryland governor) Spiro Agnew—had obtained a job as an aide to Agnew.[83] Perhaps because of his government position, perhaps because the Supreme Court's opinion had declared that the ". . . *News Review* was performing its wholly legitimate function as a community newspaper when it published full reports of these public debates in its news columns,"[84] Bresler opted not to pursue the lawsuit, and the case against the *News Review* was dropped.[85]

Ocala Star Banner v. Damron (1971)

Leonard Damron had been mayor of Crystal River, Florida, for thirteen years in 1966, when he decided to run for tax assessor of Citrus County.[86] In April 1966, the *Ocala Star Banner* published an article that said federal perjury charges had been filed against Damron.[87] The newspaper had the right story, but the wrong Damron. The story identified Mayor Leonard Damron as the person facing perjury charges when the defendant actually was his brother, James.[88]

According to the newspaper, the mistake occurred when a newly hired editor, who had never heard of the mayor's brother, changed "James" to "Leonard" after the reporter phoned in the story.[89] However, despite the assertion of unintentional error, and despite the fact that the newspaper published a retraction, Damron believed the article was a deliberate attempt by the newspaper to discredit him and hamper his efforts to win the tax assessor's race. He noted that Lucy Ware, the author of the story, had correctly identified his brother as the perjury defendant in a story several months earlier. In addition, he said Ware had become "a bitter enemy" because he had reprimanded her for interrupting city council meetings she was covering. Finally, Ware was the mayor's next-door neighbor; he believed that she knew the difference between him and his brother.[90]

After Damron lost the election for tax assessor, he sued the *Star Banner* for libel. At the trial, Damron was awarded $22,000 in damages. The newspaper appealed, but the Florida District Court of Appeals agreed with the trial court and ruled in favor of Damron. The newspaper appealed to the state supreme court, which refused to review the case. The newspaper then pushed its fight with Damron to the U.S. Supreme Court, which in 1971 struck down Damron's $22,000 award and sent the case back to the Florida courts.[91] By this time, Mayor Damron decided he had enough. He had spent all the money he could afford to spend and chose not to pursue a second trial.[92]

Time, Inc. v. Firestone (1976)

In late 1967, a Florida court dissolved the marriage of tire company heir Russell Firestone and his wife, Mary Alice Firestone. On December 22, 1967, *Time* reported the final divorce decree, saying Russell Firestone had been granted the divorce on the grounds of "extreme cruelty and adultery."[93] Mary Alice Firestone sued Time, Inc., for libel, saying that the *Time* article falsely accused her of adultery.[94] Indeed, *Time* had made a mistake; the divorce had not been granted on grounds of adultery.

After a series of appeals of pretrial rulings, Mrs. Firestone's libel suit went to trial in the Florida state courts. A jury awarded Mrs. Firestone $100,000 in damages. Another series of appeals followed the jury verdict; the case finally ended up at the Supreme Court of the United States. In 1976, the Supreme Court ruled in favor of Mrs. Firestone on a key point—it said she was not a public figure for purposes of the libel suit—and sent the case back to the Florida courts.[95]

By the time the U.S. Supreme Court sent the case back to the Florida courts, the *Time* article was nine years old. Mrs. Firestone had married John Asher, another wealthy entrepreneur, and had no desire to "have her name and the issue of adultery dragged through the courts anymore."[96] Mrs. Firestone felt she had made her point by winning a jury verdict in Florida, and as far as she was concerned, justice had been done.[97] The case could have gone to trial a second time, but Mrs. John Asher—the former Mary Alice Firestone—let the case drop instead.

WOLSTON V. READER'S DIGEST (1979)

Ilya Wolston was a naturalized U.S. citizen born in Russia. In July 1958, he faced contempt of court charges for failing to appear before a grand jury in New York City investigating a Soviet spy ring. Wolston had tried to persuade authorities not to require him to travel from his Washington, D.C., home to New York for questioning because he was suffering from depression.[98] Wolston pleaded guilty to the contempt charge and received a one-year suspended sentence and three years' probation. At no time was Wolston indicted for espionage.

In 1974, *Reader's Digest* published a book written by a member of its staff, John Barron, that chronicled Communist spy activities since World War II. Barron's book, *KGB: The Secret Work of Soviet Secret Agents,* briefly mentioned Wolston and identified him as a "Soviet agent in the U.S."[99] Wolston sued *Reader's Digest* for libel in federal court, arguing that he was never a Soviet spy. The district court dismissed the suit, and the U.S. Court of Appeals affirmed the dismissal. Wolston appealed to the U.S. Supreme Court, and in June 1979 the Supreme Court reinstated the lawsuit, declaring that Wolston was a private figure who should have a chance to establish his libel claim at trial.[100] Wolston died shortly after the Supreme Court decision, and because his survivors chose not to pursue the case, his libel dispute with *Reader's Digest* died with him.[101]

PHILADELPHIA NEWSPAPERS V. HEPPS (1986)

The sale of beer in Pennsylvania in the 1960s and 1970s was heavily regulated by the state legislature. People who wanted to buy beer had to buy it from a beer distributorship.[102] In the 1960s, Maurice S. Hepps went into direct competition with the other beer distributorships by pioneering the first supermarket beer stores in Pennsylvania.[103] The other beer distributors did not like Hepps's new beer-selling concept; many believed his franchising idea was "skirting the edge of the law."[104] His competitors argued that Hepps's Thrifty Beverage chain was illegal and a potential monopoly that could drive independent operators out of business.[105] Hepps's competitors also were suspicious of Hepps's relationship with Pennsylvania state senator Frank Mazzei, a Pittsburgh Democrat and convicted felon.[106]

The *Philadelphia Inquirer,* owned by Philadelphia Newspapers, Inc., published five articles in 1975 and 1976 suggesting that Hepps and his beer chain had ties with organized crime. The articles also implied that Hepps had improperly used Mazzei's political influence to gain competitive advantages over other beer distributorships.[107] Hepps, who said the articles were false, sued the *Inquirer* for libel.[108]

At the trial, the question of burden of proof arose. Was it up to Hepps to prove that the *Inquirer* articles were false, or was it up to the newspaper to prove that the articles were true? Under Pennsylvania law, the burden of proving truth was on the defendant.[109] Accordingly, Hepps's attorneys asked the judge to instruct the jury that the *Inquirer* would win only if it could prove that its articles were true and accurate. However, the judge—ruling that the state's burden-of-proof law was unconstitutional—declared that Hepps would win only if he could prove that the articles were false. Based on the judge's instructions, the jury returned a verdict in favor of the newspaper, and Hepps appealed.[110]

Because the trial court decision involved a ruling that a state statute violated the U.S. constitution, Hepps's appeal bypassed the Pennsylvania appeals court and went directly to the state supreme court.[111] The Pennsylvania Supreme Court ruled unanimously that the trial judge was wrong in ruling that the state statute governing the burden of proof in a libel case was unconstitutional. The court ordered a new trial.[112] The *Inquirer* appealed to the U.S. Supreme Court, which overruled the Pennsylvania Supreme Court. A public figure such as Hepps could not win a libel suit unless he could prove that the alleged defamation was false, the High Court said.[113]

In essence, the U.S. Supreme Court had upheld the ruling of the trial judge, which had led to a verdict in favor of the newspaper. The case was returned to the Pennsylvania appellate courts so that Hepps could pursue his appeal on matters other than the burden-of-proof question. However, more than a decade had passed since the *Inquirer* first suggested that Hepps was linked with organized crime, and Hepps decided it was useless to continue the suit.[114] He dropped the case.

DISCUSSION

Retracing the twenty-two media-related libel cases that reached the Supreme Court of the United States between 1965 and 1990 shows that the High Court is not always the final stop in the judicial process. Seventy-three percent of these cases—almost three of every four—did not end with the Supreme Court's ruling. Typically, it took several more months or even years before the cases finally were resolved, either by a definitive lower-court decision, an out-of-court settlement, or a decision to simply drop the dispute altogether.

This chapter's findings debunk the myth that the U.S. Supreme Court is the "court of last resort," at least with respect to media-related libel cases. This is not to suggest that the Supreme Court is an insignificant step in the judicial process, however. In many cases the High Court proved to be instrumental in steering the parties to the dispute toward a final resolution.

Cases such as *Keeton v. Hustler*, *Calder v. Jones*, *Schiavone v. Fortune*, and *Milkovich v. The Lorain Journal Co.* hinged on questions of law or procedure (e.g., jurisdiction, statute of limitations, fair comment) that had to be decided before the case could be tried on its merits. Once the U.S. Supreme Court resolved the issues of law or procedure, the context for resolving the dispute was established and the parties could weigh whether it was to their interest to settle the case or take it to trial. The course the dispute ended up taking—an out-of-court settlement or a trial—was influenced by the decision of the Supreme Court.

In several cases, litigants opted not to pursue their disputes after a Supreme Court ruling on a point of law or procedure that favored the other side. The litigants' decisions to drop the cases may have been an acknowledgment that, although the Supreme Court did not deal with the cases directly on their merits, the High Court's ruling for all practical purposes made the outcome of a trial obvious.

The study on which this chapter is based traced the twenty-two libel disputes from the first appearance of the media content that triggered the dispute to the final resolution of the dispute. Readers who are interested in details about the social patterns that developed as the disputes evolved may wish to consult the full study.[115]

NOTES

1. The study examines all media-related libel cases that reached the Supreme Court after *New York Times v. Sullivan*, 376 U.S. 254 (1964), through the end of 1990.

2. Anthony Lewis, *Make No Law: The Sullivan Case and the First Amendment* (New York: Random House, 1991), pp. 171–182.

3. See, e.g., *Wolston v. Reader's Digest*, 443 U.S. 157 (1979), or *Schiavone Construction Co. v. Fortune*, 477 U.S. 21 (1986).

4. Insightful discussions of the legal aspects of the six cases in which the Supreme Court's decision was final can be found in any of the standard media law textbooks. See, e.g., Donald M. Gillmor, et al., *Mass Communication Law: Cases and Comment*, 5th ed. (St. Paul, Minn.: West Publishing, 1990); Kent R. Middleton and Bill F. Chamberlin, *The Law of Public Communication*, 3rd ed. (New York: Longman, 1994); Don R. Pember, *Mass Media Law*, 6th ed. (Dubuque, Iowa: Brown and Benchmark, 1993).

5. Telephone interview with Emile J. Hodel, June 21, 1991.

6. Telephone interview with C. Harold Hanks, June 12, 1991.

7. "Hanks on Top in Libel Suit," *Raleigh Register,* June 1, 1966, p. 1; Telephone interview with Jack Mann, attorney for Beckley Newspapers Corp., June 10, 1991.

8. *Beckley Newspapers Corp. v. Hanks,* 389 U.S. 81 (1967); Hanks interview; "Supreme Court Throws Out Hanks' $5,000 Libel Suit Against BNC," *Raleigh Register,* November 6, 1967, p. 1.

9. *Hanks v. Beckley Newspapers Corp.,* 172 S.E.2d 816 at 817 (Sup.Ct.W.Va. 1970).

10. 172 S.E.2d at 818.

11. Hanks interview.

12. "Civil Rights: Dawdling on the Corner," *Time,* November 24, 1961, pp. 15–16.

13. Telephone interview with Frank Pape, May 31, 1991.

14. *Time, Inc. v. Pape,* 401 U.S. 279 (1971).

15. Telephone interview with Patrick Dunne, attorney for Frank Pape, May 15, 1991.

16. Dunne interview.

17. Pape interview; Dunne interview.

18. Alan Stang, "Frame-Up: Richard Nuccio and the War on Police," *American Opinion,* April 1969, pp. 1–18.

19. Peter Irons, *The Courage of Their Convictions* (New York: The Free Press, 1988), p. 333.

20. 418 U.S. 323 at 351–352.

21. 418 U.S. at 352.

22. Telephone interview with Elmer Gertz, May 9, 1991.

23. *Gertz v. Welch,* 680 F.2d 527 (7th Cir. 1982).

24. CBS News, "The Selling of Colonel Herbert" (transcript), *60 Minutes,* vol. 5, Number 9, February 4, 1973; Barry Lando, "The Herbert Affair," *Atlantic Monthly,* May 1973, pp. 73–81.

25. Telephone interview with Mike Wallace, senior correspondent, CBS News, June 4, 1991; telephone interview with Jonathan W. Lubbell, attorney for retired Lt. Col. Anthony Herbert, May 29, 1991.

26. *Herbert v. Lando,* 441 U.S. 153 (1979).

27. *Herbert v. Lando,* 596 F.Supp. 1178 (S.D.N.Y. 1984); Alan Kohn, "Ex-Army Officer Loses Appeal in Suit Against CBS, Magazine," *New York Law Journal,* January 16, 1986, p. 1.

28. *Herbert v. Lando,* 476 U.S. 1182 (1986).

29. Telephone interviews with Alma G. Smith, retired editor, *Laconia Evening Citizen,* June 11, 1991, and with Lawrence J. Smith, retired managing editor, May 23, 1991.

30. Alfred D. Rosenblatt, "Out of My Head," *Laconia Evening Citizen,* December 11, 1958, pp. 23–24.

31. Telephone interview with Brenda Baer, June 14, 1991. Brenda Baer is the daughter-in-law of Frank Baer.

32. Alfred D. Rosenblatt, "Out of My Head," *Laconia Evening Citizen,* February 14, 1959, p. 8.

33. Alfred D. Rosenblatt, "Out of My Head," *Laconia Evening Citizen,* January 29, 1960, pp. 2, 12.

34. Brenda Baer interview.

35. Brenda Baer interview.

36. Telephone interview with Arthur Nighswander, Alfred Rosenblatt's lawyer, May 30, 1991.

37. *Rosenblatt v. Baer,* 383 U.S. 75 (1966).

38. Nighswander interview.

39. 401 U.S. 266; Douglas A. Anderson, *A "Washington Merry-Go-Round" of Libel Actions* (Chicago: Nelson-Hall, 1980), p. 82.

40. Telephone interview with Stanley M. Brown, attorney for Alphonse Roy, May 23, 1991; *Roy v. Monitor-Patriot Co.,* 109 N.H. 441, 254 A.2d 832 (1969).

41. 401 U.S. at 270.

42. Anderson, *A "Washington Merry-Go-Round,"* p. 192.

43. *Monitor Patriot Co. v. Roy,* 401 U.S. 265 (1971).

44. Anderson, *A "Washington Merry-Go-Round,"* p. 192.

45. Shirley Jones, Marty Ingels, and Mickey Herskowitz, *Shirley and Marty* (New York: William Morrow and Co., 1990), pp. 15–16, inside front cover.

46. Ingels withdrew from the lawsuit. Telephone interview with Paul S. Ablon, attorney for Shirley Jones and Marty Ingels, May 15, 1991.

47. *Calder v. Jones,* 465 U.S. 783 (1984).

48. "Sorry Shirley, and Surely Sorry," *Time,* May 7, 1984, p. 92.

49. Ablon interview.

50. Ablon interview; *Time,* May 7, 1984, p. 92.

51. *Time,* May 7, 1984, p. 92.

52. Telephone interview with Kathy Keeton, June 27, 1991.

53. Keeton interview.

54. *Keeton v. Hustler Magazine, Inc.,* 465 U.S. 770 (1984).

55. Ibid.; Keeton interview.

56. Telephone interview with David Branson, attorney for Jack Anderson, May 8, 1991.

57. Nora T. Cannon, "Sieg Heil," *Comment,* October 1991, pp. 2, 4.

58. Branson interview; telephone interview with Michael Sullivan, attorney for Jack Anderson, June 24, 1991.

59. *Anderson v. Liberty Lobby, Inc.,* 477 U.S. 242 (1986); "High Court Overturns Scalia in Libel Case," *Publishers Weekly,* July 11, 1986, p. 18.

60. Branson interview; Sullivan interview.

61. Branson interview; Sullivan interview.

62. Sullivan interview.

63. Telephone interview with Theodore Geiser, attorney for Schiavone Construction Co., May 28, 1991.

64. Roy Rowan, "The Payoff Charges against Reagan's Labor Secretary," *Fortune,* May 31, 1982, pp. 80–87.

65. "Schiavone Partners Denied Libel Suit against Magazine," *The New York Law Journal,* June 19, 1986, pp. 1, 3.

66. "Schiavone Partners Denied Libel Suit."

67. Geiser interview.

68. Geiser interview; "A Time to Fight and a Time to Settle," *Newsweek,* August 29, 1988, p. 5.

69. Telephone interview with Ted Diadiun, March 28, 1991.

70. David Margolick, "How a '74 Fracas Led to a High Court Libel Case," *New York Times,* April 20, 1990, p. B8, col. 3.

71. Diadiun interview; Margolick, "How a '74 Fracas Led," p. B8.

72. Diadiun interview.

73. Scott also sued, but his suit was unsuccessful.

74. *Milkovich v. The Lorain Journal Co.,* 497 U.S. 1 (1990).

75. "Milkovich Lawsuit Finally Settled," *Presstime,* May 1991, p. 44; Diadiun interview.

76. "The Next Step," *Greenbelt News Review,* November 30, 1972, p. 3A.

77. Telephone interview with Mary Lou Williamson, editor, *Greenbelt News Review,* June 5, 1991.

78. Dorothy Sucher, "School Site Stirs Up Council: Rezoning Deal Offer Debated," *Greenbelt News Review,* October 14, 1965, pp. 1, 3.

79. Sucher, "School Site Stirs Up Council."

80. Telephone interview with Elaine Skolnik, news editor, *Greenbelt News Review,* June 20, 1991; "Charles Bresler Files $2,000,000 Suit against *News Review,*" July 28, 1966, p. 1.

81. Williamson interview; Skolnik interview.

82. 398 U.S. at 15.

83. Theo Lippman, Jr., *Spiro Agnew's America* (New York: W. W. Norton, 1972), p. 89.

84. 398 U.S. at 13.

85. Williamson interview.

86. Telephone interview with Leonard Damron, July 9, 1991.

87. Damron interview; 401 U.S. 296, fn. 1.

88. Damron interview.

89. 401 U.S. at 297; *Wallace Dunn, Ocala Star Banner v. Damron,* On Writ of Certiorari to the District Court of Appeal, First District, State of Florida (Brief of Respondent), May 4, 1970, p. 5.

90. Damron interview.

91. *Ocala Star Banner v. Damron,* 401 U.S. 295 (1971).

92. Damron interview.

93. "Milestones," *Time,* December 22, 1967, p. 77.

94. Time, Inc., should have been on notice to take extra care with stories about Mrs. Firestone. A year before the erroneous report about her divorce, *Life* magazine—also published by Time, Inc.—published a cover story about electronic eavesdropping. The story featured a photo of Mr. and Mrs. Firestone and a second photo of a private investigator. The caption for the photos asserted that the Firestones were using private investigators to spy on each other. John Neary, "The Big Snoop," *Life,* May 20, 1966, pp. 38–46. Mrs. Firestone sued for libel and won $30,000 in damages, but the award was overturned on appeal. Telephone interview with Joseph Farish, attorney for Mary Alice Firestone, July 15, 1991; *Firestone v. Time, Inc.,* 414 F.2d 790 (5th Cir. 1969).

95. *Time, Inc. v. Firestone,* 424 U.S. 448 (1976).

96. Telephone interview with Edna L. Caruso, attorney for Mary Alice Firestone, July 9, 1991.

97. Telephone interview with Robert Montgomery, attorney for Mary Alice Firestone, July 12, 1991.

98. 443 U.S. at 162.

99. John Barron, *KGB: The Secret Work of Soviet Secret Agents* (New York: Reader's Digest Press, 1974), pp. 188, 462.

100. *Wolston v. Reader's Digest,* 443 U.S. 157 (1979).

101. Telephone interview with Sidney Dickstein, attorney for Ilya Wolston, June 4, 1991.

102. Telephone interview with Ronald H. Surkin, attorney for Maurice S. Hepps, June 17, 1991.

103. Telephone interview with Maurice S. Hepps, June 23, 1991.

104. Ibid.

105. William Ecenbarger, "How Mazzei Used Pull, Kept Beer Chain Intact," *Philadelphia Inquirer,* May 5, 1975, p. 1A; Surkin interview.

106. Ecenbarger, "How Mazzei Used Pull," May 5, 1975, p. 2A.

107. Ibid, p. 1A; Surkin interview; Hepps interview.

108. Hepps interview.

109. Telephone interview with Sam Klein, attorney for Philadelphia Newspapers, Inc., June 13, 1991.

110. Surkin interview.

111. Ibid.

112. *Hepps v. Philadelphia Newspapers, Inc.,* 506 Pa. 304, 485 A2d. 374 (1984); Surkin interview.

113. *Philadelphia Newspapers, Inc. v. Hepps,* 475 U.S. 767 (1986).

114. Hepps interview.

115. Eddith A. Dashiell, "Getting to the Supreme Court of the United States: The Social Characteristics of Supreme Court Media-Related Libel Cases Since *Times v. Sullivan,*" unpublished Ph.D. dissertation, Indiana University, 1992.

13

The Future of Media
Accountability

DAVID PRITCHARD

The first chapter of this book stressed that media accountability is a process that can be understood only through careful research into what Emerson called "the actual forces at work." Toward the end of greater understanding, this volume's empirical studies examined the "actual forces at work" in a variety of contexts. The goal of this final chapter is to summarize what has been learned from the empirical studies and then to apply their lessons to the question of whether the American system of media accountability can be improved.

In a sense, of course, it is misleading to talk about a single American system of media accountability; what exists is a variety of mechanisms of media accountability that are largely ad hoc, unorganized, and idiosyncratic. The fragmented, partial, and diffuse nature of media accountability may be inevitable, given the strong ideology of autonomy among American journalists and, more generally, the fact that political and social processes in the United States tend to be local and diverse rather than national and uniform.

The media accountability process begins with citizens. If no citizen makes a claim, a media organization never learns that it caused a problem. The intermediate stages of media accountability often involve various kinds of ethical norms and forms of self-regulation established by media organizations. Looming vaguely and somewhat ominously in the background is law, not only in the form of litigation but also as a set of rules and doctrines intended to outline media rights and responsibilities.

Citizens, ethics, and the law, in other words. This conclusion will discuss them in that order.

CITIZENS

Despite the often pious pronouncements of news industry leaders about their concern for the public, ordinary citizens do not seem to be taken very seriously by the news media. Journalists engage in low-level deception routinely and often without much thought, as the study of the television news staff showed in chapter 2, and then they compound the error by failing to reveal their news-gathering tactics to the people in their audience. Newspapers report so sloppily that they regularly make factual errors (chapter 3), but in the rare instances when a citizen calls the newspaper to ask for a correction, journalists are reluctant to provide one unless the caller is prominent (chapter 4). Little wonder, then, that most ordinary people who experience problems because of shabby journalistic treatment try to solve the problems themselves rather than asking the news organization to do so.

The turn-of-the-century crisis of media credibility may well be related to the accumulation of these kinds of events. Almost every such event, taken by itself, is fairly trivial. However, if they happen as often as chapters 2, 3, and 4 suggest—perhaps thousands of times a day across the United States, hundreds of thousands of times every year—the cumulative effect is massive. Journalistic carelessness may be killing journalism's credibility, little by little.

Many journalists have come to understand that accuracy is a problem. A Pew Research Center survey of 552 journalists and news media executives in the late 1990s revealed that about half of them said that factual errors and sloppy reporting are on the rise.[1] Whether the journalism industry is willing to take steps to improve the accuracy of news reports, however, is an open question, given that some industry leaders see declining credibility more as a public relations challenge than as a central issue of the quality of the news product. The Newspaper Association of North America, for example, plans a $6 million public relations campaign to improve the public's view of news credibility. The Freedom Forum has invested more than $1 million to investigate ways in which the press and the public can understand each other better.[2]

ETHICS

Everyone agrees with the general statement that the media should be ethical. What it means to be ethical, however, is something of a quandary. Part of the challenge is ideological. Mainstream American journalists worship at the altar of a curious ideal of objectivity, one that rejects conscious commitment to all but the most abstract of value systems. If journalists did align themselves with a meaningfully concrete system of moral values, they would risk contradicting a fundamental tenet of "objectivity."

In the absence of meaningful value systems, many news organizations have adopted ethics codes or have created ombudsman positions to enhance accountability. Published or broadcast media criticism also focuses on questions of media ethics and accountability much of the time. In addition, news industry groups in a few regions of North America have established news councils, which are bodies designed to serve more or less as informal, voluntary ethical courts. Each of these mechanisms of media accountability merits some discussion.

ETHICS CODES

At first glance, a news organization's ethics code would seem to be intended as a guide for how journalists should behave. Research, however, has been unable to demonstrate that ethics codes have any discernible influence on the behavior of journalists.[3] Some news organizations may be more ethical than others, but when that is the case, ethics codes are not the reason for the difference.[4] Surveys show that journalists' actual views of ethics are sharply different from what is found in their news organizations' codes of ethics.[5] Journalists and other media workers may have ethical sensibilities, but they do not factor them into their routine work in any coherent fashion. This is true even in the high-profile area of crime coverage; journalists regularly ignore guidelines intended to preserve criminal suspects' fair-trial rights.[6] The study of the television news staff in chapter 2 suggested that deceptive news practices are routine, especially among younger journalists, and that they occur without much discussion or reflection. What is more, even when reflection does precede the use of deception as a reporting tool, the reflection generally is not based on identifiable ethical principles, ethics codes, or any set of clear guidelines for ethical decision-making.

Left to their own devices, in other words, journalists seem to be fairly insensitive to ethical concerns and fairly superficial in their thinking about them. That journalists pay scant attention to ethics codes may be related to the fact that such codes often are intended more as tools of public relations—as attempts to persuade the public that the media are ethical—than as meaningful guides for media conduct. This strong public relations component of ethics codes has been documented in analyses of codes pertaining to newspapers,[7] broadcasting,[8] advertising,[9] and film.[10]

NEWS OMBUDSMEN

An ombudsman is a direct and public link between citizens and a news organization. News organizations that have ombudsmen provide ordinary citizens with an identifiable person whose principal job is to receive and attempt to resolve complaints. The examination in chapter 5 of the news ombudsman at the *Louisville Courier-Journal* concluded that an ombudsman can be a meaningful agent of accountability, especially if he or she writes a regular column for public consumption, and especially if the ombudsman has the freedom to criticize his or her own news organization. Ethics codes can be criticized for being nothing but fluff, mere words on paper that have no impact on the journalists whose work they supposedly govern. Ombudsmen who efficiently and effectively resolve the public's complaints also serve the public relations interests of the news organizations that employ them, but the work of ombudsmen is more than mere fluff. They attempt to solve real problems of real people.

Although there is little evidence that ombudsmen have much effect on the journalists who work at their news organizations,[11] their principal function is dealing with the public. The public seems to like the idea of a contact person at a news organization. Ombudsmen receive lots of communication from the public. The *Washington Post*'s ombudsman, for example, receives about 15,000 telephone calls a year.[12] And studies show that people who contact a news ombudsman tend to be satisfied with the results of the contact.[13]

MEDIA CRITICISM

The pioneering study in chapter 6 of the content and influence of a journalism review is a blow to those who would see organized media criticism as a meaningful mechanism of media accountability. Most of the content of the *St. Louis Journalism Review* was not of a type that could foster meaningful reform of news practices; most St. Louis journalists said the review was not very influential on their thinking about what constituted good journalism. National journalism reviews were even less influential.

Perhaps part of the problem is that the intended audience for journalism reviews traditionally has been journalists, a situation that may inhibit the publication of articles sharply critical of well-established news practices. In June 1998 a new national journalism review aimed at a mass audience was founded by Steven Brill, the media entrepreneur who had founded Court TV and *The American Lawyer*. Brill anticipated that the new journalism review, *Brill's Content,* would have a circulation of about 500,000 copies a month. In addition to its own critiques of the media, *Brill's Content* has an ombudsman who writes critiques of the magazine's content.[14] A study of the influence of *Brill's Content* should be high on the agenda of future research in media accountability.

NEWS COUNCILS

In the abstract, news councils seem like appealing exercises of social responsibility on the part of the news industry. Although they are funded by the news industry, all of the news councils in North America include members both from the media and from the public, generally equal numbers of each.[15] They gather evidence; they allow all parties to a dispute to be heard. In addition, there is some evidence that news councils may reduce the number of libel actions filed against the news media.[16]

However, there are problems with news councils, as the study in chapter 7 of the Quebec Press Council documented. News councils take a long time to act. Even worse, they make decisions on a case-by-case basis, with the result that decisions often are not based on clear principles of ethics and accountability and sometimes even contradict decisions made in earlier cases that presented identical issues.[17] The fact that news councils are financed by the media leads to continual doubts about their impartiality.[18] None of these flaws, however, has prevented a renewal of the debate about the wisdom of re-creating the National News Council in the United States, an organization that existed from 1973 to 1984.[19]

LAW

In theory, law should be a powerful tool of media accountability, a force that media workers routinely factor into their decisions. After all, multi-million-dollar judgments against news organizations are not uncommon in the United States. The Federal Communications Commission has the authority to impose sanctions against broadcasters, up to and including revocation of their licenses. Certain criminal statutes (e.g., obscenity) may be activated against the media.

In practice, however, law is at best a peripheral influence on journalists and others who produce media content. This is partly because the law is used only rarely to hold the media accountable. Individuals are not inclined to use the law, both because they often think they can solve the problems caused by media themselves, as chapter 2 suggested, and because it takes time, money, and expertise to engage in litigation.[20]

Ordinary people generally lack the resources to do legal battle. It is only when citizens organize into interest groups that their accountability demands are taken seriously. Chapter 8, the study of the letter-writing campaign to the FCC in protest of a raunchy radio show, clearly demonstrated this phenomenon. For better or worse, however, relatively few Americans belong to organizations that make a priority of taking concerted action related to media accountability.

Whether or not a lawsuit is likely, legal standards ideally should help establish the boundaries of media work. But that can happen only if media workers know the law. Unfortunately, ignorance of relevant legal standards is widespread among media workers. Chapter 9, the case study of regulation of local cable access programming, illustrated this state of affairs well, as did the review in chapter 11 of interactions between newspaper journalists and the lawyer for a state press association.[21] Chapter 10 showed that news organizations often consult lawyers, but more to define and solve problems than to learn about legal standards or to engage in litigation. Actual lawsuits were very rare.

Media law in the United States is horribly complex. Libel laws, for example, "have become complicated almost beyond human comprehension," wrote a leading media law scholar.[22] The simple question of whether an allegedly libelous statement was true is rarely a central issue in libel cases in the United

States. Rather, resolution of the cases is based on interpretation of a dense web of constitutional and procedural issues. Once those issues are resolved, litigants may be so exhausted—or may have exhausted so much of their resources—that they never resolve the key issues of accuracy and harm, as chapter 12's study of libel cases that had reached the Supreme Court showed.

CONCLUSION

The world is changing rapidly. The forces that dominate social and political life in the United States—governments, corporations, the media—appear ever more distant and unreachable. Western societies are grappling with a paradigm shift from citizenship and democracy as central organizing principles to consumerism and markets as central organizing principles. The noble ethics of the public interest threatens to yield to the dubious ethics of whatever the public may be interested in. The very meaning of democracy sometimes seems under siege, though the pressures on democracy are difficult to perceive because the forms of democracy still exist.

Forms of media accountability exist, too, though this book paints a rather gloomy picture of how well many of them work. Various mechanisms of media self-regulation can seem to be an appealing compromise between the heavy hand of government regulation and the anarchy of market forces, but ethics codes, media criticism, and news councils often fail to live up to the claims made by their supporters.[23] Law—costly, cumbersome, and complex—fares even worse as a means of media accountability.

At its core, the problem of media accountability is a problem of democracy. How can the media, which must have freedom from most forms of governmental regulation in order to fulfill their roles in democratic societies, be held accountable for their behavior? We believe that a realistic answer to that question has two parts.

The first has to do with corporate self-interest. Effective procedures for responding to complaints about media content result in very positive public relations. There are ways to do this without having an ombudsman, but as chapter 5 showed, ombudsmen can act as meaningful agents of media accountability while performing an important public relations function for their companies. Media organizations that do not institute effective accountability procedures may need to be reminded that such procedures are in their corporate self-interest.

The second part of the answer has to do with citizens. The message of the study in chapter 8 of the letter-writing campaign to the FCC is that organized citizen action can make a difference. The key is organization. Without it, concerted economic action (e.g., boycotts) or political action (e.g., pressure on regulatory agencies) is impossible.

Ultimately, media accountability depends upon citizen participation. The same, of course, is true of democracy. We choose to be optimistic about both media accountability and democracy, in part because the alternatives are so unpalatable, but also because we believe that a stronger system of media accountability and a stronger democracy are in everyone's self-interest.

NOTES

1. Dylan L. McClain, "More Journalists Are Critical of the Media," *New York Times,* April 5, 1999.

2. Thomas Winship, "Journalists Uniting to Take Action," *Editor & Publisher,* May 17, 1999.

3. David Pritchard and Madelyn Peroni Morgan, "Impact of Ethics Codes on Judgments by Journalists: A Natural Experiment," *Journalism Quarterly* 66 (1989): 934–941.

4. David E. Boeyink, "How Effective Are Codes of Ethics? A Look at Three Newsrooms," *Journalism Quarterly* 71 (1994): 893–904.

5. Philip Meyer, *Ethical Journalism: A Guide for Students, Practitioners, and Consumers* (New York: Longman, 1987).

6. James W. Tankard, Jr., Kent Middleton, and Tony Rimmer, "Compliance with American Bar Association Fair Trial–Free Press Guidelines," *Journalism Quarterly* 56 (1979): 464–468; Dorothy J. Imrich, Charles Mullin, and Daniel Linz, "Measuring the Extent of Prejudicial Pretrial Publicity in Major American Newspapers: A Content Analysis," *Journal of Communication* 45 (Summer 1995): 94–117.

7. Meyer, *Ethical Journalism,* p. 19.

8. Joel Persky, "Self Regulation of Broadcasting—Does It Exist?" *Journal of Communication* 27 (Spring 1977): 202–210; Louise M. Benjamin, "Birth of a Network's 'Conscience': The NBC Advisory Council, 1927," *Journalism Quarterly* 66 (Autumn 1989): 587–590.

9. Quentin J. Schultze, "Professionalism in Advertising: The Origin of Ethical Codes," *Journal of Communication* 31 (Spring 1981): 64–71.

10. John Dimmick, "Canons and Codes as Occupational Ideologies," *Journal of Communication* 27 (Spring 1977): 181–187.

11. David Pritchard, "The Impact of Newspaper Ombudsmen on Journalists' Attitudes," *Journalism Quarterly* 70 (1993): 77–86.

12. Linda Fibich, "Under Siege," *American Journalism Review,* September 1995, pp. 16–23.

13. James M. Bernstein, "The Public's View of Newspaper Accountability," *Newspaper Research Journal* 7 (Winter 1986): 1–9; Barbara W. Hartung, Alfred JaCoby, and David M. Dozier, "Readers' Perceptions of Purpose of Newspaper Ombudsman Program," *Journalism Quarterly* 65 (1988): 914–919.

14. Robin Pogrebin, "Watchdog for Media Watchdogs," *New York Times,* March 11, 1998.

15. An exception to the 50-50 rule is the Quebec Press Council. Only 7 of its 19 members come from the public. The rest come from the ranks of media managers and journalists.

16. Ronald Farrar, "News Councils and Libel Actions," *Journalism Quarterly* 63 (1986): 509–516; Dennis Hale, "ADR and the Minnesota News Council on Libel," *Dispute Resolution Journal* 49 (June 1994): 77–81.

17. Ulric Deschênes, "Légitimation et système normatif: Une étude de la jurisprudence du Conseil de presse du Québec," *Communication* 17 (December 1996): 169–187.

18. David Cassady, "Press Councils—Why Journalists Won't Cooperate," *Newspaper Research Journal* 5 (Summer 1984): 19–25.

19. See, e.g., Evan Jenkins, "News Councils: The Case for . . . and Against," *Columbia Journalism Review,* March/April 1997, pp. 38–39.

20. Robert Martin, "Libel and Class," *Canadian Journal of Communication* 9 (1983): 1–14.

21. Other studies also have documented gaps in media workers' knowledge of media law. For example, relatively few journalists knew whether their state protects them from having to furnish confidential information to law-enforcement authorities. Vince Blasi, "The Newsman's Privilege: An Empirical Study," *Michigan Law Review* 70 (1971): 229–284. Only 15 percent of high school principals and 10 percent of high school newspaper advisers had heard of a major federal appeals court decision regulating high school press in their area. Robert Trager and Donna L. Dickerson, "Prior Restraint in High School: Law, Attitudes and Practice," *Journalism Quarterly* 57 (1980): 135–138. Most editors of newspapers with more than 25,000 circulation did not know that in a libel suit, courts treat letters to the editor no differently than other published material. Steve Pasternack, "Editors and the Risk of Libel in Letters," *Journalism Quarterly* 60 (1983): 311–315, 328. Station managers in Washington state could apply political broadcast regulations correctly only 44 percent of the time. Elizabeth Krueger and Kimberly Corrigan, "Broadcasters' Understanding of Political Broadcast Regulation," *Journal of Broadcasting and Electronic Media* 35 (1991): 289–304. Kansas editors, as a group, could correctly apply libel principles only about two-thirds of the time. Matthew D. Bunker, "Application of Libel Law Principles by Kansas Editors," *Newspaper Research Journal* 13 (Summer 1992): 13–24.

22. Donald M. Gillmor, *Power, Publicity, and the Abuse of Libel Law* (New York: Oxford University Press, 1992), p. 165.

23. For a broad overview of this issue, see Angela J. Campbell, "Self-Regulation and the Media," *Federal Communications Law Journal* 51 (1999): 711–772.

CONTRIBUTORS

Kristie Bunton is associate professor of journalism at the University of St. Thomas in St. Paul, Minnesota. With her colleagues, she is author of *Writing across the Media,* a textbook with a video guide and interactive World Wide Web site published by Beford/St. Martin's. She is a frequent commentator for the Minnesota news media on journalism ethics issues.

Eddith A. Dashiell is an associate professor in the E. W. Scripps School of Journalism at Ohio University. She has been on the faculty since 1992, after earning her doctorate from Indiana University. Her teaching interests include broadcast journalism, communications law, and information gathering.

Tom Luljak is former news director at WTMJ-TV, Milwaukee. He received a George Foster Peabody Award for investigative reporting and was honored as the Associated Press broadcast journalist of the year in Wisconsin. Currently, Luljak is director of corporate communications for Blue Cross & Blue Shield United of Wisconsin. He also is a part-time instructor in the Department of Journalism and Mass Communication at the University of Wisconsin–Milwaukee.

Neil Nemeth is an assistant professor of communication at Purdue University Calumet in Hammond, Indiana. He teaches news reporting, news editing, law, ethics, and other mass media courses. He worked as an education and city hall reporter at the *News Journal* in Mansfield, Ohio, and as a special projects reporter at the *Times* in Hammond, Indiana.

Patrick O'Neill teaches in the Department of Broadcast and Electronic Communication at Marquette University. His primary research interests are telecommunication policy and First Amendment law. He received a Ph.D. in telecommunications from Indiana University and has chaired the Law and Policy Division of the Broadcast Education Association.

Lindsy E. Pack chairs the Department of Communication and Theatre Arts at Frostburg State University in Maryland, where he is an associate professor. He also chairs the History Division of the Broadcast Education Association. He holds Ph.D.s in telecommunications from Indiana University and in American history from Texas A&M University. His scholarly interests include telecommunications law, broadcast history, and video production.

David Pritchard is a professor in the Department of Journalism and Mass Communication at the University of Wisconsin–Milwaukee. His research interests include media law, press coverage of crime, and Canadian journalism. A former Fulbright scholar and visiting professor at Laval University in Quebec, Professor Pritchard is the lead author of *Les journalistes canadiens: Un portrait de fin de siècle* (Presses de l'Université Laval, 1999). He has published more than three dozen scholarly articles and essays.

Craig Sanders is an assistant professor in the Department of Communications at John Carroll University in Cleveland, where he teaches journalism, public relations, and communications law. Sanders earned a Ph.D. in mass communications at Indiana University. His research interests include the interaction of journalists and attorneys, and the work of newspaper ombdusmen.

INDEX